The Renaissance Man

is nowhere better exemplified than in the life and work of Thomas More. Wit, statesman, husband, father, friend, scholar, controversialist, poet, and—in the end—martyr for the sake of conscience . . . In this volume, every facet of Thomas More's personality emerges. John P. Dolan's fast-paced translation of *Utopia* makes that classic of the imagination live. The English works, edited by James J. Greene for the modern reader, show the place of More in the development of English prose and reveal the deep humanity that underlay his learning and achievement.

Includes a general introduction to More by Professor Greene, as well as discussions of the individual works.

UTOPIA
and
Other Essential Writings
of
Thomas More

Selected and Edited by
James J. Greene and John P. Dolan

in modern translation

A MERIDIAN CLASSIC
NEW AMERICAN LIBRARY
NEW YORK AND SCARBOROUGH, ONTARIO

Library of Congress Catalog Card Number: 83-73478

This book was published in a Mentor edition under the title
The Essential Thomas More.

MERIDIAN CLASSIC TRADEMARK REG. U.S. PAT. OFF. AND FOREIGN COUNTRIES
REGISTERED TRADEMARK—MARCA REGISTRADA
HECHO EN WINNIPEG, CANADA

SIGNET, SIGNET CLASSIC, MENTOR, PLUME, MERIDIAN
AND NAL BOOKS are published *in the United States* by
New American Library, 1633 Broadway, New York, New York 10019,
in Canada by The New American Library of Canada Limited,
81 Mack Avenue, Scarborough, Ontario M1L 1M8

First Meridian Classic Printing, May, 1984

1 2 3 4 5 6 7 8 9

PRINTED IN CANADA

Contents

Introduction

Introduction

In a very real sense the best introduction to any writer is the verbal legacy he has bequeathed to posterity. The historical figure we know as Thomas More, however, while revealing much of his richly complex self in what he wrote, remains more than the sum of his written works.

Before offering some remarks and guidelines to the complexities—even downright contradictions—of More's remarkable literary output and even more remarkable life, it would be wise to record the knowable facts of that life (one is tempted to say lives). He was a devoted father and husband, who also wrote a tract defending the common sharing of wives; a successful lawyer and holder of the highest judicial office in England; the bosom companion of the same Henry VIII who was later to order his execution for treason; a thinker open to entertaining radically unconventional ideas; a writer of vituperative theological tracts and a ferocious hounder of heretics; a man who died in defense of the freedom and autonomy of conscience; a canonized saint of the Roman church.

No one is sure of the year in which Thomas More was born. According to our present knowledge, the date of his birth is either the sixth or the seventh of February, 1477 or 1478. Of his birthplace and parentage we are more certain. He was born in London, the son of Agnes Granger and John More, Gentleman. In an epitaph he composed for his tomb at Chelsea, More described his family as not famous but honest. They were also relatively prosperous. His father was a successful lawyer who rose high in his profession and who, toward the end of his life, became a judge of the King's Bench.

The young More received his early Latin-centered education at St. Antony's school in London and, around the age of twelve, went to live in the home of the powerful and learned prelate Archbishop Morton. This was not an unusual custom at that time. (Readers of *Utopia* will recall the deft compliment More paid to his former patron and benefactor through the mouth of Hythloday in Book One.)

After some two years in Morton's home, More entered Oxford, and at about sixteen, at his father's urging, entered one of the Inns of Court—New Inn, an institution devoted exclusively to the training of lawyers. These law schools need not be thought of as the antihumanist training centers Erasmus once suggested they were. Recent scholarship has tended to suggest that these Inns actually constituted England's unofficial "third university." At eighteen More passed on to the more advanced legal training offered by Lincoln's Inn, one of whose officials was the young man's father.

More's legal career was eminently successful, culminating in his appointment as Lord Chancellor the highest judiciary post in the realm, in 1529. More's legal studies and later professional obligations did not interfere with his immersion in the humanistic culture of the day. In 1499 Erasmus, soon to become the acknowledged leader of European humanism, paid his first visit to England and met the young More. The two men formed a friendship which was to last through their lifetimes. (Erasmus' *Praise of Folly* was written during a period of convalescence in More's Chelsea home.) For several years More served as a Reader in Law at Furnivall's Inn and toyed with the idea of entering the monastic life, going so far as to sample that life by living with the London Carthusians for a time.

During these years—his early twenties—More immersed himself in the exciting new intellectual import of the day, Greek studies. One immediate result was a translation of Greek epigrams into Latin. He also delivered, according to Erasmus, a series of public lectures on Augustine's *The City of God*. In 1504 we find More a member of Parliament, the last one of Henry VII's reign. In 1505 he married Jane Colt, and the same year the first of his four children, Margaret, was born. (The others were Elizabeth, Cecily, and John.) In 1511 Jane More, the woman described in an epitaph as *cara uxorcula*, his "dear little wife," died; and her husband, left with four young motherless children, married that same year a certain Alice Middleton, a widow seven years his senior.

The reason for the hasty second marriage may have been somewhat less than romantic. In the words of More's son-in-law, William Roper, "He rather married [her] for the ruling and governing of his children, house and family than for any bodily pleasure." Dame Alice More and Erasmus did not, we are told, get on well, but More, according to Roper, "lived a sweet and pleasant life with her."

More became increasingly involved in the political life of England. By 1515, he had risen high enough in the estimation of King Henry VIII to be sent on a special embassy to the Netherlands. This journey, with its many empty hours, provided him with the opportunity to compose a major part of *Utopia*, which he published the following year. By 1517 he was fully immersed in the life of politics, having been appointed one of Henry's special councillors.

To claim, as many beginning with Erasmus have, that Thomas More was lured into government service against his will is to oversimplify a complex matter. Erasmus' assertion in a letter to Tunstall in 1518 that More was "enticed" into the court is echoed in even stronger terms in his letter to Von Hutten: "King Henry . . . would never rest until he dragged him into his court. 'Dragged,' I say, and with reason, for no one was ever more ambitious of being admitted into a court than he was anxious to escape it." Against such statements, which possibly were colored by Erasmus' own distaste for political service, there is evidence to suggest that More—typically—may very well have been of two minds on the subject. William Nelson, an authority on the literature of Tudor England, has pointed out that

> . . . in 1509, the year Henry VIII ascended the throne, More joined the crowd of eager flatterers who sought place and wage under the new king, dedicating to him a volume of epigrams beautifully inscribed in a vellum manuscript illuminated with white and red roses and the pomegranates of Queen Katherine. . . . To ask whether More desired that place [at court] or whether it was forced upon him is futile. Very likely he was not himself of one mind.

According to Ammonius, another humanist employed by Henry, More at one time literally haunted the person of the powerful Cardinal Wolsey, hoping presumably to gain recognition and preferment. More's attitude toward political involvement seems to have been ambivalent. It would not, perhaps, be fanciful to look upon the debate between the characters More and Hythloday in Book One of *Utopia* as a literary projection of More's internal dialogue with himself. Hythloday, arguing against the intellectual's involvement in the political order, insists, "There is no room for philosophy in the courts of princes," to which the character in the dialogue named More answers:

> Yes, there is . . . but not for that academic philosophy which fits everything neatly into place. There is, however, another, more sophisticated philosophy which accommodates itself to the scene at hand and acts its part with polish and finesse. . . . The same . . . holds for the commonwealth and the councils of kings. You do not, simply because you are unable to uproot mistaken opinions and correct long-established ills, abandon the state altogether. In a storm, you do not desert the ship because you are unable to control the winds. . . . You must try to use subtle and indirect means, insofar as it lies in your power. And what you cannot turn to good, you must make as little evil as possible. To have everything turn out well assumes that all men are good, and this is a situation that I do not expect to come about for many years.

By 1517, less than two years after composing that apologia for the intellectual in politics, More was a member of the king's Privy Council. Thus began a political career which, by any standard, must be judged eminently successful. Advancing through a number of government positions, he was knighted in 1521, became Speaker of the House in 1523, and Lord Chancellor in 1529. More resigned the chancellorship in 1532, offering ill health as his reason, but it is clear that the growing rift between More and King Henry the Eighth over the validity of Henry's marriage to Catharine had much to do with his decision to leave government service. Even then, however, he was not safe from Henry's relentless pursuit or his increasingly strident demands that More, as one of the most prominent men of the time, speak his mind on the subject. The king's ex-chancellor, on the other hand, insisted on the right to the privacy and autonomy of his conscience. He was willing, as he revealed in one of his letters to Cromwell, to acknowledge Anne Boleyn as queen, but on the question of the validity of Henry's marriage to Catharine, he remained silent, a silence that cost him his life.

Despite the demanding claims of his political activities, More was not completely "lost to literature," as Erasmus feared he would be. Aside from the correspondence that he managed to maintain with the luminaries of European humanism, the bulk of More's writing during his later years was directly inspired by the great event of the age: the Protestant Reformation.

As early as 1523, writing under the pseudonym of Guilielmus Rosseus, More had written a Latin treatise defending King Henry against the abusive attacks of Martin Luther. More's book consists largely of vituperative invective, which was the accepted controversial style of the age. In 1528 the English hierarchy, disturbed over the increasing flow of Protestant books into England, commissioned More, then Lord Chancellor, to take up his pen in defense of orthodoxy against the attacks of the reformers. Cuthbert Tunstall, Bishop of London, wrote to Chancellor More: "I send you their mad incantations in our tongue and as well some of Luther's books whence these monstrous ideas have sprung." And then comes the invitation which led to More's shouldering the burdensome task of theological controversy:

> Because you, dear brother, are able to emulate Demosthemes in our vernacular tongue no less than in Latin, and are wont to be an ardent defender of Catholic truth whenever you hear it attacked, you cannot spend your leisure hours—if you can steal any from your official duties—better than in composing in our own language such books as may show to simple and unlearned men the cunning malice of the heretics, and fortify them against those impious subverters of the Church.

More apparently agreed with his friend's assessment of the situation, for within a year he had completed the first of his English controversial works, the *Dialogue Concerning Heresies*. It was published in June, 1529. Other works poured from More's prolific pen in the ensuing years, until the very day before his execution, July 6, 1535.

So much for the factual record, the bold outline of a life. What remains is the more difficult task of assessing that life, of attempting to clarify its mysteries, its ambiguities, its paradoxes—if for no other reason than that the problems and ideas which concerned More over four hundred years ago are excitingly, troublingly relevant to us today. More explored such vital questions as the common ownership of property, divorce, euthanasia, capital punishment, religious tolerance, the conduct and ethics of warfare, the problems of educating the masses, clerical celibacy, and the relationship of the intellectual to politics.

For these and other reasons Thomas More remains one of the significant figures of our past. The modern mystique of More is undoubtedly more sophisticated than its Counter-Reformation counterpart. The end result, however, is frequently the same: uncritical adulation. As one of the forgers of the modern critical, skeptical spirit, More surely deserves better treatment. He deserves to be seen, insofar as this is possible, for precisely what he was: a remarkable human being. But human beings, even (perhaps especially) the great ones, are frequently bundles of antitheses, of weaknesses and strengths, fears and hopes, timidity and valor, self-service and altruism. Frank and Fritzie Manuel in their recent study of the Utopian idea in western thought state the matter with a cogent simplicity: "Five hundred years after More's birth we are still perplexed by him."

That Thomas More did achieve at least a measure of greatness few have denied; and those few were, for the most part, such theological opponents as William Tyndale and John Foxe, who derided More in the polemical heat of ferocious religious controversy. (Tyndale described More as "that gleering fox," who had "hardened his heart against the truth." And Foxe called More, among other things, "a bitter persecutor . . . of good men," "a wretched enemy against the truth of the gospel.") One of the fascinating facts about the More story, however, is that those who, unlike Tyndale and Foxe, have seen greatness in the man have rarely agreed on the grounds of that greatness.

To Erasmus, Thomas More was "the most delightful character in the world," a man "born and made for friendship." "There is nothing in the human situation," he wrote, "in which he does not find pleasure." He was, for Erasmus, the embodiment of the humanists' values and ideals. The gentle and learned English humanist John Colet spoke of More as England's only true genius. More's contemporary Richard Whittington applied the traditional rhetorical commonplace to him when he described him as "a man for all seasons," the title for Robert Bolt's play about More. Even his theological opponents, Luther and Melancthon, were appalled that Henry VIII had ordered More's execution. Jonathan Swift revered More as the only great man to have appeared since antiquity. Joseph Addison, writing in *The Spectator*, refers admiringly to "this great and learned man [who] was famous for enlivening his ordinary discourse with wit and pleasantry." The nineteenth-century Marxist Karl Kautsky looked upon More as one of the founders of European socialism. Peter Viereck sees Thomas More as a perfect example of the "unadjusted man . . . a new liberator . . . a bad mixer, scandalously devoid of education for citizenship." And, finally, the Roman Catholic Church officially lists the name of Thomas More in its calendar of saints among those humans whose piety and virtue ought to be emulated.

Thomas More was, indeed, a many-sided man, a man of many careers, values, interests, drives. He was also a man whose life was radically divided by that great cultural watershed of his age, the Reformation. His life and thought are characterized by polarity and, at times, inconsistency. But, as Eric Bentley remarks in *A Century Of Hero Worship*, "Our greatest teachers are not those who gave us doctrines or systems of metaphysics. They are the interrogators and the protesters and conondrum makers . . . whom we . . . reward by crucifixion or . . . by slander. The word for such a teacher is Paradoxical, not Profound, or Confused. . . . Such teachers are notoriously inconsistent." Such men, to a greater degree than ordinary mortals, must always remain an enigma.

It is not our present task to sort out and evaluate the various strands and skeins of the More enigma, the More paradox. It is not so much that we have a higher tolerance for mystery and inconsistency than a former, more rationalistic age might have had, because it is more than a modish flirting with paradox that enables us to live, sometimes uncomfortably, with a fundamental truth about human behavior: human beings, at their most human, are characterized by ambivalence, by paradox, and sometimes by downright inconsistency. They live poised delicately, precariously, at the center of polarity. Regardless of how this duality is expressed —the absurd and the intelligible, nature and supernature, history and eternity, the tragic and the comic, the farcical and the sublime, the quintessential self and the role-playing self—the fully conscious person must, by definition, live within the tension of ambivalence. I am suggesting, in short, that somewhere at the heart of the inconsistency that marked the life of Thomas More, "the man for all seasons," lies his essential greatness. It is, I am convinced, a greatness profoundly linked to a comic vision, a vision which can only express itself through a superb irony. And More's vision was nothing if not essentially comic, and his irony is legendary.

There are those who have insisted upon the inherently close relationship between the skeptical, paradoxical view of reality and the sense of the comic, of the absurdity as well as the seriousness of life. In fact, it might be argued, the two are identical. A contemporary sociologist, Peter Berger, defines such an outlook as "alternation," a "precarious vision," the very essence of the comic spirit, a necessary function of the skeptical mind. As Berger puts it, "The perception of society as dramatic fiction may be shocking at first. Further reflection about it reveals the deeply comic aspect of social existence. There is a liberating quality to this revelation. . . . The . . . challenge to the status quo begins by not taking it as seriously as it takes itself."

The British critic H. A. Mason has suggested that this kind of tension was the ultimate source of Thomas More's comic view of existence. He offers an explanation of More's wit that, though the perspective is different, has much in common with Berger's notion of precariousness: "More . . . strikes me as being admirably balanced—but not in the least static. I see in him two violent pulls: More was drawn powerfully to enjoyment of life; he was drawn even more powerfully to reject that enjoyment. His wit, as I see it, was generated from the violence of this conflict, from his ability to see life from opposing points of view."

Thomas More's famous wit and irony were more than rhetorically useful and entertaining modes of expression. His ironic wit, his comic spirit, provided the texture as well as the ground of his view of the human condition. His ironic wit is the verbal counterpart of his double vision of the human situation. The man who enjoyed along with its author the punning in the title of Erasmus' famous work *The Praise of Folly* (the Latin *Encomium Moriae* means both praise of folly and praise of More); the man whose own masterpiece *Utopia* means in Greek both "no place" and "the happy place" (*u-topos, eu-topos*); the man who in the midst of a solemn theological controversy pauses to recount a "merry tale"; the man who is reported to have ended his life with a series of quips—this is the man whose vision is "precarious," whose consciousness and experience are marked by "alternation."

Men like More are a threat and a scandal to the singlemindedly earnest, to the "true believers." Erasmus could chuckle admiringly over his friend as one who "from boyhood . . . was always so pleased with a joke that it might seem that jesting was the main object of his life." The solemn sixteenth-century chronicler Edward Hall, on the other hand, was righteously indignant at the thought of a man whose response to death as well as to life was a witticism. Blunt, honest, earnest Hall could only mutter, "He [More] was too much given to mocking, which was to his gravity a great blemish." "I cannot tell," he says in another place, "whether I should call him a foolish wiseman or a wise foolishman."

This is the response that the singlemindedly solemn predictably makes to the ironist. To such a mind anyone who attempts to encompass the polarities of existence threatens the neatness of ideology. The ironic perspective, which sees through the essentially fictitious nature of the social structure, the comic vision which sees simultaneously both the absurdity and the usefulness of our social fictions and rituals, must sooner or later clash with those who cannot live so precariously poised. The man who punctures artifice with ironic laughter, who insists upon saying *no* as well as *yes*, must be forced to mount the scaffold on Tower Hill to face the absolutist's ultimate weapon: the headsman's axe. Men like More are both wise and foolish, and many other things as well. If a Henry VIII should force upon such a man the terrible choice of either/or, the Thomas Mores can only answer: both/and. More's last recorded words were, it will be recalled: "I die the king's good servant, but God's first." As Frank and Fritzie Manuel point out in *Utopian Thought in the Western World*, "Only a psychology that is undaunted by polarities and ambivalences and contrarieties and paradoxes can presume to make sense of Thomas More without decapitating him psychically as the executioner did physically."

Thomas More's wit and irony characterized his life and thought: he was the canonized saint who wrote bawdy epigrams; the loyal servant and friend of the king who translated politically subversive poems; the amasser of substantial real estate holdings who described private property as the source of all political and social ills; the thinker who examined the attractiveness of religious tolerance and who also advocated the burning of heretics; the congenial lover of life who beneath his chancellor's robes wore a hair shirt.

The most perceptive of More's contemporaries understood and valued the dialectical play of More's mind; they saw in him that intensely human quality that Huizinga calls *Homo Ludens*, man the player, in his fascinating book of the same title. As Erasmus put it in a letter to More which was frequently printed as a preface to *The Praise of Folly*, "Comical matters may be so treated that a reader of ordinary sense may possibly reap more advantage from it [*sic*] than from some more serious, more solemn argument." Or, as More put in his *Apology*, "A man may sometimes say full sooth [truth] in game." In another of his English works, More puts into the mouth of one of the characters the following description of himself: "Ye use to look so sadly when ye mean merrily, that many times men doubt whether ye speak in sport, when ye mean good earnest." A man of our own time, Dietrich Bonhoeffer, who, like Thomas More, was imprisoned for his beliefs and finally executed by the Nazis, was at one with More when he wrote from prison, "Absolute seriousness is not without a dose of humor."

The either/or men will never understand and be easy with a man whose view of life is both serious and facetious, reverent and irreverent. Those solemn Marxists, for example, are just as one-sidedly mistaken in seeing *Utopia* as a pre-Marx socialist tract as are those commentators who dismiss this complex work as a piece of frivolous horseplay. The subtle mind of More—until he became the militant controversialist, and to some extent even then—refuses to be contained in rigidly neat categories. It is simply too elusive for such containment. One suspects, incidentally, that one reason More was not canonized until four centuries after his death is that his life and writings do not fit neatly into the preconceptions and categories of official sanctity.

All of More's admirers and most of his foes are agreed on one point. His death was a heroic gesture in defense of the autonomy of conscience. There are those who believe that that conscience was a mistaken one, but among these are few who will deny the heroism of More's refusal to survive at the price of personal integrity. And the noble fact to be recorded is that More really wanted to live; he enjoyed life; he was humanly terrified at the prospect of suffering and death. A deft, casuistic political accommodation to his king's demands could easily have saved his life. Yet More, whose political instincts and abilities were shrewd and tough, refused at a certain fatal point to compromise his vision of the truth. No less firmly than Luther allegedly said, and with more immediately sinister consequences, did More adopt his own version of the traditional legal formula which the great German reformer took as his manifesto: Here I stand; I can no other; God help me.

That final tragic phase of More's life, his imprisonment and execution, was, ironically, brought about by his very success and prominence. King Henry, who had become more and more shrilly adamant in his demands for total conformity not only to his divorce and remarriage but also to his assertion of supremacy over the English Church, would clearly never have bothered with a Thomas More who had remained an obscure cipher. But the More who responded to Henry's demands with a silent refusal was far from obscure. By 1534 Thomas More had become one of the best-known and widely admired figures in western Europe. It was precisely because of the symbolic importance of his resistance to the oath that Henry's ex-chancellor had to capitulate. Failing that, Henry and his ministers had only one alternative: More had to be condemned as a traitor and die a criminal's death. In More's very prestige, his symbolic importance in a vicious ideological power struggle, lies the explanation and ultimate significance of his judicial murder.

And so, in pondering the meaning of the final act in Thomas More's life, we are confronted once again with the centrality of paradox in that life. The man whose prestige and popularity were the immediate cause of his execution; the man who died "the king's good servant, but God's first";

the man who, faced with the headsman's grisly axe, jested as he lay his head on the block, "I pray you let me lay my beard over the block, lest you should cut it"; the man who died in defense of the papacy at the command of the same king who years before had alarmed More by the ultramontanist exuberance of his king's subservience to the papacy—this is a man who in the final analysis eludes our desire for simple answers. He demands that we respect his mystery.

Before turning to the selections from his works which follow, a word should be said of *Utopia*. In any attempt to come to grips with the significance of More's life and works, the central importance of *Utopia* cannot be denied.

It is idle to speculate about what Thomas More's place in history would be had he not written *Utopia* since he did in fact compose this work—which he later somewhat regretted —and it unquestionably represents his most important contribution to the history of literature and ideas.

Not only is this the work that for the last four centuries has established More's international reputation; More clearly intended *"libellus vere aureus"* (this little golden tract) to be seen as a powerful manifesto in the humanists' program for European reform. He asked Erasmus to arrange to have a series of laudatory letters and commentaries from the leading European scholars and statesmen to be printed with the first edition, which was published in Paris in 1516. This rather large body of prefactory material represents something more than mere puffery by members of a clique lauding one of their own. These letters and verses, along with the text of *Utopia*, represents a trenchant, at times even radical, assault on the institutional corruption of the age.

Launched with such fanfare and written in Latin, the international language of the humanist elite, *Utopia*, for all of its wit, sly word play, and irony, was obviously intended to be taken as a major statement of humanist concerns.

The intellectual urge to set up an ideal state (although More continually reminds us that his imaginary commonwealth is far from perfect) obviously stems, consciously or unconsciously, from a dissatisfaction with things as they are. The new voyages of geographical discovery, furthermore, were opening up options and possibilities other than those of sixteenth-century Europe. Accounts of the new world obviously stimulated More's "play" (in Huizinga's sense of the word) with the idea of what a society not based on avarice and the corruption of power might be like. More and Erasmus referred to such a place as *numquam*, no place, which it certainly was geographically and historically. It was rather a moral and intellectual perspective from which to view and criticize the decadence they saw infecting every stratum of the society in which they lived. Erasmus, in fact, in a letter to another prominent humanist reformer, Ulrich Von Hutten, wrote that far from constructing an ideal society, More was intent upon focussing attention on the widespread corruption of the times, particularly in the England which he knew so well. No one was more aware of More's intentions than Erasmus, who states unequivocally that More's objective was to point up those conditions that "occasion mischief in commonwealths, having the English constitution especially in view, which he so thoroughly knows and understands."

This call for reform, this dialectical exploration of some rather subversive ideas, was launched just prior to another reformer's attacks on what he too saw as widespread corruption. Martin Luther nailed his famous ninety-five theses to the door of the Wittenberg Cathedral one year after the publication of *Utopia*. The Lutheran revolt was not only a significant watershed in the history of Christianity; it was also a personal crisis for Thomas More, who must have responded with something like the words of T. S. Eliot's Prufrock: "That is not it at all,/That is not what I meant at all."

While the German monk's propositions were intended to be taken literally—and in fact were so taken—More's book was clearly not laying out a blueprint for an ideal state. The devices which More used to undercut the notion that *Utopia* was a model society are scattered throughout the work. The note of ambiguity is struck immediately in the title itself: *The Best State Of A commonwealth And The New Island of Utopia*. The insertion of that "and" (*deque* in the Latin) makes all the difference in the world, since it makes a distinction, however subtle, between "The Best Commonwealth" *and* "The New Island of Utopia." To claim that Utopia is *not* the perfect state based on that point alone would be frivolous. But the evidence becomes overwhelming in light of other statements in the book.

Prior to the opening of Book One, More provides a Utopian alphabet and then composes a quatrain in the Utopian vernacular, which translated, reads in part: "Ungrudgingly do I [the island of Utopia] share my benefits with others; unde-murringly do I adopt whatever is better from others." A commonwealth open to adopting "whatever is better from others" can hardly be described as the ideal society.

Then there is the matter of Raphael Hythlodaeus, whose personality is rigid, petulant, doctrinaire, unwilling to accommodate his philosophical concepts to the realities of history. And his is the voice, we must remember, which narrates Book Two, providing the detailed description of life on the fabulous island. Hythlodaeus' voice, to put it bluntly, is not More's. His name itself is a learned joke—Raphael meaning "the healing of God," and Hythlodaeus signifying "well-learned in nonsense." The audience for which More intended his book would certainly see this as a cue not to take what he says in a fundamentalist, literal fashion. Raphael too refers to the Utopians' willingness to learn from others: "You can see," he says at one point, "to what extent they capitalized on the chance arrival of a few of our people. . . . They immediately, from a single encounter, took over whatever useful discoveries we had made. . . . It is this willingness to learn, I feel, that accounts for their being better governed and happier than we are."

No reader can take seriously the proposal that the ostentatious, sumptuous display of gold and jewelry characteristic of European society could have been abolished by utilizing gold only for chamber pots and by using pearls and other precious jewels exclusively as playthings, toys, for children. It is richly ironic to recall that not many years after writing those words, the same Thomas More would be depicted in Holbeins famous portrait decked out in the magnificent robes and golden chain befitting his position as England's Lord Chancellor.

And finally the closing passage of *Utopia* clearly reinforces the spirit of irony and ambiguity which permeates the entire work:

> However, I knew that by this time he was tired of talking, and I questioned whether he would tolerate my voicing an opposite opinion. I also recalled his earlier expressed fear of censure from those who thought that finding fault in any proposal was a sign of wisdom. So

taking him by the hand and praising their way of life, and his account of it, I led him to dinner. I did say, however, that there would be another time for deeper thought on these matters and for further discussion. It is my sincere hope that this will be the case. In the meantime I must continue to hold my reservations concerning what he had to say. Yet I must admit that he is trustworthy as well as erudite and experienced. I readily admit that there is much in the Utopian commonwealth that I wish rather than expect to see realize in the cities of our own world.

And so the island which Erasmus and More referred to as *numquam*, *U-topos*, nowhere, is also referred to in one of the prefatory verses accompanying the early editions as *Eu-topia*, the happy land. Which of the Utopian customs and institutions are to be emulated and which are to be shunned? It is in the very nature of the genre More chose in which to explore his ideas—the dialogue form—to leave these questions open. And so those readers, for example, who are repelled by the Utopians' method of warfare, their imperialistic acquisition of underutilized territory, their totalitarian-like restrictions on travel by its citizens, need not, indeed cannot, conclude that these are planks in More's platform for a perfect society.

The author of *Utopia* was, in short, no Utopian. Although he coined the word *Utopia*, thereby providing a label for a huge and richly varied literary genre, he was not a utopian as the world patronizingly uses the term today—an idle, impractical dreamer who wastes his time on fantasies and unworkable schemes, an escapist who refuses to face the grim realities of the here and now. Perhaps that misunderstanding of More's term is the ultimate irony in the history of this superb ironist.

JAMES J. GREENE

Utopia

Introduction

Utopia is More's masterpiece. The country whose name means "no place" has over the centuries become the "everywhere" of humanistic hope for a society in which wisdom and justice prevail.

The two books of *Utopia* were written in reverse order: the second in 1515 while More was in Flanders on a mission for the king; the first a year later after he had returned to London. The first recounts More's meeting his humanist narrator Hythloday and contains Hythloday's reaction against England (and by extension, Europe) in the sixteenth century, where neither prudence nor justice reigns. The second—and to the modern reader easily the more interesting—describes the society that has made the adjective *Utopian* part of the English language. It is a society without private property and unemployment, a society that eschews aggressive war, punishes criminals sensibly, and has nothing but contempt for such arbitrary human values as foppish clothes, precious stones, and glittering gold. In Utopia, men value justice and share human work, cultivate learning and practice religious freedom. The odd thing is that it all makes sense; the reader may argue with details but, as he is carried along by the narrative, he more often than not agrees: This is what society should be like.

The Utopian world has not, of course, lacked critics. William Tyndale and John Foxe were two who would have agreed with Sir Thomas Smith when in 1583 he condemned all Utopias as "feigned commonwealths, such as never was nor never will be, vain imaginations, phantasies of philosophers." Not a few Roman Catholic commentators have been distressed by the central place given the pleasure principle in More's Platonic island. (A more sophisticated Catholic scholar, Edward Surtz, S.J., has ably exposed the superficial understanding that has given rise to this difficulty.)

Utopia has also had its more or less ideological misinterpreters. R. W. Chambers oversimplifies when he sees Utopia as purely pagan, a society of pure reason designed to bear witness against Christian Europe. The work is more complex—and more radical—than that. Karl Kautsky, on the other hand, conceives of *Utopia* in Marxist terms. In the process he divorces it from its own time and place, rendering it an essay in primitive socialism. The work is more complex—and less radical—than that.

John Ruskin's comment that *Utopia* is infinitely foolish and infinitely wise is more to the point. The work is simultaneously serious and playful, an essay in reform and an essay in literary elegance. More writes as a man of affairs who takes seriously, for example, his own involvement with the *de facto* society at which he levels his criticism; at the same time he can look with irony upon his criticism, as, for example, at the end of Book II when he confesses that he might well have presented many objections to Hythloday's Utopian vision.

This alternation—a concept already explored in the general Introduction—may well be useful as a key to reading *Utopia*. For this is above all an open and humanistic book, as J. H. Hexter's *More's "Utopia": The Biography of an Idea* admirably demonstrates. It is a reforming work that never loses its urbanity, an imaginative work grounded in realism, a serious work that communicates through wit. The one sure error in reading it is to do so in simplistic terms.

A NOTE ON THE TRANSLATION

Utopia was first printed at Louvain in 1516 and soon appeared in a new edition published in Paris (1517) and Basel (1518). It was translated into German in 1525, Italian in 1548, and French in 1550. It was not rendered into English until 1551.

The present translation is from the March 1518 edition. The translator has arrogated to himself certain privileges, one of them quite important. The C. G. Richards translation (1923), which reproduces quite skillfully More's Latin diction, has been slightly revised by Surtz and is readily available in the Yale edition. For this reason, the translator has felt free to attempt to capture the spirit of More's Latin—especially its relaxed, conversational tone—without at the same time reproducing its diction and syntax. Additional justification can be found in the fact that this volume reproduces a considerable selection from More's English works, which put the reader in direct touch with the author and his style. This relatively free approach will not, of course, please everyone. Nor should it. It does, however, add to the number of ways in which the modern reader can approach More's masterpiece. And that, surely, is what matters most.

JOHN P. DOLAN

Book I

Since the invincible Henry VIII of England, a king adorned
with all the princely virtues, had recently been involved in a
serious controversy with His Most Serene Highness, Charles V
of Spain, he sent me to Flanders to negotiate a settlement. My
colleague on this mission was the incomparable Cuthbert
Tunstall, who, to everyone's satisfaction, had recently been
appointed Master of the Rolls. I will not try to praise him, not
simply because the world would discount such praise from a
close friend, but because his fine qualities and learning defy
description. His fame is so widespread that praising him would
be, as they say, like lighting up the sun with a candle.

As previously arranged, the emperor's distinguished ambassadors, led by that outstanding man, the Margrave of Bruges,
met us in the city of Bruges. The real spokesman and leading
light of their group was, however, George de Theimsecke, the
Provost of Cassel, a man highly endowed by nature and by
learning, an expert in the law, and a negotiator whose innate
skill had been sharpened by long experience. After several
meetings had failed to produce any agreement, they left for
Brussels to consult with the emperor.

In the meantime, with free time on my hands, I proceeded
to Antwerp. Among those who visited me there, none was more
gracious than Peter Giles. A native of Antwerp, he was highly
respected, and rightly so, since he is deserving of the highest
honors one could bestow upon him. I know of no other young
man, in fact, whose learning and character surpass his. He is
the best and most cultivated of men, and completely honest
as well. To his friends he shows such affection, trust, and
sincerity that it would be hard to find anyone with whom to
compare him. No one is more modest and unpretentious. No
one so combines simplicity with prudence. His conversation
was so pleasant and at the same time inoffensive that its charm
helped me to forget my homesickness. At that time I had been
away from home for over four months.

One day after attending services in Notre Dame Church, by
far the most beautiful and well-attended in the city, I was about

to return to my quarters when I happened to see Peter talking
to a stranger, a man bent with age, with a weather-bitten,
bearded face, and clothed in a long coat that hung loosely from
his shoulders. From his appearance I judged him to be a sea-
man. When Peter saw me he approached and greeted me.
Before I could answer him, he took me aside and, indicating
the stranger, said, "Do you see that man? I was just about to
introduce you to him."

"For your sake, he would be very welcome," I replied.

"Yes," he answered, "and for his own sake, if you only knew
him. No man alive can tell you as much about unknown peoples
and places as he can. I know you'd be extremely interested in
hearing about these things."

"Then," I replied, "I was not wrong in sizing him up, since
I took him to be a man of the sea."

"No, you are quite mistaken," he said. "He has sailed, all
right, not as a Palinurus, but as a Ulysses, or better yet, as a
Plato. For this Raphael, whose surname is Hythloday, while
not unversed in Latin, is very proficient in Greek. He has
applied himself more to Greek than to Latin because he is
completely dedicated to the study of philosophy, and there is
nothing important in this area written in Latin but the writings
of Seneca and Cicero. So eager was he to see the world that
he divided his inheritance among his brothers back in his native
Portugal and joined Americus Vespucius on three of his four
voyages, accounts of which are now in everyone's hands. Hythloday was his constant companion until the last trip, when he
decided not to return. Instead, he prevailed upon Vespucius to
leave him with the twenty-four others who were to stay behind
in the farthest outpost of the expedition. For one more concerned with travel than with the tomb, being left behind in this
manner was a gratifying experience. He used to remark, in fact,
that the heavens cover one who has no grave, and that the way
to the great beyond is equidistant from all places, a fantasy that
would have been dearly paid for had not God favored him.
After Vespucius and the others had departed, he left the fort
with five companions and traveled through many regions until,
with amazing good luck, he arrived first in Ceylon and then
in Calcutta. Here he found some Portuguese ships and, contrary to everyone's expectations, made his way back home."

After Peter had related this to me, I thanked him for his
kindness in introducing me to a man whose conversation he
knew would please me. I then turned to meet Raphael and we
greeted each other, exchanging the usual amenities. All of us
then returned to my house, and seating ourselves on a moss-
covered bench in the garden, we began to talk.

Raphael told us that after the departure of Vespucius, he and his companions, through their blandishments and generally ingratiating behavior, gradually gained the good will of the natives. Not only were they safe from harm, but they actually achieved a certain familiarity with them. Even the chief (whose name and country now escape me) came to look upon them favorably and supplied them generously with whatever they needed. He also provided them with means of travel, rafts for the water and wagons for land, and he gave them a trusty guide who would introduce them to other rulers. During their long journey, he continued, they discovered many large, well-established cities and republics.

On both sides of the equator, however, lie vast, parched deserts almost as wide as the distance encompassed by the orbit of the sun. The landscape is depressingly desolate and wild. The land is inhabited by wild beasts and serpents and by men no less fierce and harmful. As one progresses, however, everything gradually improves. The air is less scorching, the earth greener, the beasts less ferocious. Finally one comes upon cities and towns where the inhabitants engage in commerce among themselves and with their neighbors and carry on both a land and sea trade with distant countries. From there it was possible for Raphael and his companions to visit other countries in any direction, and they were welcomed aboard every ship, regardless of its destination. Hythloday explained that the first ships that they saw were flat-bottomed, with sails woven of wicker reeds, or in some cases of leather. Later they came upon vessels with round keels and canvas sails, exactly like our own. Their sailors were expert navigators and astronomers. He related that these mariners were especially grateful to him for demonstrating the use of the compass, an instrument about which they had known nothing. Because of this ignorance they used to sail in great fear of the sea and trusted it only in summer. Now they place such faith in the compass that they have contempt for the winter, to the point of carelessness. There is now a danger that the instrument which they thought would bring them so much good may, because of their reckless lack of caution, actually bring about harm.

It would take too much time to explain everything that Raphael told us of his experiences, nor is it my intention to do so in this work. Perhaps in another place I will say more, especially about those things which might prove instructive, such as the institutions he observed among the civilized peoples he encountered. We carefully avoided questioning him about monsters, those creatures which are, in any case, hardly novelties these days. Rapacious Scyllas, Harpies, cannibals, and monsters of this type are found easily enough, but it is difficult to discover a people who are governed both wisely and well.

Although he mentioned many things that needed reforming among these peoples, he also recounted many others that might serve as models for improving our own cities and kingdoms. This question, as I have mentioned, will be dealt with in another place. My present intention is to treat only of what he told us about the customs and institutions of the Utopians. But first I must explain how we came to discuss that commonwealth.

Raphael next spoke with great wisdom about those things that needed correcting—and certainly there are many, both among us and in those far-off places. But he spoke too of the wise institutions he found among us as well as among the new nations, conversing as though he had spent his entire life there. Peter, for one, was quite fascinated by him.

"I am amazed, Raphael," he said, "that you have not entered the service of some king, since I know of no one who would not welcome you. For your learning and your wide experience in various places and among various peoples would not only entertain a monarch but force him to listen to your advice. In this way, you would not only serve your own interests but those of your friends as well."

"As for my friends," he replied, "I am not greatly concerned about them since I feel I have already fulfilled my obligations to them. While still in my prime I divided among my friends and relatives those possessions which others do not part with until they are old and sickly, and then only regretfully, since they can no longer hold on to them. I feel that my friends ought to be content with this display of kindness and not urge me to take service with some king for their sake and thus enter into a form of servitude."

"Well said," replied Peter, "but it was not my intention that you should enslave yourself. I was thinking rather of the service you could render to a ruler."

He answered, "I think we are quibbling over words."

"I don't see," replied Peter, "how else you can make yourself useful to a people—in their capacity as both private individuals and as citizens of a state. This would, furthermore, be precisely the way in which you could make yourself happier."

"Happier?" said Raphael. "Would a way of life which I find repellent make me happier? Now I live exactly as I please, a condition which I strongly suspect does not prevail among many who wear the purple. Actually there are so many who now seek the favor of the powerful that it will be no great loss if they are deprived of me and a few others who feel as I do."

To which I replied, "It is fairly obvious that you seek neither riches nor power. I value a man with such qualities as yours much more than I do those who now hold the reins of power. I feel, however, that you would be acting in keeping with your generous and philosophical nature if you would commit your talents and efforts to public affairs, even though this is distasteful to you. There is no better way to accomplish this than by joining the council of some great prince, some ruler whom you could persuade to act nobly and justly. I know you could do this if you were in such a position. The health or the sickness of the entire populace, after all, flows from the prince as from a perennial fountain. Your learning is so great that even without your experience you would be an exceptional adviser, and your experience is such that even if you had no learning the same would be true."

"Your mistake is twofold, my dear More," he said, "first with regard to me and secondly with regard to the matter at hand. I do not have those qualities you claim to find in me, and even if I did, the public would not benefit from the sacrifice of my leisure. In the first place, most princes are more interested in warfare, in which I have no experience or interest, than they are in the arts of peace. The acquisition of more territory by fair or foul means occupies them more than the wise administration of those they already possess. Furthermore, those who make up the council of kings are so wise—or at least they think they are—that they need no advice. They agree with and even flatter those who make the most absurd statements, hoping thereby to ingratiate themselves with those who surround the king. It is only natural, after all, that one should be flattered by his own ideas. Thus the crow is pleased with its offspring and the ape with his young.

"If, in such a group shot through with jealousy and envy, someone were to bring up something that he has either read about or experienced, the others would react to this as a threat to their reputation for wisdom. To avoid looking foolish, they feel compelled to demonstrate that others' opinions are always wrong. When everything else fails, they resort to the argument that such and such was good enough for their forefathers, whose wisdom and example we should imitate. Having said this, they act as if the affair had been settled and congratulate themselves on having exposed the pretender who claimed to be wiser than our ancestors. But yet these same men rarely see what really was excellent among the ideas and practices of the past, and whenever someone suggests that a particular thing might perhaps be done better than in former times, these men cling tenaciously to that past. I have seen these absurdly conceited prejudices in many places, and even once in England."

"Were you ever in England?" I asked.

"I was," he answered, "for several months. It was soon after the western rebellion, which was suppressed with such extreme cruelty. During my stay I was much indebted to the very reverend father, John Morton, Archbishop of Canterbury and Cardinal, a man, my dear Peter (and More will confirm this), no less respected for his authority than for his wisdom and virtue.

"He was of medium height, unbent by age, with an appearance that commanded respect rather than fear. His conversation was at once serious and relaxed. He often delighted in testing the character of those he dealt with by addressing them sharply yet harmlessly. He was delighted when they reacted with spirit and vigor to his prodding—as long as they didn't become impudent—since he felt at home with such qualities of mind. Men with such traits, he felt, make the best public servants. His speech was both eloquent and forceful. Well versed in the law, he also possessed an incomparably good mind and a prodigious memory. These natural gifts he had improved by study and experience. The king frequently consulted him, and a good many of the affairs of state seemed to depend upon him when I was there.

"While still young he left school for the court and devoted his entire life to public affairs. He survived the many ups and downs of political life, and through the various changes of fortune he acquired a political acumen not easily lost when gained the hard way, as he gained his.

"Once while at dinner with him, I met a skillful lawyer who praised the severity of the laws against thieves. Executions were so widespread that he had recently seen as many as twenty hanged from the same gibbet. In view of this he found it difficult to understand the continued prevalence of thievery. At this point I dared to speak out in the cardinal's presence, saying, 'This is not surprising since this way of punishing thieves is neither just in itself nor is it beneficial to the public. It is too severe a punishment for this crime. Neither does it serve as an effective deterrent. Simple theft is not such a grave crime that it demands capital punishment, nor does it really restrain a person who has no other means of livelihood. Not only you people but almost everyone in this world seems to imitate those bad schoolmasters who would rather punish their students than instruct them. Cruel and severe punishments are inflicted upon the thief when it would be much better to provide him with the means of making a living instead of forcing him out of sheer necessity to steal and then to die.'

"The lawyer replied, 'There is sufficient provision for this

situation; there are the mechanical arts and there is farming,
by which any man can make a living, unless he prefers crime.'

"At this point I said, 'You are not going to dodge the question
that way. Let us leave aside the problems posed by the wounded
veterans of civil and foreign wars, of the uprising in Cornwall,
and before that the French war. Disabled while serving their
country, these men are no longer able to follow their former
trades, nor are they young enough to learn new ones. These,
I say, we should leave out of our discussion, since wars are
extraordinary occurrences. Rather let us turn our attention to
what takes place every day. There is a large number of nobles
who, like drones, live idly on the labors of others and who
shave their tenants down to the very skin by increasing their
rents. This, incidentally, is the only frugality they display,
because they reduce themselves to begging by their other ex-
travagances. These nobles are surrounded by a large crowd of
idlers who have never bothered to learn a trade by which they
could support themselves. Then when the head of the household
dies, or when they themselves become ill, they are thrown out,
for the masters prefer to feed idlers rather than the sick. Frequently too the heir is not able to support as large a group as
his father had. Their only alternatives, consequently, are either
starving or stealing. What else can they do? When they have
worn out their clothes and ruined their health and then appear
with gaunt faces and torn garments, men of high standing do
not care to take them in. The farmers dare not do so for they
know that one who has been brought up in idleness and
pleasure and has been accustomed to strutting about armed
with sword and buckler, looking down his nose at the entire
neighborhood, would hardly be inclined to work with a shovel
and spade for a poor man for a small wage.'

"To this the lawyer replied, 'These people ought to be especially favored among us, for in time of war with their bravery
and high spirits, in contrast with the workers and farmers, they
form the very backbone of the army.'

"To this I answered, 'You might as well admit that we should
favor thieves because of wars, for you will never be lacking
in the former as long as you have the latter. For the two pro-
fessions are so closely related that thieves sometimes play the
role of brave soldiers and soldiers the role of industrious thieves.
The practice of keeping too many hangers-on is only too common among you and is widespread in other countries. France,
however, is afflicted with an even more troublesome pestilence,
for the entire kingdom is filled with mercenaries who are maintained in time of peace, if one can call it peace. The French
use the same argument you do to justify these lazy, idle hang-

ers-on. The so-called wise men insist that public safety requires that a strong army, preferably of veterans, be in constant readiness. Since they feel that inexperienced troops are not reliable, they sometimes even provoke wars in order to keep their soldiers and cutthroats in shape. They follow Sallust's maxim: The hand and spirit lose their vigor in idleness.

"'The French, however, have learned to their regret how dangerous it is to keep such beasts. What occurred in Rome, Carthage, Syria, and elsewhere also demonstrates the same thing; not only the governments, but the cities and fields of these countries were ruined by these standing armies. That this is not necessary is proved by the fact that the French, although they train their troops from an early age, did not distinguish themselves against your raw recruits. I won't flatter you by elaborating on that fact. But neither your urban nor rural workers seem to fear the idle followers of the nobility, unless, of course, their physical strength is not equal to their valor or unless their morale is broken by seeing their families lacking in life's necessities. There is, consequently, no danger that those once strong and robust (for our gentry corrupt only the elite) but now weakened by idleness and softened by womanish occupations—there is no danger that such persons would become effeminate if they were to be trained in some useful trade and exercised in manly labors. As things now stand, it certainly does not seem right to me that you maintain a large group in anticipation of a war, since there is no war unless you want one anyway. You should, in short, be more concerned with maintaining peace than with stirring up war. I do not believe, however, that the need to steal arises from this alone. There is another reason which is peculiarly English.'

"'What is that?' inquired the cardinal.

"'Your sheep,' I said. 'Once they were gentle and ate little, but now I hear that they have become so greedy and wild that they are devouring the human population. They devastate and depopulate fields, homes, and entire towns. For wherever in this kingdom they produce a softer, and therefore more expensive wool, the nobility, the gentry, and even the holy abbots are no longer content with the rents their predecessors were satisfied to increase. They are no longer content to live in splendid idleness, contributing nothing to society; they are actually bent upon harming the common good. They leave no land for tillage, enclose pastures, destroy houses, and level villages to the ground. Only the churches are left standing and these are used as sheep sheds. As if it were not bad enough that the amount of arable land has been gradually reduced by forests and game preserves, these same men have turned homes and fields into a desert. With a single hedge one insatiable glutton, like a plague on his country, can enclose thousands of acres. Some tenants are forced off their land by fraud or violence and others, worn out with indignities, must sell all their possessions.

" 'By such means these miserable people, men and women, husbands and wives, orphans, widows, parents with small children, families large rather than rich because of the demands of farming, are forced to leave their familiar hearths with no place to receive them. Their household goods, which would not bring a decent price even if they could await a prospective buyer, they are compelled to sell for little or nothing. As soon as what little they have is spent, what is left for them to do but steal? For which they will, justly no doubt, be hanged. And if they are caught at vagrancy and begging they will be imprisoned. Even though they are anxious to work, none will hire them. The lack of arable land renders impossible the type of work to which they are accustomed. One herdsman can take care of a flock of sheep grazing in an area that, if cultivated for grain, could support many people.

" 'For this same reason, the price of grain has gone up in many localities. Even the price of wool has risen so that many who were accustomed to making cloth are no longer able to purchase it, thus increasing unemployment. Since they began increasing the amount of grazing land, a plague has carried off innumerable sheep, as if God were avenging the avarice of the owners. Justice would have been better served had this happened to the owners themselves. And yet, the rising number of sheep does not bring a corresponding decline in the price. Although this does not constitute a monopoly, since one person does not control the sale, it is nevertheless an oligopoly. The few wealthy owners, since there is no competition or need, sell only when they are guaranteed the greatest profit. The price for other kinds of cattle is even higher because with so many farms destroyed and farmers ruined, there is no longer any breeding. The rich, who do not breed the cattle as they do the sheep, purchase scrawny animals from abroad at a low price, and after fattening them up in their pastures, sell them at exorbitant prices. As yet, however, the ill effects of this practice do not seem to be in evidence. They are scarce only in the areas where they are sold but when they are brought up faster than they can be bred, a shortage will occur in these areas and soon become widespread. Thus, the selfishness of a few will endanger your island, which appears to be especially blessed in this area.

" 'Furthermore, the high price of the crops entices the wealthy to evict as many as possible from their farms. And what, may I ask you, can they now do, except beg or even steal—for which they are more temperamentally suited. Sloth and wastefulness combine to make this destitution even worse. Not only the servants of the nobility, but even the craftsmen, the workers, and to some extent the farmers now indulge in flamboyant dress and gourmet dining. Take for example the disreputable eating places, the houses of prostitution, the taverns, the gambling, and the places of amusement. Is there any doubt that such diversions soon eat up their money and force them into robbery? Get rid of these evils and force those who have ruined the farms and villages to restore them or give them to those who will. Restrain these land-grabbing policies and the monopolistic practices of the rich. Bring fewer up in idleness. Restore agriculture and the manufacture of wool, and labor will be provided for those who have been compelled by their circumstances to a life of thieving. Indeed, unless you remedy these evils, any attempts to justify the severity of your laws against theft will be in vain. In spite of appearances they are neither just nor useful. If you permit people to be poorly educated, and allow their morals to be corrupted from a tender age, and then when they have reached adulthood, punish them for the very crimes for which this early training has prepared them, what else is this, I ask you, than making them thieves and then punishing them for it?'

"Before I finished speaking, the lawyer, typical of most men in his profession, began to prepare a rebuttal, more like a summation than an actual retort, since lawyers consider the memory as our chief faculty. He began by saying, 'You speak well for a stranger, but unfortunately your remarks are based more on hearsay than actual observation, as I shall presently prove to you. But first I shall enumerate in proper sequence what you have said. Then I shall point out your ignorance of the matter before us and, finally, I will break up all your arguments. Therefore, as I promised: four things, it seemed to me . . .'

" 'Hold your tongue!' said the cardinal, 'for if you begin this way we will be here all day. We will spare you the trouble of answering for the moment and postpone it until our next meeting which will be tomorrow if it is agreeable to both you and Raphael. Meanwhile, my dear Raphael,' he continued, 'I would like to know why you think that theft should not be punished by death, and what other punishment you propose would better serve the common good? Certainly you don't think that theft should go unpunished. Since death has been proved not to be a deterrent, what other power could restrain men from crime if they felt that their necks were safe? As I see it, any relaxation of the punishment would merely be an inducement to further crime.'

" 'It seems to me, most kind father,' I said, 'that it is extremely unjust to take a man's life for a little money. I cannot conceive any good results comparable with life itself that might accrue from such an act. If they say that the punishment is not because of the money, but because justice has been violated, then cannot extreme justice be considered extreme injury? Surely we shouldn't condone the death penalty. Nor should we follow the Stoic view, which makes no distinction in the gravity of crimes. To do so would be to consider purse-snatching equal to homicide, which has been condemned by God himself. For what reason, then, do we so facilely put a person to death who has stolen only a small amount of money? If human laws have so modified the command of God regarding killing that it rests on our discretion, what is to prevent similar legislation that would legalize prostitution, adultery, or perjury? God has not given man the right to deprive another, or even himself, of life. Would it not be placing human laws above God's law if men agreed by mutual consent to free themselves from the divine law forbidding homicide? This puts them in the position of determining the extent to which divine laws are binding. The Mosaic law is severe and, intended as it was for an enslaved and stubborn people, nevertheless punished theft with a fine rather than death. Let us not think that God in his new law of mercy, whereby he assumes the role of a father toward a son, has given us a broader license for eliminating one another. For these reasons I think it is illegal, and there is no one, in my opinion, who does not realize the need to make the punishment fit the crime. Will not the thief also murder his intended victim if he knows that the punishment will be the same in any event? As long as the punishment remains the same, there is greater security in murdering and greater hope of concealing the crime by disposing of the witnesses. Thus while we attempt to intimidate the thief with excessive cruelty, we actually incite him to kill the innocent.

" 'Why should we doubt the effectiveness of the method of punishment that was long used among the Romans, who were noted for their ability in matters of government? They condemned those convicted of major crimes to work in quarries and mines for the rest of their lives. As far as I am concerned, however, I prefer the type of punishment that I observed while traveling in Persia among what we call the Polylerites. They are a well-established nation, prudently governed and subject to their own laws except for an annual tribute they pay the king of Persia. Located some distance from the sea and almost completely surrounded, they are quite content with the fruitful products of their own country, and consequently have little trade with other nations. By long-established custom they do not pursue an expansionist policy, and protected by the mountains and the tribute they pay, they remain safe from invasions and the entanglements of war. They live in comfortable though not pretentious surroundings. Since they are content to pursue happiness rather than notoriety, I doubt that they are even known by name except by their closest neighbors. Anyone among them who is found guilty of theft is obliged to make restitution to the owner and not, as is the case elsewhere, to the ruler, who they think has no more right to the stolen object than the thief. In a case where the thing stolen no longer exists, restitution is made from an estimation of the value of the thief's property, the remainder of which is given to the thief's wife and children. Unless the theft was carried out with violence, those convicted are sentenced to serve in public work projects, but are not imprisoned or chained. Those who are indolent or simply refuse to work are whipped rather than chained; those who perform their tasks are not reprimanded. Only after roll call in the evening are they confined to their rooms.

" 'Except for assiduous labor, there is nothing burdensome in their lives. They are well provided for by the state out of the public fund, which varies depending upon the area where they are working. In some places they are supported by charity, which, because of the generous character of the people, proves to be more than ample. In certain places public revenues are set aside for them, and in other areas they are supported by a poll tax. In some cases they do not perform public work, but are selected from the marketplace and hired out on a daily basis, receiving a wage only slightly below that of the ordinary worker. If the hireling fails to earn his fee, he may be flogged.

" 'They are all dressed in the same color, their hair is closely cut above the ears but not shaved, and a small portion of each ear is cut off. Their friends are permitted to give them food, drink, and even clothing, provided, of course, the color matches. However, to give them money means death for both the prisoner and the donor. It is equally criminal to take money from slaves, who are likewise not allowed to handle weapons. In each region they are marked with a different sign and it is a capital offense for them to remove this brand, to leave their own district, or to communicate with a slave from another region. Planning escape is considered tantamount to escape itself and to aid in such a plan means death for the slave and servitude for the free man. Conversely, informers are rewarded, money for the free man and freedom for the slave, and for both pardon and immunity from any punishment. Thus it will always be safer to repent of an evil plan than to carry it out.

" 'Their humanity and practicality are plainly demonstrated by the prevailing law and order. It is their intent to eliminate crime and thereby save human lives. Criminals are treated in such a way that they see the necessity of good action and make amends for their past by persevering. So remote are the possibilities of slipping into their former ways that cross-country travelers prefer them as guides; changing them at the boundaries of each new district. Being unarmed, the slave would not have the means with which to carry out an intended robbery, and besides it is a crime for him to have any money in his possession. His clothes would set him off as a fugitive unless he fled naked and even then his clipped ear would give him away. Therefore, with no hope of escaping he would soon be arrested and punished. You might ask whether there is a possibility that the slaves would form a conspiracy against the government. This might present a danger, but since the success of such a plan would require communication between the slaves in various areas, which (as I pointed out earlier) is forbidden, the conspiracy would be doomed from the start. And who would take such a risk when there are so many advantages for those who might betray the secret? In addition there is always hope of being freed if they conduct themselves properly and indicate that they will improve their lives in the future. Each year a few are rewarded for their patience by being pardoned.'

"Having said all this, I added that I saw no reason why the same practice could not be adopted in England, and with much greater success than the justice advocated by the famous lawyer.

"The lawyer responded by saying that to do so would expose the state to the gravest danger. He then shook his head, bit his lip, and held his peace; and all of those who sat at his feet seemed to agree.

"The cardinal replied, 'It is not easy to predict the success of such a system, which has not been tried. The prince might suspend a death sentence in favor of this practice without, of course, the right of sanctuary. If it proved to be practical, then it could be established as law. Otherwise the execution would be carried out as before, since it would be no more unjust than if the man had been condemned when sentence was originally passed, and he would not be a source of danger. I think that it would be better if vagrants were treated in this way, also. Previously laws have been passed against them, but to no avail.'

"They eagerly approved of what the cardinal said, although they had rejected the same ideas when I presented them. This was particularly true of what he added about vagrants.

"I don't know whether I should tell you about what was

next said, since it was quite ridiculous. However, it was not really malicious and does pertain to the subject at hand.

"There was a certain hanger-on in the group who so desired to play the role of the fool that he actually appeared to be one. So dead were his attempts at humor that he was laughed at more than his jokes, though at times, it must be said, he did come up with something witty. As the old proverb goes, if you throw the dice often enough, you are bound to come up with a lucky roll. One of the group, then, spoke up, saying that as I had in my speech provided for the thieves, and the cardinal had taken care of the vagrants, it remained only to provide public care for the poor who could no longer be employed because of sickness or old age.

" 'Let me take care of that subject,' interrupted the fool, 'and I will see it through. There is no other type of person I would rather have out of my sight. As often as they have approached me with their pitiful pleas, not once have I given them a single cent. For either I have no intention of giving them anything or, when I am so inclined, I haven't the money to give. When they see me coming now they discreetly pass in silence, knowing that their efforts would be wasted on me. In fact they expect no more from me, by Hercules, than if I were a priest. I would recommend that a law be passed requiring that all vagrants be sent to monasteries, the men to the Benedictines to become lay brothers, and the women to be nuns.'

"The cardinal smiled, taking it as a joke, and the others reacted likewise. However, a certain friar, who was a theologian and by nature serious to the point of severity, was so taken up with what he heard about the priests and the monks that he began to laugh. 'You will never rid yourself of beggars unless you take care of us friars also,' he said.

" 'You have already been taken care of!' said the leech. 'The cardinal has included you in his proposal to force the vagrants to work. Certainly you must be the greatest vagrants of all.'

"When the group, their eyes fixed on the cardinal, saw that he took this in a humorous way, they too began to laugh, all except the friar. To no one's surprise he was so filled with indignation that he could not be constrained by the group. He denounced the man as a good-for-nothing, a detractor, a slanderer, and damned his soul, citing terrible threats from Scripture.

"Without delay the jester began to ridicule in earnest, as he was clearly on his own ground. 'Don't be angry, my dear friar,' he said, 'for the Scriptures say, "In patience shall you possess your souls." '

"In answer to this the friar said (and I quote him), 'I am

not angry, you gallows-bird, or at least I am not committing any sin, because the psalmist says, "Be angry and sin not." '

"Having been gently cautioned by the cardinal to compose himself, the friar replied, 'I spoke only out of zeal, my lord, as I am supposed to do. Holy men have always had great zeal, for thus it is said, "The zeal of thy house consumed me," and in church we sing: "Those who mocked Elisha for being bald, as he went to the house of God, felt the effects of his zeal." In this way perhaps this fool, this obscene detractor, shall feel it.'

" 'Perhaps you are acting with good intention,' replied the cardinal, 'but it seems to me that you would be wiser, if not holier, if you restrained yourself, so as not to get involved in a foolish argument with a fool.'

" 'No, my lord,' he answered, 'I could not possibly act more wisely, for Solomon himself, the wisest of all men, once said, "Answer a fool according to his folly." This is exactly what I am doing and I am showing him the pit into which he will fall unless he listens to me. For if the mockers felt the zeal of Elisha, who was only one bald man, how much more shall this detractor of friars feel it, among whom there are so many bald pates. In addition, we have a papal bull by which all who deride us are excommunicated.'

"When the cardinal saw that this discussion was not about to end, he nodded to the parasite to leave, and directed the conversation to another matter. Soon after, he rose from the table, and dismissing us, turned his attention to the affairs of his clients.

"I have burdened you, my dear More, with an awfully long story. This would have embarrassed me except that you were so anxious to hear it, and you appeared to listen as if you did not want to miss a word. I did not condense it, in order to illustrate that what I had to say was at first rejected by this group, and then, with an about face, completely accepted when proposed by the cardinal. They were so excessive in their flattery that they seriously accepted what he had only approved as the witticism of a jester. Now maybe you can understand how little value courtiers would place on either me or my advice."

"My dear Raphael," I replied, "you were so erudite that it was a pleasure to listen. As you spoke I seemed not only to be taken back to my own country, but also to relive my own youth in the pleasant company of that cardinal in whose court I was raised. Great as my affection is for you for other reasons, you will find it hard to believe how much it is increased by the manner in which you honor his memory. Nevertheless, I am still unable to change my opinion that if you could overcome your aversion to court life, you might be of great service to mankind through the advice you have to offer. There is nothing more incumbent upon you in fulfilling your duty as a good man. Your Plato thinks that the only happy republics will be those where philosophers are kings and kings philosophers. It is little wonder that we are so far from happiness when philosophers do not find it worthwhile to assist kings with their counsel."

To this Raphael replied, "They are not so ungrateful that they would not do this gladly. As a matter of fact, many have already done this through the books they have published. It remains only for those in high places to avail themselves of their good advice. There is little doubt that Plato foresaw that unless rulers took to philosophy themselves, they would not listen to the advice of philosophers. Instead they would remain under the influence of the evil doctrines that they had been exposed to since childhood. Plato experienced much the same thing at the court of Dionysius. Don't you think that if I were at the court of some king, and proposed reasonable laws, attempting to draw him over to my way of thinking, he would have me thrown out or expose me to ridicule?

"Imagine me at the court of the king of France. The king himself presides, while his wise counselors earnestly discuss methods and intrigues whereby he may retain Milan, and recover elusive Naples. After this, there are plans for the subjection of all Italy, Flanders, Brabant, Burgundy, and the other realms he has already planned to invade. One man advises an alliance with the Venetians as long as it is expedient, even going to the extent of sharing plans and spoils with them, the latter of course being retrieved when things go according to plan. Another advises the hiring of German mercenaries and the neutralization of the Swiss with cash payment. Another proposes propitiating the divine will of His Imperial Majesty with a votive offering of gold. Meanwhile, another suggests that peace should be concluded with the king of Aragon and Navarre. A further suggestion entangles the prince of Castile with the hope of a marriage alliance, while winning over some of his courtiers with a promise of pensions. The most difficult problem of all is the treatment of the English. A treaty of peace as strong as possible must be drawn up with them. For a weak society demands a particularly strong treaty. Although labeled friends, they must be suspected as enemies. The Scots must be constantly mobilized to attack them, even at the first sign of reneging. Also a certain exiled pretender to the throne of England must be given secret support (treaties prevent open action on this). This will bring pressure to bear on the English king and hold him to the treaty.

"Can you imagine a simple person like me standing in the midst of such turmoil, with so many great men planning how best to carry out a war, urging them to change their schemes, leave Italy alone and stay at home? France is large enough, with its bureaucratic government beyond the capacity of one man, without his trying to govern others. Suppose that I were to tell them about the great decree of the Achorians, who inhabit an island to the southwest of Utopia. Their king had inherited through marriage an ancient claim to another kingdom, and these people fought a war many years ago in an attempt to acquire it. Once having conquered it, they found keeping it no less a problem. The threat of internal revolt and outside invasion continually increased. Consequently, their new subjects were either fighting for or against them and the state was in a perpetual state of mobilization. Meanwhile, Achorians were bled white by the heavy taxes. Their money was being drained out of the kingdom and their blood shed for the small glory of foreigners. With little hope of peace there was a moral breakdown at home, as their lust for plunder and violence was confirmed. The laws were held in contempt since their king, distracted with the cares of two kingdoms, could not give proper attention to either of them. Realizing that the situation was only going to get worse, they held a conference and petitioned the king to choose between the two kingdoms. They declared that the nation was too large to be governed by half a king, just as no man was willing to share his mule-driver with another. Thus, this good king was forced to be content with the old kingdom and turned the other one over to a friend who, incidentally, was a short time later deposed.

"Imagine, finally, that I informed the council that because of these wars entire nations would be thrown into confusion, treasuries exhausted, the population destroyed, and that in the end bad luck might still frustrate the entire effort. Imagine that I informed the king that he should look after his own kingdom and improve it to the best of his ability, that he should love his own and be loved by them, that he should live in union with them, and govern them wisely, and not be allowed to govern other kingdoms when it happens that his own is already too large? What, my dear More, would be the reaction to such a proposal?"

"It would certainly not be favorable," I answered.

"Let's carry this a little further," he said, "by assuming that the counselors were together with the king devising a plan which would increase the treasury. One person suggests inflating the money when the king pays his debts and deflating it when he collects his revenues. Another recommends that, under the guise of a threat of war, money be extorted and then conclude a peace settlement. This of course the people would attribute to the piety of the prince, who has mercifully spared them the shedding of blood. Still another person suggests that old, long-forgotten laws be reenforced and fines imposed for their violation. No way of collecting money is more profitable and honorable than that which parades under the banner of justice. It is also proposed that laws be passed which forbid, under severe penalties, such activities which are not in the best interest of the people. Later, the king will suspend them, for a fee of course, thus making a double profit as well as pleasing the people. On the one hand he can impose severe fines on those who, out of a desire for profit, have broken them, and on the other, by selling licenses at an exorbitant price, he can create the impression that he is deeply concerned with the people's welfare, since he places such a huge sum as an obstacle to any exception to the law.

"Another counselor urges that judges be forced to pass only judgments favorable to the king. They should be called frequently to the royal court in order that the king may hear them argue cases affecting him. Thus, there will be no case, regardless of how blatantly unjust it is, that will be decided against him. Loopholes will be found to twist the truth, either through a love of argument, shame at appearing to agree, or desire to win the king's favor.

"Thus, while the judges argue among themselves, what was obviously a cut-and-dried case is now questioned, and sufficient reason is found for the king to step in and interpret the law to his advantage. The dissenting judges will be persuaded to concur, through either shame or fear, and the tribunal will hand down a decision upholding the king. It will be argued that equity supports his position, that the wording of the laws are on his side, or that there seems to be some ambiguity.

"In rendering their decision, the judges will follow the maxims of Crassus: The prince's gold is never sufficient, since he must support his army; a king does nothing unjustly even if he wants to; all property, including that of his subjects, belongs to the king; whatever property one does happen to possess comes through the king's kindness; the little that people are allowed should be kept to a minimum to insure the king's position, for wealth and freedom are an obstacle to the submissiveness of the people when confronted with an unjust law. Deprived of wealth, people are much more docile and less inclined to revolt against oppressive laws.

"Suppose that after this I should stand up and assert that such advice was both dishonorable and threatening to the king, since his honor and even his security depend more upon the people's wealth than on his own? Suppose further that I were to demonstrate that they choose the king for their own sake, not for his, that by his effort and endeavor they may live safely and free from injury? Therefore a prince should take care of the welfare of his subjects rather than his own. It is just like the duty of a shepherd, who, insofar as he is a shepherd, must place the good of the flock before his own. It would be a grave mistake to think that the poverty of the people is a safeguard of peace. Where do you find greater discord than among beggars? Who strive more to bring about changes than those who are least satisfied with their present status? Who is bolder in his haste to stir things up than one who has nothing to lose and everything to gain? If a king is so despised and hated by his subjects that there is no way to rule them but with abuse, plunder, and confiscation, which reduces them to begging, it would be better to abdicate his throne than to retain it by measures by which he keeps the name of power but loses majesty. It befits the royal dignity less to rule over beggars than over wealthy subjects. Fabricius, a man of upright and sublime spirit, claimed that he would prefer ruling rich men to being rich himself. Any ruler who is forever running after pleasure and amusement while those all about him are complaining and groaning is not a king, but a jailer. He is a poor physician indeed who cannot cure a patient without producing another ailment. A king who knows no other way to improve the lives of the citizens than by depriving them of the ordinary pleasures of life ought to confess his inability to govern free men. He must change either his laziness or his pride, for these vices are what cause the people to condemn and hate him. Let him live on his own income without harming anyone and limit his expenses to his revenue. Let him put a stop to crime and through proper laws prevent, rather than allow to increase, what he must later punish. Let him not heedlessly revive laws that custom has abrogated, especially when they are long forgotten or were never desired. Let him never confiscate property as a forfeit for a fine when a judge would regard a private citizen who did so as wicked and fraudulent.

"Here, suppose that I go on to tell the king and his advisers about the law of the Macarians, a race who live near Utopia. On the day he ascends the throne, the king is compelled to solemnly swear that he will never have more than a thousand pounds of gold in his treasury, or its equivalent in silver. This law was, they claim, enacted by a worthy king who was more concerned with the prosperity of his country than with his own wealth. Its purpose was to prevent his accumulating so much treasure that he would impoverish the people. He reasoned that this amount would be sufficient to suppress a rebellion against the king or a foreign invasion, but not enough to encourage the invasion of other territories. This last was the chief reason for the law. Another reason was that this provision would insure sufficient money to carry on daily business. When a king is obliged to pay from the public treasury whatever is received above the legal amount, he will avoid doing injustice to anyone. Such a king will be feared by evildoers and loved by the good. If I should force these and other similar views upon men strongly inclined to the contrary, how deaf would the listeners be?"

"Without a doubt, they would be very deaf," I replied. "Nor, by Hercules, does this surprise me. To be quite honest, it does not seem that you should make speeches of this sort, or offer this kind of advice, when you are certain it will not be considered. For how can such radical suggestions be useful, or influence the minds of those who are already committed to different ideas? Among friends in casual conversation this speculative philosophy is pleasant enough."

"That's just what I have been saying," he said. "There is no place for philosophers among kings."

"Yes, there is," I answered, "but not for that academic philosophy which fits everything neatly into place. There is, however, another, more sophisticated philosophy which accommodates itself to the scene at hand and acts its part with polish and finesse. It is this philosophy that you should use. Otherwise, it would be as if, while a comedy by Plautus were being acted, and the slaves were joking among themselves, you were suddenly to appear in a philosopher's garb and recite the passage from the *Octavia* where Seneca debates with Nero. Would it not be better to take a part without lines than confuse tragedy with comedy? You ruin and subvert a play when you introduce irrelevant material, even though the lines you brought be better. Give your best to whatever play is on stage and do not ruin it merely because something better leaps to mind.

"The same advice holds for the commonwealth and the councils of kings. You do not, simply because you are unable to uproot mistaken opinions and correct long-established ills, abandon the state altogether. In a storm you do not desert the ship because you are unable to control the winds. Nor should you, on the other hand, impose unwelcome advice upon people whom you know to be of opposite mind. You must try to use subtle and indirect means, insofar as it lies in your power. And what you cannot turn to good, you must make as little evil as possible. To have everything turn out well assumes that all men are good, and this is a situation that I do not expect to come about for many years."

"The only trouble with this approach," he said, "is that while I would tend to save others from insanity, I would myself become mad. If I wish to speak the truth, there are certain things that must be said. Whether the philosopher may utter lies, I do not know, but certainly it is not my way. Although what I have to say may seem out of place and irritating, I don't see why it should be considered absolutely absurd. If I should urge what Plato imagines in his *Republic,* or what actually obtains among the Utopians, conditions far superior to what I have described, then these might seem strange, for here property is owned privately, while in those places everything is in common. To be sure, what I have to say will displease those rushing in an opposite direction, since it calls them back and points out the dangers. Yet what is there in my speech that not only could not, but should not, be said anywhere?

"If we are to exclude as crude and absurd all that the perverse customs of mankind have found strange, we will have to conceal even among Christians most of what Christ taught. He wanted this to be shouted from the housetops rather than whispered. Most of his teachings are more at variance with our present way of life than what I have proposed in my discourse. However, I feel that the clever preachers have followed your advice, for when they find it difficult to adapt human morals to Christ's, they accommodate his norm to human standards. In reaching such a reconciliation they make the law of God a dead letter, with the apparent end result being that they become more deeply rooted in evil. This is as far as I could go among the advisers of kings, for either I would think differently than they, in which case they would have no use for me, or I would agree with them and be, as Terence's Mitio says, an aid to their madness. I see no value in your advice to take a subtle approach and to make the best of a situation by at least preventing it from going from bad to worse. There is no place here for concealing the truth and acquiescing. In such a case a man would be obliged to approve the worst advice and the most terrible decrees or run the risk of being accused of sedition and treason if he only grudgingly approved. Of what good is the person who has fallen among companions who are more apt to corrupt him than be corrected by him? He will either slip into their evil practices or, if he remains firm and innocent, be blamed for the malice and foolishness of the others. It can be seen, then, how remote the possibilities are of improving any situation by indirect methods.

"For this reason Plato, in a lovely simile, explained why wise men should not involve themselves in affairs of state. They see crowds who lack the sense to come in out of the rain but remain indoors themselves since they know that if they went out they would accomplish nothing other than getting wet. They cannot remedy the foolishness of others, but can at least save themselves.

"However, if I may be honest with you, my dear More, I don't believe that a republic can be prosperous or justly governed where there is private property and money is the measure of everything. Unless, of course, you feel that it is fair for the worst men to receive the best things, and that it is a sign of prosperity that everything be divided among a few, in which case even those few are not really well off when the rest live in misery.

"For this reason I turn our attention to the extremely prudent and sacred institutions of the Utopians. With the aid of only a few laws, they have organized things so well that virtue has its reward and from the goods of the community all are well provided for. As a contrary example, take those numerous nations that constantly pass new legislation yet never satisfactorily order their affairs. In them everyone calls whatever is in sight his private property but all the laws on the books are not sufficient to enable him to obtain, defend, or adequately distinguish what he considers as his very own from that of another. This fact is borne out by ever-increasing and seemingly endless litigations. Considering these things, I become more inclined to favor the opinion of Plato and admire his refusal to make laws for those who will not share their goods equally. Being the wisest of men, he readily foresaw that the common good was to be found in common property. Where property is held privately I do not see how the common good can be achieved when each individual, by various titles, accumulates as much as he can. A few rapacious and evil men divide everything among themselves, abandoning to poverty the rest of the masses who are generally more deserving. By virtue of their daily industry these simple and unpretentious men better serve the common good than themselves.

"It is my conviction that unless property in this sense be abolished, there can be no equitable distribution of wealth or any real happiness in the human condition. As long as this situation exists the largest and finest segment of society will be burdened with a heavy and inescapable weight of cares and anxieties. Although the burden may be alleviated somewhat, I maintain that it cannot be totally removed. Laws might be passed limiting the possession of land and money to specific amounts, or preventing the king from holding too much power and the populace from becoming too aggressive. Legislation might be enacted to prevent seeking after or selling offices or to lessen the financial burden of higher offices. Otherwise, those in office are tempted through fraud and theft to line their own pockets, and wealth rather than ability becomes the criterion for filling important positions. The effect of such legislation would be like the application of medicinal remedies to those whose sickness seems incurable. The treatment would lessen and mitigate the effects of the illness, but there is little hope of full recovery as long as one remains in complete control of his own property. While you attempt to cure one part, the sickness in other parts becomes worse. So the cure of one evil only produces another, since you cannot give something to one person without depriving another."

"I believe just the opposite," I said. "For men cannot live in harmony where everything is held in common. How can there be an abundance of everything where there is no incentive to work? The prospect of gain will not motivate them, and reliance on the industry of others will make them lazy. If men are stirred by want, and no one can legally protect what he has earned, would there not be constant slaughter and sedition, especially when respect for authority and public officials are taken away? I cannot imagine how there will be any authority among those who share all without distinction."

"It does not surprise me," said Raphael, "that you should come to this conclusion, since you have no idea, or a false one, of such a state. However, had you been with me in Utopia, where I lived for over five years observing the customs and institutions, you would have to admit that you had never seen a people so well ordered."

"You will have difficulty," said Peter Giles, "in persuading me that these people in that new land are better ordered than are we in our old world. For we are not lacking in ability and our government, I believe, is older than theirs. Long usage has provided us with much that makes for pleasant living, and we have discovered certain things by experience which no amount of mental effort could have produced."

"As to the antiquity of the states," answered Raphael, "you might have a better idea if you were to read the histories of this region, which, if they can be believed, indicate that they had cities before our land was inhabited. Advances by way of natural ability or chance discovery can be said to have taken place there as well as among us. Even though we certainly have surpassed them in natural ability, when it comes to effort and industry they leave us far behind. Except when a ship was wrecked off the island twelve hundred years ago, their records indicate that they heard nothing of the men beyond the equator —as they call us—until we landed there. A few surviving Romans and Egyptians were cast ashore and the islanders seized the opportunity to improve themselves. There was nothing of the useful arts and crafts of the Roman Empire that they did not learn from their shipwrecked guests, whether by direct questioning and explanation, or by reconstructing it with a few scraps of knowledge. You can see to what extent they capitalized on the chance arrival of a few of our people. If any from their country should have, by a similar accident, come here, it has been completely forgotten, as no doubt my having been there will be. Just as they immediately, from a single encounter, took over whatever useful discoveries we had made, so it will be a long time, I feel, before we accept any of their accomplishments which far surpass our own. It is this willingness to learn, I feel, that accounts for their being better governed and happier than we are, even though we surpass them in ingenuity and wealth."

"Then, my dear Raphael, I insist that you describe this island. Do not attempt to be brief, but explain in order, the fields, rivers, cities, people, customs, institutions, laws, and finally everything you think we should know. Spare us no details for you may assume that we want to know everything."

"There is nothing I would rather do," he said, "for it is on the tip of my tongue. However, it will require some leisure time."

"Let us dine first and then, afterward, we can arrange a convenient time," I said.

"As you wish," he replied, and so we proceeded to dinner.

Having eaten, we returned to the same place, seating ourselves on the same bench. Then, after giving orders to the servants that we not be disturbed, Peter Giles and I besought Raphael to carry out his promise. When he saw us eager and anxious to hear, he paused in deep thought for a few minutes and then began to speak in this way. . . .

Book II

The island of Utopia measures two hundred miles at its middle and widest part; most of it is not much narrower, except for the ends which gradually narrow as they turn toward each other. These ends, as if completing a curve of five hundred miles, give the entire island the appearance of a crescent moon. A channel flowing between these two horns of the island separates them by eleven miles and then spreads into a huge bay. Surrounded on all sides by land which protects it from the wind, the bay resembles a vast lake, quiet and tranquil. Thus, much of the bay is a harbor from which vessels have easy access to every part of the island (much to the advantage of the Utopians). The entrance to this harbor, with shallows on one side and rocks on the other, is terrifying. Almost in the center of this inlet, on the one rock that rises above the water, the Utopians have built a tower manned by a garrison. The other rocks are hidden and treacherous. Since the Utopians alone know the channels, it seldom happens that any foreigner penetrates to the inner coast without a Utopian pilot. Even these pilots would not be able to enter the harbor, without the aid of certain navigational marks on the shore. If these marks were shifted, the Utopians could easily lure an enemy fleet, no matter how well prepared, to destruction. Although there are many ports on the other side of the island, the coast is so well guarded by man-made or natural defenses that a few defenders would be able to repel an enormous force.

Utopia, however, was not always an island. Utopus (whose name is borne by the island which had been called Abraza) was responsible for the high level of civilization in which the people find themselves today. After taking possession of this land by conquest, he immediately commanded the removal of the fifteen-mile section of land joining the island to the continent. He forced the natives to do this work; but, to prevent them from thinking this labor shameful, he also commanded his own soldiers to assist them. Since the work was divided among such a large number, it was completed with incredible speed. The natives, who at the beginning had regarded the

53

work as vain folly, were now awe-struck at its successful completion.

Utopia has fifty-four spacious and noble cities, identical in language, customs, institutions, and law. Within the limits of their location, all have similar plans and sites. The cities are at least twenty-four miles apart, but none is so isolated that a traveler cannot walk from one city to the next in a day's time. Each year three elders from each city meet in Amaurot to decide questions of common interest to the island. Amaurot, because of its central location, is considered the leading city of Utopia. The fields assigned to each city are spacious, twenty miles or more on each side, and no city desires to increase its lands, as the Utopians regard themselves as cultivators rather than landlords of that which they possess.

Well-designed houses, stocked with farm tools, are found in every part of the countryside. Each citizen in his turn must reside there. Each country household has no less than forty men and women and two bondsmen. Two mature adults are responsible for each household, and every thirty households has one Philarch. Twenty persons from each household who have completed two years in the country return to the city every year and are replaced by an equal number of city dwellers who are taught by those who have been in the country for a year and are more expert in country life. These in turn teach others the next year. This is done because if all were new to farm life, the annual yield would suffer through their inexperience. This custom of changing the farm workers is carefully followed so that no one is forced to endure the strenuous country life for too long a time. Many Utopians, delighted by the study of country things, request more time at rural tasks.

These workers care for the land, feed the animals, and hew wood, which they transport to the city. They raise an immense number of chickens by a marvelous system: The hens do not sit on the eggs, because the Utopians incubate them by gentle heat and bring a great number to maturity. As soon as they hatch, the chicks identify humans with their mothers and follow them about.

Only a few high-spirited horses are bred, and the sole use of these is in training the Utopian youth in the art of horsemanship. Oxen alone are employed for the work of cultivating and hauling. Although the Utopians are aware that horses are more powerful, they appreciate the endurance and health of oxen. Also, oxen are cheaper, require less care and food, and when too old for work, they may be used for food.

Grain they use only for bread, and they drink wines made

from grapes, cider from apples and pears, and sometimes plain water. Often they distill honey or licorice, which they have in abundance. As a result of careful study, they know just how much grain a city and its surrounding district consumes. They sow more grain and raise more cattle than necessary for their own use, however, and share the rest with their neighbors. Whenever the country dwellers need things from the cities, they easily obtain these from the city magistrates without any monetary payments. One day each month many of them go to the city for a holiday. When harvest time draws near, the country Philarchs notify the city magistrates as to the number of helpers needed. These harvesters are there at the appointed time, and they are usually able to harvest the entire crop in one day.

THE CITIES: ESPECIALLY AMAUROT

To know one of their cities is to know them all; for they are completely alike insofar as the land allows. So I shall describe one of them—which one doesn't matter. But why choose a city other than Amaurot, as there is none more worthy, for it is the seat of the Utopian Senate. Also, I know it best, having lived there for five years.

Amaurot is situated on a gentle slope. It is almost rectangular in shape, about two miles wide beginning just below the crest of the hill and extending down to the Anydrus River. The side along the river is somewhat longer. The Anydrus rises from a small spring about eighty miles above Amaurot but is so swollen by streams running into it that it is almost a half-mile across as it passes the city. Soon it is wider still, and after sixty miles, it reaches the ocean. In the space between the city and the sea, and even six miles above the city, the swift river alternates between low- and flood-tide every six hours. When the sea enters the river for thirty miles, its waves fill the Anydrus and drive back the fresh water. The ocean pollutes the river with salt water a little beyond this point, but the fresh water glides unmixed past the city, and flooding back again, runs pure and unspoiled to the river's mouth.

The city is connected to the opposite bank of the river by a beautifully arched bridge of dressed stone, placed at the part of the city farthest up-river to enable ships to navigate the whole of the city unhindered. There is also another river, not as great, but very gentle and pleasing, which rises from the hill on which the city stands and flows through the middle of the city, finally mixing with the Anydrus. The Amaurotans have fortified the fount of this river (which springs up a short way outside the city) to prevent an enemy from diverting or spoiling the water supply of the city. This water is drawn by brick canals to the lower parts of the city. Where the slope of the land prevents this, they collect rain water in deep cisterns.

A high, wide wall girdles the city with many towers and bulwarks. The three sides of these fortifications are surrounded by a deep, thorn-filled ditch. On the remaining side the river itself serves as a moat.

The city streets are planned for carriage travel—they are at least twenty feet wide—and protected from the wind. The houses are very attractive and front on the streets in a long unbroken line. Behind the houses are spacious gardens, and each house has a door to the garden as well as one to the street. Since the two leaves of these doors open by a push of the hand, and close by themselves, anyone who wishes may enter. Nothing in their homes is private property, and the houses themselves are changed by lot every ten years. The Utopians place great value on their gardens in which they grow fruits, herbs, and flowers. These gardens are extremely well arranged and cared for, and I have never seen anything more suitable for the pleasure of the citizens. The founder of the republic seems to have had nothing for which he cared more than the gardens.

They attribute the planning of the entire city to Utopus himself. Utopus saw, however, that even a lifetime would not be enough to complete this work; and so he left its finishing to those who came after him. The chronicles of the island's history for the 1,760 years since its capture show that the buildings in the beginning were like peasant cottages, made of any wood at hand, with mud-spread walls and thatched roofs. Now all the buildings are well-designed, three stories high and finished with stone, cement, or brick. The flat roofs are covered with an inexpensive, fire-resistant plaster which surpasses lead in withstanding the elements. Glass is often used in the windows, but sometimes they dip linen in oil and use this as a window covering, as it admits more light and less wind.

THE MAGISTRATES

Each year a magistrate is elected by every thirty households and is called a Syphogrant (Philarch in their modern language). A Tranibore (Protophilarch) rules ten Syphogrants and their households.

The two hundred Syphogrants, sworn to vote for the most able, choose the prince by secret ballot from the four candidates selected by the people—one from each quarter of the city. The chief magistrate holds his office for life, unless it is suspected that he will become a tyrant. The Tranibore is elected yearly, as are the other magistrates. The Tranibores meet with the prince every third day to review state affairs and settle the few private disputes which arise. Each day two different citizens accompany the Syphogrants into the Senate, where all matters concerning the republic must be debated for three days before any policy may be decided. The Utopians consider it a capital offense to hold discussions outside the public committees or Senate. That restriction, it is said, is to prevent the prince and Tranibores, if they should succeed in suppressing the people by tyranny, from conspiring to change the nature of the republic. When anything of great importance is to be decided, it is referred to the council of the Syphogrants, who declare the proposal to their households, consult among themselves, and announce their decision to the Senate. At times a special question is placed before the whole island for a solution.

The Senate also has a custom of discussing nothing on the day it is proposed, waiting until the next meeting to take up the matter. The reason for this is to prevent anyone who blurts out an opinion from contriving reasons to support his rashness. They realize that some would sacrifice the public good to their own pride, attempting to defend their lack of foresight. In the Utopian Senate, the emphasis is on speaking wisely rather than quickly.

CRAFTS AND PROFESSIONS

Agriculture is the one art common to all, and all are educated in it from their youth by lessons both in the schools and in the fields; thus, their knowledge is practical as well as theoretical.

Besides agriculture, everyone is taught a particular skill of his own, usually the making of linen or woolen cloth, masonry, metalworking, or carpentry.

Their clothing is the same throughout the island, and by it the married are distinguished from the unmarried. Although the style does not change, their clothing is pleasing, flexible, and suitable for both summer and winter. Every household makes its own clothing. The men and women also learn another craft. The women, being weaker, practice the lighter crafts of working with wool and linen, while the heavier skills are exercised by the men. Everyone is usually trained in the craft of his father, since he is often inclined this way by environment. But if he desires to learn another skill, then his father and the magistrate see that he is assigned to a household specializing in that skill and headed by an honest householder. The same method is followed if anyone skilled in one art wishes to learn another. After he has learned both, he works at the one he wishes, unless the city has a greater need for one of his skills.

The principal task of the Syphogrants is to see that no one is idle and that everyone works diligently at his own craft. Still, no one should exhaust himself in continual labor from early morning until late at night as if he were a beast of burden. (This is far worse than slavery; yet, except among the Utopians, this is the life of the workers almost everywhere.) The Utopians labor only six hours out of the twenty-four: They work for three hours before noon, after dinner they rest for two hours, and then end their three hours' afternoon labor with an evening meal. They go to bed before eight o'clock and spend eight hours in sleep. Each one is allowed to use the time not given to work, sleep, and meals as he wishes. This time is not wasted in debauchery and sloth, because, freed from work and following the bent of their own minds, the Utopians employ themselves in other studies. Many spend these free periods in reading. It is a custom to have daily public lectures in the mornings, but only those who have chosen to follow studies are required to attend. A great number of men and women of all classes attend these lectures voluntarily, each attending the lecture which interests him most. Anyone wishing to devote his time to his own craft (as often happens with many who are not inclined toward the study of some liberal science) is not forbidden to do so and is praised as being of service to the common good.

After supper, they spend an hour in recreation—in summer in the gardens, in winter in the common halls. This recreation is usually music or conversation, as they are not acquainted with dicing or any of those silly and harmful games. They have two games which resemble our chess: one, a battle of numbers in which one number preys upon another; the other in which the virtues and vices fight in battle formation. This game shows very cleverly the strife which the vices have among themselves, and it makes clear which vices are opposed to which virtues, with what weapons they assail the virtues, and how they attack by secret maneuvers. One can also see how the virtues break the strength of the vices, how they evade the traps, and how they are victorious in the end.

To prevent misunderstanding, we must now look closely at one point: Since the Utopians work for only six hours, you might think that some lack of necessary goods would result. This time, however, not only suffices to supply all goods needed, but it even produces a surplus. This can be easily understood if you consider how many people in other countries are idle. First, almost none of the women produce goods, and this accounts for half the population. If any of the women are busy, the men are idle. To this number, add the priests and religious men—how great and idle a crowd they are. Then count all the rich, especially the lords of estates, whom the vulgar call gentlemen and nobles, and their black flock of swaggering hangers-on. Finally, the strong, healthy beggars hiding their idleness under a pretext of sickness. Surely, you will find that those whose labor produces those things used by men are much fewer than you at first thought. Ask yourself which of those workers are following necessary crafts. Indeed, where everything is measured by money, it follows that many unnecessary skills are practiced, serving only dissolute pleasure. If the supply of workers were busied at the arts which necessity demands, there would be such an abundance of needed goods that the prices would be almost too low for the craftsmen to live. But if all presently engaged in useless trades (as well as that whole crowd that now languish idle and slothful—any one of whom consumes as much as two workers) were relocated in useful occupations, you can easily see how little time would be required to supply all those things which either our necessity or convenience demands. Even if you add the requirement of a task which would be true and natural, there still would be an overabundance of goods.

The situation in Utopia makes this obvious to us: Less than five hundred men and women in each city who are able to work are exempted from labor. Among these are the Syphogrants, who, though exempted from labor by law, still work in order that their labor may encourage others to do the same. This immunity from labor is enjoyed by those whom the people, on the recommendation of the priests and a secret ballot of the Syphogrants, exempt for the pursuit of studies. If anyone fails to live up to expectations, he is returned to his craft. On the other hand, as often happens, a tradesman may study so zealously and diligently in his free hours that he is exempted from labor and promoted to the class of scholars. From this group are chosen the priests, legates, Tranibores, and even the prince himself (called Barzane—Ademus in the new language).

Since almost all are neither idle nor engaged in useless

business, it is easy to estimate how much good work can be done in a few hours. Besides, they also need less work in the necessary arts than other people. First, the construction and repair of buildings elsewhere requires the incessant labor of so many because the buildings of the father are allowed to deteriorate by the heirs, and the successor is forced to restore the building from the ground up at great cost. Indeed, it often happens that the heir, with his more aesthetic taste, spurns his father's house; it collapses in a short time, and he builds elsewhere at great expense. Since the Utopians have a well-ordered and established society, it is seldom that a new area must be selected for building. Both present and imminent defects in their buildings are remedied quickly, so that they last a long time and leave the builders with little to do. These builders, in the meantime, hew timber and square stones so that, when the need arises, homes can be built quickly from pre-formed materials.

Notice how little work they must do to produce their clothing! First, when at work they wear casual clothing made of leather, which lasts for seven years. When they appear in public, they cover this with a cloak—thus hiding their rude apparel. On the island all cloaks are of one color, a natural tone. Therefore, much less woolen cloth suffices, and the cloth that they use is inexpensive. Linen cloth is in wide use, since it requires little work to produce. The Utopians concern themselves only with the whiteness of their linen and the cleanness of their woolen cloth; they do not place any value on the fineness of the thread. In other lands, five woolen cloaks and five silk cloaks are needed by one man (for the delicate, ten of each are not enough). In Utopia, however, everyone is content with one cloak which often lasts two years. Really, there is no reason for wanting more than this; if a man had more than one, he would not be better protected or better dressed.

Since the Utopians concern themselves only with useful crafts, there is an abundant supply of all things. When they produce a surplus, they organize a large work-force to repair the public streets, and when this work is not necessary they publicly announce fewer hours of work for all. The magistrates do not force the citizens to do superfluous work, since the republic has always desired that all citizens should spend as much time as possible in cultural activities. For in this they think the happiness of life is to be found.

SOCIAL AND BUSINESS RELATIONS

Now I must explain the social structure, internal commerce, and system for the distribution of goods. Since the city is made up of households, most individuals live with blood relations. Married women join the household of the husbands; male children and grandchildren remain in their own households and must obey the eldest parent unless he is senile. In that case, the next oldest parent runs the household.

In order to stabilize the urban population, no city may exceed six thousand households (excepting those in the immediate district) and no household may include fewer than ten or more than sixteen adults. No limit is set on the number of children but the rule is easily kept by transferring those who increase the larger households to those with fewer children. If a city exceeds its maximum limits, households are transferred to smaller cities.

If the whole population grows beyond the capacity of the island to support it, they choose citizens from every city to plant a colony under their own laws on the nearby continent. The natives there have more land than they can use, so some of it lies fallow. The Utopians permit the natives to live in the colony if they wish, since their acceptance of Utopian laws and customs means they are easily assimilated, which benefits both peoples. The Utopian way of life makes the land fruitful enough for both groups, though previously it was too poor and barren for either. All natives who refuse to live under Utopian law are driven out of the colony and war is waged on the natives who resist. Utopians regard a war as just if it is waged to oust a people who refuse to allow vacant land to be used according to the very law of nature. If the population of a Utopian city declines so that it cannot be refilled from other parts of the island, then its population is restored to a normal level by re-emigrants from the colonies. They claim this has happened only twice in their history, both times from a great raging plague. Utopians would prefer that their colonies perish rather than that any of the cities of the island decay.

But let us return to the way the citizens live together. As I said before, the eldest parent rules each household. Wives serve their husbands, children their parents and generally, the younger serve the elder. Each city is divided into four equal sections and in the middle of each of these there is a marketplace with all kinds of provisions. The households bring together all their products at certain depots, which distribute the goods to their proper stores. The head of each household seeks what is needed from these stores and takes away the merchandise without paying money of any kind. For why should anything be denied him? There is an abundance of all products and no fear that any will take more than they need. Why would individuals take an excess, when they are assured that nothing will ever be lacking? The fear of being needy makes for greed in all kinds of animals, but in man alone pride makes him think it glorious to surpass all others in an extravagant show of material things. But this kind of vice has no place in the customs of Utopians.

Adjoining the storehouses I have just mentioned are food markets in which are displayed not only herbs, fruit, and bread, but also fish, meat, and fowl. These products have to be taken outside the city to places where they can be cleaned in running water. Slain cattle are brought for washing by bondsmen only. Utopians are never allowed to become accustomed to the slaughter of animals, because they fear that the habit of compassion, the most human affection of our nature, would perish little by little. Nothing dirty or unclean may be brought into the city which might pollute the air or spread disease.

Equidistant from each other throughout the city are spacious halls in which live the Syphogrants. Thirty households are assigned to take their meals in each hall. The stewards of the hall gather at the marketplace at a fixed hour to request the food allotted to their particular group.

First regard is for the sick who are cared for in public hospitals. Each city has four hospitals placed outside the walls, so spacious as to equal small cities in themselves. The sick are never crowded together so that they are uncomfortable or so that contagious diseases are allowed to spread. These hospitals are furnished with all the means to restore health, and such tender and tireless care is given with such expert doctors that no one refuses medical treatment there. Anyone in the whole city suffering from bad health would prefer the hospital to his own home. When the steward of the sick has received the foods prescribed by the doctors, then the best is distributed among the halls according to the numbers, except when some special attention is paid to the prince, Tranibores, legates, or strangers. The small number of visitors have certain well-constructed houses prepared for them.

The Syphograncy, except for those in hospitals or who lie at home, are called by the blare of a brass trumpet at fixed hours. After a satisfactory meal at the hall, no one is ever forbidden to take food home from the market, for no one would do this without reason. No one is forbidden to eat at home, but no one does so because it would not be honorable and it would be stupid to take the labor of preparing an inferior meal at home rather than eat one so splendid and rich at the neighboring hall. All dirty and difficult serving in the hall is left to the bondsmen. Only the women, taking turns, prepare the food and arrange the meals. The diners sit at three or more long tables; the men gathered on the side near the wall, the women on the outside. Thus, the women can attend their children without disturbing the others at their meal.

Nurses remain with breast-fed children in a designated room. There is always fire, clean water and also cradles in which to lay the infants. When the nurses wish, they can free the children from their swaddling clothes and refresh them with play. Each mother nurses her own child unless prevented by sickness. When that happens the wives of the Syphogrants quickly look for nurses, who are not difficult to find. For women who can nurse offer themselves willingly because they are praised highly and the children nursed look upon them as their mothers. All boys under five sit in the room with the nurses. All other minors younger than marriage age either serve the diners or look on in silence if they are not old enough to help. Children eat what is given to them from the tables and do not have any separate time for their meals.

The Syphogrant and his wife sit in the middle of the first table, which is raised and placed crossways in the dining room. Everyone thus falls under their gaze. The two oldest are placed with them, for they always sit four to a table. If there is a church in the neighborhood, the priest and his wife sit with the Syphogrant so that they preside together. People of different ages are mingled together so that the dignity of the elders and the reverence due them will inhibit the younger people from excessive behavior. The food is served first to the eldest and then to the rest equally. When the supply of something is not abundant, the eldest share with those sitting near them as they please. Thus, the honor of the elders is served, yet equal comfort comes to all.

They begin each dinner and supper by reading of conduct and morals, briefly so as not to bore. After this the elders engage in decent conversation omitting topics sad and unpleasant. They do not monopolize the conversation for they freely hear the young. Indeed, the young are encouraged to talk in order to give proof of the talents, which show themselves more easily during meals. Their dinners are short because of the work that follows, but their suppers are longer and followed only by sleep and quiet, which is thought conducive to healthy digestion. No meal passes without music and sweets are never missing from dessert. They burn incense and spray perfume in order to delight the diners. They believe that no pleasure should be forbidden if no harm follows. Though this is the way they live in the city, in the country those that live far from neighbors eat in their own homes. A rural household never lacks food, for the whole supply of the city comes from the country.

TRAVEL

If anyone wishes to see another city, or visit friends there, he easily obtains permission from the Syphogrants and Tranibores, unless good reason prevents. Utopians are allowed to travel in groups with a passport from the prince, which includes the day of return. A wagon and bondsman-driver is given them, but unless there are women in the group it will often be sent back as a burden. They take nothing with them on their journey, for they never lack anything, being at home everywhere. Anyone staying in a city for more than a day follows his craft there and is welcomed by his fellow craftsmen. If anyone leaves his district without permission or passport he is led back as a fugitive, treated with scorn, and sharply punished. A second such offense and he is bound into slavery.

An individual may travel through the fields belonging to his own city if he has his father's permission and his wife's consent. But no matter where in the countryside he is, he can obtain no food without having finished his work. Thus, citizens may go anywhere within the limits of their own city-district and still be as useful as if they were within the city.

So there is little opportunity for loitering and little pretext for laziness. There are no taverns, no brothels, no opportunities for corruption and no secret meeting-places. Since everyone sees everyone else, all necessarily perform their work or spend their time in decent leisure.

Since this is the ordinary way of life for the people, naturally an abundant supply of everything results. Since all share equally, no one is needy or must beg. In the Senate at Amaurot (to which, as I said, every city sends three men annually) they determine which districts have a surplus of goods and which are poor and then they transfer the excess from one district to the other. Nothing is charged the poor districts for this service and as each gets what it needs from the others, the whole island is treated as if it were one household.

After provision has been made for two years' supply of

goods (because of the uncertainty of next year's crops) their surplus of grain, honey, wool, lumber, dye stuffs, hides, wax, tallow, livestock, and leather is exported. One-seventh of their exports is given as a gift to the poor and the remainder sold at moderate prices. From their foreign commerce they bring back what they lack (mostly iron) and a great amount of gold and silver. Because of their many years of prosperity, few outsiders would believe the quantity of precious metals in Utopia. They need money so little today that most of their exports are used to build up credit. Commercial transactions are handled by the city, backed by public faith and credit. When debts are paid, the money is put into the city treasury. But demands for repayment are seldom made, for Utopians think it hardly just to take something that is needed away from someone.

However, if the Utopians need to make a loan to some other people or must support a war, they will demand their money. Only for this last reason do they maintain a large treasury at home, so that it will be a protection in extreme peril or sudden danger. The money is useful when they hire mercenaries (whom they use in battle rather than their own people), or attempt to buy off enemies, or cause trouble in the enemy camp.

Shame deters me from explaining how they keep a large treasury, since I fear no one will believe me. I realize that I would not have believed, unless I had seen it with my own eyes. For it seems almost inevitable that the more unfamiliar the information reported, the less it is believed. A wise observer, seeing that the rest of their customs are so different from ours, would not be surprised that their use of silver and gold is more adapted to their ways than ours.

They use no money themselves, but keep it in the treasury for emergencies so that, since it is there, it may never have to be used. They hold gold and silver among themselves, but do not value it more than their nature deserves. Who cannot see how inferior these metals are to iron? By Hercules, men could not live without iron any more than they could live without fire and water, while nature has not given to gold and silver any use that we could not easily forgo, if the stupidity of men had not put value on rarity. Indeed, like the most indulgent parent, nature has placed the best of everything out in the open, like fire, water, and the earth itself. Those things of vanity and no profit are hidden. If these metals were hidden in some tower, there might be some suspicion (foolish reasoning of a vulgar crowd) that the prince and Senate might attempt to deceive the people in order to profit themselves. If made into plate by skilled artisans, these metals might have to be melted down to pay for soldiers and men would be reluctant to give up objects of beauty they had begun to appreciate.

To prevent this, they thought out a solution as consonant with the rest of their customs as it is exceedingly abhorrent to ours (since precious metal is so valued by us and so diligently hoarded) that it would not be believed except by those who have been to Utopia. They eat and drink out of earthen and glass vessels, beautifully made but of small value. But they make chamber pots and other common vessels for both their dining halls and homes out of gold and silver. They make their chains and heavy fetters, used to restrain bondsmen, out of the same metals. Finally, they weigh down their criminals with heavy golden chains, collars, rings, and bands. While other peoples surrender these metals no more willingly than they would surrender their intestines, Utopians would feel small loss if all their gold and silver were snatched away.

They find pearls on their shores and diamonds and rubies on certain cliffs. When found (by chance, for they never search for them) the stones are cut and polished. They are given to children, who glory and take pride in such ornaments. But when the children have grown, they put these things away, along with their rattles, toys, and dolls, since only children have use for such trifles.

Utopian laws, so different from the rest of mankind's, have caused many diverse comments. I have never been so clearly aware of this as in the case of the Anemolian ambassadors. While I was at Amaurot, these men came to discuss matters of great weight, and so three citizens came to meet them from each city. All the legates of neighboring people who had landed before were experienced in the customs of Utopia, and understood that they did not hold sumptuous apparel in honor; since they knew that silk was despised and gold was considered shameful, they came dressed as modestly as possible. But the Anemolians, who lived a long distance away and had little contact with Utopia, heard of their simple clothing and concluded that the Utopians lacked the things they did not use. Being more proud than wise, they decided to dazzle the Utopians by presenting themselves like gods in gorgeous apparel. The ambassadors entered with a hundred servants, many in silk and all in various colors. The legates themselves, nobles in their own country, were in gold cloth with great collars, necklaces, gold earrings, gold rings on their fingers, weighted brooches on their caps, which flashed with pearls and gems. They were completely decorated with all those things which among the Utopians were reserved for slaves or children. It was worth the price of all their preparation to see how high they held their heads when they compared their ornate clothing with that of the Utopians who swarmed out into the streets. It was no less amusing to consider how far their hopes and expectations were shattered, how far they were from the stunned impression which they thought their passage would leave behind. In the eyes of the Utopians, except those who had traveled to other lands, the whole splendor of their clothing seemed shameful. The Utopians saluted the most commonly attired as lords, and they passed over the ambassadors themselves without honor, thinking them from their use of gold to be slaves. You should have seen the children, who had thrown away their gems and pearls, when they saw the caps of the legates. They began to nudge their mothers and say: "O mother, what a great silly fool uses pearls and gems as if he were a little boy."

But the mothers answered them seriously: "Be quiet, son. I think he is one of the ambassador's jesters."

Others found fault with the golden chains, pointing out that they were of no use since they were so thin that any slave might break them and flee whenever he wished.

It is true, though, that the legates' spirits subsided when they had been there for a day or so and had seen such a great amount of gold held in such low esteem. They saw it was as scorned in Utopia as it was honored among themselves and they noticed that the chains and fetters of one slave amounted to more than the gold on any three legates. After they became familiar with the Utopians and learned their customs and opinions, they put aside all that clothing in which they had arrogantly exalted themselves. Indeed, the Utopians marvel that a man who could look up at some star and even the sun itself could be so earthbound as to find delight in the dubious brilliance of a stone. They wonder that any man is so insane as to deem himself nobler on account of the fineness of his woolen threads, since a sheep once wore this same thread and was never anything but a sheep. They marvel that gold, which is by its nature so difficult to use, is now so esteemed by all people that man, whose use of gold gives it all of its value, is himself valued at much less than gold. They marvel that this is so even to the point that any blockhead who has no more intelligence than a post and is even more wicked than stupid, should nevertheless hold many wise and good men in bondage only because he happens to hold a great heap of golden coins. If luck or a legal trick (which no less than fortune affects all alike) transferred his coins to the lowest rascal of all his servants, he would submit himself as a servant to his onetime servant just as if he were a mere appendage to his money. They also marvel at and detest those who are insane enough to pay nearly divine honor to the rich, not because they owe them anything, or are in danger from them, but for no reason than that they are rich—and who do this even when they know that, while the despicable and avaricious rich live, not one piece of that great mass of money will come to them.

These and other opinions have taken root among the Utopians partly from their upbringing, since they were reared in that republic whose customs are so far removed from the stupidities of other nations, and partly from their education and reading. Even though there are not many in the city who are exempt from other labor and assigned to learning (that is, those who have shown from their childhood an extraordinary talent, excellent intelligence and inclination of the soul to the arts of the mind), nevertheless, all children are instructed in letters. The larger number of people, men and women alike, through their whole life devote hours free from labor to good reading. They learn the sciences in their own tongue, which is plentiful in words not unpleasing to the ear, and there is no other language more faithful in expressing their minds. This language pervades almost all that region of the world, but everywhere else it is more or less corrupted.

Before we arrived, the renown of all those philosophers whose names are celebrated in our world had never come to their attention. Still, in the sciences of music, logic, arithmetic, and geometry, they have found almost the same truths as these great men. Although they equal the ancients in almost everything else, they are still far behind in the recent discoveries of logic. For they have not invented even one rule of all those restrictions, amplifications, and suppositions most acutely excogitated in the little logic manuals which our children study everywhere. Moreover, second intentions are so far from their minds, though they have tried to investigate them, that, even when we pointed it out with our finger, none was able to see what is called man-in-common, which as you know is clearly colossal and greater than any giant. However, they are learned in astronomy. They have skillfully created models from which they have most exactly understood the motions and positions of the sun, moon, and other stars seen within their horizons. But they have not dreamed of ascribing friendship and enmity to the planets and of the whole imposture of divining from the stars. They do predict the rains, winds, and vicissitudes of the weather by signs whose meaning they have determined from long practice. As for cosmological studies and the nature of the tides, they follow our ancient philosophers. In this they constantly disagree among themselves as to the origin of things.

In moral philosophy their position is much the same as ours. They inquire into the qualities of the soul, the body, and the external world, without distinguishing whether good is characteristic of all these or an attribute only of the soul. Virtue and pleasure are treated, but the main controversy revolves around one question: Where is the felicity of man rooted and in how many ways is it manifested? Here, however, they seem too inclined to the school of thought which places human happiness in pleasure. It amazes me that they find support for such a soft doctrine in their religion, which is so somber. In discerning happiness they always base their philosophical reasoning on religious principles because, according to them, reason alone cannot grasp the nature of true happiness. These religious principles are as follows: The soul is immortal and is destined by the goodness of God for happiness, and in the afterlife virtue and good will be rewarded and sin punished. Although these principles are based upon religion, the Utopians nevertheless think that man should be compelled by reason to accept and submit to them. Should anyone reject these principles, his efforts would be considered foolish. Failure to avoid lesser pleasures that obstruct the greater brings only sorrow. They think it insane to follow a harsh and difficult virtue which demands putting aside the consolations of this life. For how can there be true enjoyment if you expect nothing after death? However, they do not pretend that happiness consists in every pleasure, but rather in what is good and decent. Virtue draws our nature to these as its highest good, though another school of thought feels that virtue is its own reward. The virtuous life is consonant with nature, as ordained by God himself. He follows the path of nature who allows reason to master his passions. Reason first enkindles in us mortals love and adoration of the Divine Majesty to whom we owe what we are and what we will ever be. Secondly, reason shows us the possibility of and excites in us the desire for leading a life that allows the least anxiety and the greatest happiness for ourselves, a life dedicated to mutual help. Although he may have pointed out the hardships involved, there was never anyone so scrupulous in virtue and disdainful of pleasure that he did not at the same time advocate alleviating the needs and sufferings of others. It is a humane practice to relieve the sufferings of others and, when their sadness is gone, to lead them to a life of pleasure. But why should not nature stimulate everyone to do the same for himself?

They reason that if a life of pleasure is not intrinsically evil, then advice to others should also be applied to oneself. Complete altruism is not required. When nature compels you to be good to others, this does not mean that you should humiliate yourself in the process. Consequently, they feel that nature has prescribed pleasure as the ultimate end of all our actions. They define virtue as living according to the dictates of nature. Furthermore, the nature of joyful living is such that a certain mutual sharing is necessary. It is an affair of the entire community. Nature warns you at the same time not to follow your own pleasure to the extent of making life unpleasant for others. They think that not only should the agreements entered into by private individuals be observed, but also the laws which the good prince has justly decreed. The common good determined by the populace must dictate the distribution of pleasurable goods. If these laws are not broken, all must promote the common welfare as well as their own interests. To rob others of the pleasures in life by an inordinate self-gratification is certainly an injury. On the other hand, what we generously give of our own to others, in a spirit of humanitarianism and kindness, is never more than what we receive in return. There is always recompense in the exchange of benefits. The satisfaction of giving and the memory of the love and good will of the beneficiary gives more pleasure than what is sacrificed in the effort. The soul that freely assents to religion holds that ultimately God repays this small and momentary pleasure with an immense and never-ending joy. So, after weighing the matter carefully, they claim that all our actions, including virtue, have pleasure as the ultimate end.

Pleasure they consider every physical and spiritual condition to which nature freely attracts them. It is not by chance that this appetite of nature is included in their notion of pleasure. For both the senses and right reason pursue that which is pleasing to nature and not that which tends to self-damage, or results in the less pleasurable, or in pain. So the Utopians claim that all those things which mortals vainly conspire to interpret as being pleasant, so long as they are beyond the bounds of nature, are deceptive. Once these false ideas have been accepted, they so occupy the whole soul with a false notion of pleasure as to leave no place for true and genuine delight. Thus pleasure in intrinsically evil things is often mistaken for the highest good.

Included among these pseudo-pleasure seekers are those whom I mentioned earlier, men who think that clothes make the man. These poor fellows err twice: They are no less deceived when they think their clothing better than when they think themselves to be so. When you consider the purpose of clothing, why should the finer thread of wool be superior to the coarser? Still, they carry their heads high as if they were especially endowed by nature and mistakenly think that something precious has come to them when actually they have been duped. So the honors which they would not have hoped for in a cheaper attire, they demand when they are more elegantly clothed. When they are slighted, they become indignant.

Is it not just as foolish to be so affected by vain and profitless honors? For what genuine pleasure does the curtsy or the bared head of another afford? Will they cure an arthritic knee or alleviate a headache? It is amazing how those who congratulate themselves on their so-called noble birth are absorbed in this fancied pleasure. They have been deceived into this belief because they happen to have been born of an ancestry that was simply a long series of rich men (for now there is no other nobility), especially those of the landed gentry. Yet, they think themselves no less noble when they have failed to inherit any money or have subsequently squandered their bequests.

Included in this group are those who, entranced by gems and precious stones, think themselves unique in discovering a rare one particularly prized by their contemporaries. It must be taken out of its golden setting so that it can be viewed in its pristine form. Moreover, the jeweler must guarantee that the stone is genuine, so solicitous are they that no imitation pass as a real one. Why should the sight of an imitation bring less pleasure when your eyes cannot distinguish between the two? A blind man could distinguish as well.

What of those who pile up superfluous wealth, without any really useful purpose? Is this not self-deception? What is to be said of those who go to the other extreme and hoard their gold, yet are filled with anxiety over its possible loss? For what is it other than a loss anyway, when by burying it in the ground they deprive not only others but also themselves of its use? Yet when they have buried their treasure, their hearts leap for joy like a soul that is already safe in heaven. But what if it were stolen and they were ignorant of the fact until ten years later? Would it make any difference? Whether the money was safe or not, one would still get the same profit from it.

To these foolish pleasures the Utopians add gambling (their knowledge of which is based on hearsay and not experience) and also hunting and fowling. What pleasure is there, they ask, in throwing dice on the table? If there were any pleasure initially, it would soon lose its fascination. How can the howling and barking dogs be pleasant to anyone's ears? Is the enjoyment greater when the dog pursues the hare rather than another dog? For the same action occurs in both instances if running appeals to you. But if it is blood lust that compels you to witness the slaughter of a harmless hare, would not mercy be more humane? The Utopians have rejected hunting as unbecoming a freeman. Butchering, as I have said before, they leave to the bondsmen. They insist that hunting is the lowest form of butchery, and kill animals only when forced by necessity. It is thought that pleasure in observing death either arises from a naturally cruel disposition or results from imperviousness to brutality. Thus the Utopians feel that, although hunting and the other sports of this kind may please the mob, there is nothing really pleasant in their nature. Although to the world at large these actions—and countless other ones like them— have a certain pleasurable appeal, the Utopians find it revolting. For perverse habit and not the nature of the thing itself causes the pleasure. This vice occurs when the bitter is exchanged for the sweet, as when a pregnant woman thinks that pitch and tallow are sweeter than honey to her tainted palate. Still, a judgment distorted by such an attitude or custom cannot change the nature of pleasure.

The Utopians point out that true pleasure is divided into various kinds. Some they attribute to the soul and others to the body. To the soul they assign intelligence and the satisfaction that comes from the contemplation of truth. To this they add the sweet memory of a life well spent and the hope of a good future. They separate the pleasures of the body into two classes, the first of which floods the senses with its transparent sweetness. Sometimes this happens in the restoration by food and drink of the organs which the natural heat within us has exhausted. Other times this occurs when the body rejects a surplus, as in the case of bowel movements, sexual orgasm, or common scratching. Other pleasures they identify neither with the sating of appetites nor the alleviation of pressure but with a certain delectable inner movement. Music they place in this category.

The other kind of physical pleasure occurs when the body is in a state of quiescence or equilibrium; that is, when its health is not affected by disease. If nothing painful exerts itself, health takes delight in itself, even though no external pleasure is applied. In spite of the fact that it calls less attention to itself and offers less to the senses than do eating or drinking, many still take health for the greatest pleasure. Almost all Utopians admit it is the foundation for all the rest, so that even in and of itself it can make our life placid and tranquil. Once health is lost, however, all other pleasure ceases. They say that unless health is present, the mere absence of pain is stupor rather than genuine pleasure. They have long rejected the opinion that robust health cannot be considered a pleasure since its presence cannot be felt except by contrast.

But against this opinion, they seem generally to agree that health occupies the first place among all pleasures. They argue that just as in sickness there is pain (which is as implacable an enemy to pleasure as sickness to health) so in health there should be pleasure. They do not distinguish between sickness and pain; the results are the same. For whether health is pleasure in itself or brings pleasure in the same way that fire generates heat, in either case where health is present, pleasure cannot be absent. Furthermore, when we experience hunger what else is it but health demanding food to satisfy this desire? As we gradually regain strength, the ensuing revival is nothing else but pleasure. So should not health, which delighted in the conflict, rejoice when victory has been won? Is there not a consciousness of victory in that which is pleasurable? They reject as sheer nonsense the claim that health cannot be felt. For what man, when he is awake, does not sense his healthy condition, unless he is ill? Who is so sunk in stupor or lethargy that he does not admit the pleasure of being healthy and vigorous? What else is this but pleasure?

The Utopians give priority to the pleasures of the soul, for they consider these the basis of all the others. They feel that most of these pleasures arise from the practice of virtue and the consciousness of a good life. Among physical pleasures, health holds first place. They contend that the satisfaction of eating and drinking or similar pleasures should not be sought except for the sake of health. For such things are pleasant in themselves only insofar as they help maintain health.

Just as no one seeks medicine for its own sake, so the prevention of sickness cannot be considered a pleasure. Otherwise, one would find happiness in constant hunger, thirst, and itching. It is evident that such a life is not only disgusting but miserable. Indeed, these are the lowest kinds of pleasure, being the least unmixed, since they never occur unless joined by their corresponding pains. For to the pleasure of eating there is united hunger, and not on an equal scale. Just as the pain is more intense, so it lasts longer. Preceding pleasure, it does not terminate except in the common death of pleasure.

Such pleasures, they feel, are to be valued only so far as necessity demands. Still, they enjoy these things and gratefully acknowledge the leniency of mother nature, who coaxes her little children to what is needed. How tedious life would be if, as with other rare diseases, the daily sickness of hunger and thirst had to be driven off by potions and bitter drugs.

Beauty, strength, and agility—these they willingly cherish as the proper and pleasing gifts of nature. The pleasures of the five senses, which in man offer something beyond the mere sustaining of life, they value in aesthetic terms. In all matters they follow a definite standard of values. But they certainly consider it ridiculous to condemn comeliness of form, to dissipate one's strength, to change agility into sluggishness, to exhaust the body with penance, to injure health, and to reject all the other demands of nature. In the case where a person exhausts himself for the public good they make an exception since an eternal reward is anticipated. But they regard as cruelly unnatural and insane anyone who afflicts himself with hardships to achieve a dubious reputation for virtue or to strengthen himself against uncertain future adversity.

This is their view of virtue and pleasure: The ultimate truth attained by human reason must be aided by revelation to find a better. Whether they are right in this, time does not permit us to examine, nor is it necessary to do so; for we have only undertaken to describe the structure of their lives, and not to defend it.

Still, I am convinced that whatever validity the Utopians' ideas may have, there never was a more outstanding people or a happier commonwealth. They are agile and sprightly in body, of greater strength than their stature indicates, yet not underdeveloped. Even if their soil is not especially fertile nor their climate very healthy, yet they guard themselves against the atmosphere with such temperate living, and improve their land by such industry, that nowhere are the bodies of men more supple and subject to fewer diseases. Not only are they adept in the ordinary practice of agriculture, but in some cases they transplant entire forests. The reason for this is not to increase supply but to facilitate transport, that they might have the wood nearer to the sea, the rivers, or the cities themselves. For it is less work to carry grain than wood for a long distance on land. The people are easygoing, good tempered, creative, fond of leisure, but prepared for physical labor when need demands. They are tireless in the pursuit of knowledge.

When they had heard from us of the literature and sciences of the Greeks (besides the poets and the historians there was nothing of the Latins which was likely to be of any interest) it was wonderful how zealously they sought permission to master them from our own instruction. At first we began by reading at great length, so that we would not appear to refuse the labor, though we had little hope that there would be any benefit for them. But their diligence soon showed us that our efforts would not be in vain. It was almost miraculous how fast they learned the alphabet, the pronunciation of words, and were able to commit to memory what they had learned. No doubt, it was because most of them were scholars of the highest rank. They had undertaken the task, urged by their own inclination, as well as by order of the Senate. In less than three years there was no phase of the language in which they were not well versed, and their recitations of the authors were flawless wherever the text allowed.

Indeed, I surmised that they grasped the Greek language more easily because it was somewhat related to their own. I suspect that the people originally came from Greece, because their language, in other ways almost Persian, preserved traces of some Greek words in the names of their cities and magistrates. I had stowed a rather good-sized bundle of books on board in place of merchandise when I sailed on my fourth voyage since I had decided never to return for a merely brief stay. So they received from me most of Plato's works and many of Aristotle's as well, not to mention the volume on plants by Theophrastus, which I am sorry to say was mutilated in part. For while we were sailing, it was left about rather carelessly and a playful monkey jumped on the book and mischievously tore out some of the pages here and there by ripping them with his teeth. Of the grammarians they have only Lascaris, for I had not brought Theodorus with me, nor any dictionaries except Hesychius and Dioscorides. They consider Plutarch's books quite charming, and were captivated by the clever sayings and wit of Lucian. Of the poets they have Aristophanes, Homer, and Euripides, and also Sophocles in the small print of the Aldine press. Among the historians they have Thucydides, Herodotus, and Herodian. My companion Tricius Apinatus carried with him some small works of Hippocrates on medicine and the *Microtechnes* of Galen, which they hold in great esteem. Indeed, while they need the science of medicine the least of all people, medicine is nowhere held in greater honor, for they number the knowledge of it among the most beautiful and useful parts of philosophy. When they scrutinize the secrets of nature by the help of philosophy, it seems to them that they not only receive an admirable pleasure from it but also enter into the favor of its Author and Maker. They think that he in the manner of other architects has exposed the visible machine of this world to be looked at by man whom alone he enables to grasp such an excellent thing. So he holds dearer to himself the curious and attentive observer and admirer of his works rather than him who, like an irrational animal, stupidly neglects so great and so wonderful a spectacle.

The natural genius of the Utopians, given direction by their

learning, is wonderfully conditioned for all those inventions
of man's ingenuity which bring some new advantage to the
good life. Still, they owe to us two things, printing and the
making of paper. When we showed them the pages of books
impressed with the Aldine letters and spoke about the material
for making paper and the art of printing those letters, we described more than we could explain. Yet, on their own, they
immediately grasped the entire process. Although previously
they had only written on parchment, bark or papyrus, now they
attempted to make paper and print letters. However, at first
things did not go well, but by experimentation they soon
mastered both. They have succeeded so well that if there were
copies of the Greeks available, no books would be lacking.
But now they have nothing more than those that they received
from me, in spite of which they have published thousands of
copies.

They receive with open hearts and minds any travelers who
have acquired a knowledge of distant places and things. It was
for this reason that we were so gratefully received. However,
it might be mentioned that they do not have many traders
stopping off. For what can traders bring to Utopia except
iron—unless gold and silver, which they would rather take
home than bring to the Utopians! They also have a prudent
policy stipulating that all exports be carried in their own ships.
Because of this they have become great explorers, thus preserving their maritime prowess.

SLAVERY

They do not make slaves of prisoners of war, unless captured by themselves, nor of the sons of slaves, nor finally of
those who had been in slavery when acquired from some other
people. Among themselves, they enslave those guilty of vicious
crimes, or (as is more often the case) those in other countries
sentenced to death for some atrocity. Of these they have many
whom they bought for a low price. Often, they simply ask for
them and bring them back without charge. This class of bonds-
man they not only keep in continual work, but also enchained.
In the case of local criminals, the treatment is more harsh.
They consider them deplorable and their punishment a deterrent to further crime. Although excellently instructed in virtue
by a superior education, they still could not be restrained from
crime. There is another kind of slave, occasionally a common
servant of another people, poor and heavily burdened with
labor, who chooses of his own free will to serve among the
Utopians. If any of them should wish to return (which is

seldom the case) they are not held against their will or sent away empty-handed. Except for imposing a little more work on them, since by background they are more suited to labor, they treat them as well as their own citizens.

They care for the sick with great affection, as I have mentioned, and omit nothing by which these can be restored to health, either by way of medicine or special diet. They console the incurably ill by sitting and talking with them and by alleviating whatever pain they can. Should life become unbearable for these incurables, the magistrates and priests do not hesitate to prescribe euthanasia. Since the priests are looked upon as the interpreters of God, this is considered a pious and holy deed. When the sick have been persuaded of this, they end their lives willingly either by starvation or drugs that dissolve their lives without any sensation of death. Still, the Utopians do not do away with anyone without his permission, nor lessen any of their duties to him. They are convinced that in acting in this manner, they have acquitted themselves honorably. But anyone who inflicts death upon himself when his cause is not approved by the priests and the Senate, is considered worthy neither of the earth nor of fire, but is cast unburied into some stinking marsh.

Women do not marry before the age of eighteen, and men, not until twenty-two. If a man or a woman is convicted of illicit intercourse before marriage, he or she is gravely punished— they are never allowed to marry unless they are pardoned by the prince. Both the father and mother of the individuals involved suffer great infamy since they have failed to instill in their children a proper set of values. The crime is punished this severely because they realize that unless people were restrained from promiscuous relations, few would come together in conjugal love. Marriage is permanent; its trials must be borne for a lifetime.

Moreover, in choosing wives, they seriously and strictly observe a practice which at first seemed to us most improper and ridiculous. A worthy and decent matron presents the woman, virgin or widow, naked to her suitor; in turn, some upright man shows the suitor naked to the woman. When we laughed at this custom and dismissed it as foolish, they, on the contrary, wondered at the extraordinary stupidity of all other nations. For in buying a colt, where only a little money is involved, men are so cautious that, although it is already almost bare, they will refuse to buy until they not only take the saddle off, but also remove the trappings lest some defect be hidden. But in choosing a wife who is to be a companion for a whole life in good times and bad, they act so carelessly when they judge the whole woman from her face (for the rest of the body is covered by clothing) and marry her with the risk of living together badly. For not all men are wise enough to consider a woman's behavior alone; even in the wives of the wise, physical endowments offer no little addition to the virtues of the soul. Surely, some foul deformity could hide under these wrappings and immediately alienate a man's mind from his wife after it is too late to be separated corporally from her. If by chance such deformity arises after the marriage is contracted, it is then necessary that each one bear his lot. So before marriage, lest a man be deceived by some guile, he should be protected by law. This precaution must be taken because the Utopians are the only ones in that part of the world who are content with a single spouse. Marriage among them is rarely dissolved except by death, unless adultery is at issue, or some troublesome disposition that can no longer be borne. The one offended is allowed to change mates; the other party is looked upon as infamous and bound to the celibate life forever. They will not permit in any way the repudiation of an unwilling spouse in whom there is no blame, simply because some calamity of the body has occurred. For they judge it to be cruel to desert anyone when he needs consolation most; and especially to act with weak and uncertain fidelity at the time of old age, which brings sickness and is in itself a sickness. Sometimes it happens that a married couple who are incompatible find others with whom they can live more sweetly, and after willingly separating, contract new marriages. Yet, this cannot be done without the sanction of the Senate, which does not permit divorce until the senators and their wives have diligently examined the case. Indeed, they do not allow this easily, since they know that there is little hope in reconciling the two involved if they have before them the prospect of a new marriage.

People who violate the marriage bond are punished with the most burdensome slavery. If both are married, those who have suffered the injury, after they have repudiated the spouse in adultery, may if they wish be married to each other, or to anyone whom they find pleasing. But if the injured party persists in the love of such an evil, undeserving spouse, the marriage may continue undissolved, provided this one is willing to follow the other in the work of the condemned. Occasionally it happens that the repentance of the one and the dutiful zeal of the other move the prince to compassion, and he grants them their liberty again. But if the guilty one relapses into the same crime, he is punished with death.

As regards other crimes, there is no prescribed penalty;

rather, the Senate decides the type of punishment on the basis of the gravity of the crime. Husbands punish their wives and parents punish their children unless the crime is such that a public punishment would benefit public morality. Most serious crimes are punished with slavery. This is felt more advantageous to the public good and less distasteful to the criminal than his immediate destruction or removal. Enforced labor is far more profitable than execution of the criminal and it further deters others from crime. However, if the criminals remain recalcitrant, they are executed as incorrigible. This does not mean that prisoners remain in a hopeless state. If after a long period of probation, they indicate that the punishment is more an evil than their crime, their imprisonment is shortened by the authority of the prince or by popular vote. To induce someone to sin is considered equal to the actual performance of the crime. In all criminal cases, an attempted crime is equal to a committed crime.

They take great delight in fools, but it is considered thoughtless to ridicule the fool, yet it is permissible to get pleasure from his foolishness. This foolishness they feel is beneficial to the fool as well as to others, and they do not entrust a fool to anyone who is not moved to laughter by his antics. Ridicule of a deformed or mutilated person reflects on the person who ridicules, as he thoughtlessly reproaches as a failing something that the man could not possibly help.

Whereas the failure to guard one's natural beauty is looked upon as indolence, the Utopians consider the use of cosmetics an affectation. They realize that in a wife virtuous living is to be valued more than physical appearance, for they know from experience that, although beauty captivates, it does not hold.

In addition to discouraging crime through punishment, they encourage good citizenship through public recognition, placing statues of famous citizens in public places. They both glorify them and incite others to follow their example. Anyone aspiring to office is discouraged from campaigning. The magistrates live together in common accord. They are willingly paid honors that they do not seek or demand. The prince is not known by his apparel, but only by a little handful of grain carried before him. Similarly, the high priest is recognized by a candle-bearer who proceeds him.

Since they are such a well-educated society, few laws are required. Their disapproval of others is based primarily on inability to govern themselves with a multiplicity of laws. It is thought criminal to be governed by laws too numerous to be read and too obscure to be understood. They exclude from their country absolutely all lawyers since these plead cases with cunning and slyly dispute the laws. They believe that every man should be able to plead his own cause and tell the judge what he would have told his lawyer. The truth prevails, they feel, when the case is not confused by lawyers' tricks. In this way, the judge is also unencumbered in his role as arbiter and can help the unsophisticated against the crafty. The accumulation of laws elsewhere makes this an impossibility. In Utopia, however, all excel in legal knowledge. With very few laws, they easily arrive at an interpretation which is obviously the most just. Since all law is promulgated in order to remind people of their duties, a subtle interpretation would go beyond the masses and fail in its purpose. Since law is aimed at the majority of the people, there would be no difference between having no laws and having ones too complicated to understand. The common people have neither the time nor the training to comprehend a set of complicated laws.

Although the neighboring peoples are free and independent, they have selected officials from among the Utopians, some to serve for as long as five years. At the end of their service, they are often exchanged for others. The honors bestowed upon them are a reward for valuable service. These officials are chosen in Utopia for their good morals. These men take an excellent and healthy care of their states, for the safety or destruction of the state depends on the character of the public servant. Because of the temporary nature of their duty they are above bribery and corruption, nor do they become involved in bickering, being strangers in a foreign land. It is partisanship and avarice that so often weaken justice, the strongest sinew of the state. These nations to which the Utopians supply officials are referred to as "allies," and the others to which they have given aid they call "friends."

Alliances so often violated by other nations are unknown among the Utopians. Why, they ask, is an alliance necessary when nature has already united mankind? Whoever disregards nature will not consider mere words any more valuable. This opinion is strengthened by the prevalence of unkept pacts and covenants in their part of the world. In Europe, especially Christian Europe, on the other hand, agreements are considered holy and inviolable. This is due to the justice and goodness of the rulers and also to reverence for and fear of the popes, who do not promise anything which they do not religiously observe and order all others to exactitude in the fulfillment of their commands, while those who seek to evade these behests they coerce with the severity of their pontifical censure. The popes consider it shameful if faith in alliances is lacking among those who call themselves the faithful.

In that new world whose geographic location is as far removed from us as are its customs, there is no belief in alliances. The more ceremoniously men bind themselves, it is felt, the more quickly they break their agreements. Loopholes inserted in treaties always provide an escape from even the most binding agreements. If statesmen discovered such loopholes in private contracts, they would denounce them as worthy of capital punishment; yet, they pride themselves in offering this same dishonest advice to princes. As a result, justice is viewed as an inferior virtue which ranks much lower than other virtues. Or a double standard is followed; one for the common people, and another for the royalty which, since it is set apart, is far more noble and must submit to its own self-interest. This failure of rulers to respect treaties is the reason for the Utopians' rejection of this practice. It would perhaps be modified if they lived here; yet even then I doubt if they would change their attitude.

People often behave as if they were born into opposing armies simply because they are separated by geography; they may be pacified only by treaties. Even when treaties are entered upon, the people are not united in true friendship, but prey upon one another by finding loopholes in the treaty. It is the opinion of the Utopians that one who has not injured you cannot be your enemy. They believe that the fellowship of nature is prior to any treaty and that men are more securely bound by love than by agreements. Peace is a matter of the heart rather than of words.

MILITARY AFFAIRS

War is considered utterly detestable and plainly beastlike—although there are no animals so diligent in practicing it as are men. Nothing is considered as inglorious as is the glory gained from war. Still, men and women assiduously exercise military discipline on certain days so that they will not be useless for war when the need arises. They do not go to war on mere impulse, but only to guard their own boundaries, drive out enemies who may have invaded the lands of their friends, or to liberate peoples who have been made miserable by tyranny and servitude. This is done for the sake of humanity. Sometimes they grant aid to their friends for the purpose of retaliation and vengeance. They do this only if they are consulted about the matter while it is still fresh and the offenders refuse to restore things to their original state. Then they take the initiative in starting the war. They do this not only when they see that booty has been taken as a result of enemy incursions, but also much more violently when the merchants of one country are subjected to unjust persecution in another country under the pretense of justice, either under cover of iniquitous law or the manipulation of good laws.

This was the reason for the war which the Utopians waged on behalf of the Nephelogetes against the Alaopolitans a little before our time. The merchants of the Nephelogetes had suffered damage, it seemed to them, under the pretext of law. Whether or not an injustice had been done, however, a savage war ensued in which the neighboring countries joined with all their hatred, zeal, and power. Even the most prosperous nations were shaken to the core or seriously afflicted. The troubles that fell upon the Alaopolitans finally brought them to surrender and slavery. The Utopians, who had not been seeking anything for themselves, delivered them to the Nephelogetes, whose civilization was far below that of the Alaopolitans when they were at their height.

Thus, the Utopians bitterly avenge any damage done to their friends, even in monetary matters, but do not act similarly in cases involving themselves. If they lose their goods anywhere by fraud, they only allow their anger to make them abstain from any more trade with those people until satisfaction has been made. It is not because their losses are of less concern to them than their allies', but because they feel their friends' losses more strongly than their own. For when the merchants of their friends lose their private goods the Utopians feel a personal loss; but when one of their own citizens is cheated, he loses nothing personally but only that which belongs to the commonwealth—goods that, had they not been in surplus at home, would not have been exported in the first place. Such a loss does not affect the individual, and they think it cruel to declare war and cause many deaths over a wrong in which no one feels the loss. However, if any Utopian is ever seriously injured or killed, either publicly or privately, the matter is investigated; and, if not appeased by the deliverance of the persecutor, the Utopians will immediately declare war on that nation. But if the offenders are delivered they are punished either with slavery or death.

Bloody victories cause shame among them because they think it stupid to win even precious goods with the loss of lives. If they win by skill or deception, they hold public celebrations, erect a monument just as if the victory had been gained strenuously and boast that they have achieved victory in a way possible to no other animal except man by the power of his intelligence. Bears, lions, boars, wolves, and other wild beasts can fight with brutal force; man alone with cleverness and reason.

They hope for one thing from war: to achieve that which, had it been obtained previously, would have prevented the war. But if war cannot be avoided, they punish those they consider guilty so severely that they are afraid to attempt the same thing again in the future. In this way, they place more emphasis on avoiding danger than on winning praise or glory.

Once hostilities begin, the Utopians secretly place small public notices in enemy territory promising large rewards to whoever removes the enemy prince. The removal of lesser personalities whom they consider warmongers is also rewarded. In the event the person is brought in alive, the reward is doubled. They then persuade the captured enemy to turn against his own people with the offer of money.

By this tactic they induce fear and suspicion among their enemies, as often even their leaders can be bought off. Realizing the risks involved, the Utopians do not hesitate to reward the betrayers handsomely and in relation to the risk involved, giving them large sums of money and in some cases, the titles to immense estates. Although this practice may be decried elsewhere, among these people it is considered worthy of the highest praise since it terminates warfare without bloodshed. It also benefits the common people of both countries who would have been the real victims of an actual war, had not the few guilty people been eliminated. Their sympathy extends to the people of the enemy since the Utopians realize that they do not come to war of their own accord, but are driven to it by their leaders. When this plan fails, they resort to other means of intrigue; usually by sowing internal dissension or by forging a title to the territory for their neighbors. Once war has been declared however, their aid is in matériel rather than in actual intervention. So great is their devotion to their own people that they would never exchange even one of their citizens for the greatest of the enemy. The treasury is used for this purpose and there are no limits as long as the welfare of the country is at stake. The financial holdings abroad, already referred to, are also used. In order to fight their war they utilize mercenaries from all lands. Their favorite mercenaries are from among the Zapoletans, a fierce barbarian people who inhabit the forests and mountains about five hundred miles to the east. This hardy race of nomads, unaccustomed to luxury and impervious to the vicissitudes of the weather, live off the land. These people are a nation born for war, living mainly by hunting and plundering, and they eagerly seek any opportunity to wage it. They find nothing more attractive than being employed as mercenaries, and large numbers of them have made this a way of life. As long as they are well-enough paid they will fight fiercely and loyally. However, they do not hesitate to change sides when a higher price is offered by the opposition, but will return to their original employers if a slightly higher sum is offered. It is rare that they do not engage in battle on both sides of a conflict, often facing their own friends and relatives. Casting kinship and friendship aside, they will not hesitate, for the sake of a little money, to attack their own. Although their avarice is so powerful, it does them little good because this blood money is almost immediately dissipated in riotous living.

It is for the Utopians that they fight with greatest enthusiasm since no one pays them better. In selecting this group, the Utopians feel that their eventual extermination would be a great benefit to mankind. Hence, they do not hesitate to send them into the greatest dangers with an appropriate reward.

In addition to these, they employ militia from among their allies. From their own troops they select someone noted for valor as a leader. He is backed by two others who follow in succession in the event of his death or capture. This they do to avoid the possibility of the entire army being wiped out through the loss of a commander. Recruitment in each city is entirely voluntary and no one is obliged to fight abroad; thus the danger of cowardice in the ranks is avoided. But should the enemy endanger the country through invasion, the cowardly are pressed into military service either on ships where they are intermingled with braver men or along the walls where they cannot desert. With no chance of escape and confronted with the enemy, they are made into fighting men by fear and shame.

Just as there is only voluntary service for foreign war, so there is no opposition to women's accompanying their husbands. Indeed this is encouraged and praised. The women are stationed with their husbands at the battle front. The proximity of the soldier's immediate family stimulates greater resistance. Since it is a disgrace for a man to return from battle without his wife—or for a son to return without his father—Utopian soldiers, when faced with a determined enemy in hand-to-hand fighting, often determine to fight to the death rather than retreat.

The Utopians use every prudent method to avoid danger to their own men and, if possible, let mercenaries face the brunt of the action. But, if they must enter battle, the Utopians charge with the same vigor with which they had prudently avoided danger. Their initial attack is not fierce; but their ferocity gradually increases, and their spirits are so stubborn that they prefer slaughter to retreat. This disdain for defeat arises from their not being anxious over the future of their families if they should die—an anxiety that often conquers courage.

Their military training gives them confidence and the wise national institutions in which they have been educated give them courage. Here again they observe moderation, neither throwing away their lives cheaply nor placing themselves above the honor of the nation. Once the battle is under way, the younger ones seek out the leader of the enemy and harass him until he is captured or slain. Should they rout the enemy, they prefer to take prisoners rather than to slay them. Should one part of the enemy line give way, they are careful to keep their own formations intact. They bear in mind the many occasions when by regrouping after apparent defeat, they have overcome the pursuing enemy.

They are equally adept at setting up and avoiding ambushes. One of their chief tactics is feigning both attack and retreat. Should the situation demand, they are trained in the art of strategic withdrawal. Their camps are fortified with deep ditches which they dig by hand. Since except for a few guards all are employed in this operation, they can complete great fortifications with almost incredible speed.

Their armor, though strong enough to resist blows, still allows them a great deal of mobility and even enables them to swim while wearing it. In fact, swimming in armor is part of their military training. For long-range fighting they use arrows which they shoot with great accuracy whether on foot or mounted. In close fighting, they use a sort of halberd in preference to swords. These weapons are deadly in weight and sharpness and used for stabbing and hacking. The war machines that they cleverly invent are concealed from the enemy lest they be the subjects of ridicule. They are designed for easy transport and positioning.

So religiously do they observe a truce with the enemy that they will not violate it even when provoked. Slaughter of the enemy and pillage are unknown among them. They especially avoid the destruction of crops, preserving them for later use. Unless apprehended as a spy, no unarmed civilian is harmed. Captured cities are not destroyed even when taken by storm. Only those who resist are slain and the remaining defenders are reduced to slavery. The nonparticipants they leave unmolested. Should they learn of someone who advised the surrender of the city, they share the property of the condemned with him.

The remainder is turned over to their allies as they take no booty for themselves.

Whatever expenses were incurred in the war are imposed upon the conquered rather than upon their allies. Included in this is a reserve which they set aside for similar engagements and the large estates which provide them with a constant income. This revenue drawn from many peoples and acquired for a number of different reasons has gradually grown to some seven hundred thousand ducats annually. The captured estates are administered by Utopian tax collectors who live there in great splendor in the capacity of public servants. As there is still a surplus income, it is either turned into the treasury or entrusted to the conquered nation. Seldom do they demand the entire amount, and some of the estates are turned over to those of the enemy who counseled surrender. Should any neighboring prince plan to invade them, they anticipate his move by confronting him outside their own boundaries. They are extremely reluctant to wage war at home and seldom allow foreign auxiliaries to enter their island.

RELIGIONS IN UTOPIA

Religious pluralism is evident throughout the entire island and in each city. The sun, the moon, and certain of the planets are objects of veneration. Some, however, venerate a certain individual who once appeared among them resplendent with virtue and glory, not only as a god but as the highest god. The majority and the more prudent of them give credence to none of these but rather to a certain divine majesty which is unknown, eternal, immense, and beyond human comprehension. It is diffused throughout the entire universe in power, rather than in mass. Him they call the father of all. All beginnings, increase, progression, changes, and destinies they attribute to him alone; and to him alone do they grant divine honors. In fact, although all the others have different beliefs, they are in accord in attributing to the one high God the creation and direction of the universe. He is referred to in the language of the country as Mithra. Yet there are shades of interpretation. All agree, however, that whatever the differences in their view of the supreme power, it is really that same nature which is universally recognized as possessing unique majesty and sovereignty. Little by little, however, they are coming to abandon their superstition and to unite in that one religion which in reason seems to excel all others. The earlier variety would long since have disappeared were it not for a tendency to identify certain calamities with the scorn of rejected deities.

We left them with the legacy of the name of Christ, his doctrines, his death, his miracles, and the wonderful fidelity of the martyrs whose bloodshed brought many peoples from far and wide into his fold. They were greatly moved by the knowledge of Christianity, whether through the mysterious stirrings of the spirit or through its similarity to their own heretical religion. The communal living practiced by Christ among his followers, which is still in practice in real Christian communities, may also have been a deciding factor. Many came over to our religion, and were washed in the sacred waters of baptism.

Among the four of us (of the original six, two had gone to their eternal reward), I am sorry to say, there was not a priest. The Utopians, although instructed in the rudiments, still desired the sacraments, which according to our doctrines no one but a priest can confer. They understand what these are and seek nothing more ardently. Indeed, they hotly debated whether in the absence of a Christian bishop someone among their number could receive the character of the priesthood. It seemed to them that one should be selected, but up to the time I had departed, he had not been chosen. Those who do not assent to the religion of Christ still do not discourage any from it nor attack those who are inspired by it. Only once while I was there was any of our group interfered with. He was but recently baptized, and in spite of our efforts to dissuade him, began publicly to preach the cult of Christ with more zeal than prudence. He grew so inflamed that he not only extolled our religion above all others, but also condemned the rest. He shouted that their doctrines were profane and that those who adhered to them were impious and sacrilegious and doomed to everlasting punishment. After this long harangue he was seized and found guilty, not of contempt of religion, but of inciting a riot. He was sent into exile, for it is a Utopian custom that no one suffer punishment because of his religion.

King Utopus had heard that prior to his arrival the natives had fought many religious wars. He observed that the dissension among the various sects which were fighting for their country presented him with the opportunity of conquering all of them. Thus, when he attained victory, he decreed the freedom of the individual to follow the religion of his choice. Indeed, he might convert others to his religion as long as he used reasonable methods and refrained from attacking dissenters. Force and heated discussions were forbidden. Those who are carried away with fanaticism are either exiled or forced into slavery.

Utopus was prompted to establish this law not only because he saw that the peace would be jeopardized by this assiduous contest and irreconcilable hatred, but also because religion itself would be the beneficiary of such a decree. Discretion dictated that he not define anything concerning the details of religion, since he was uncertain whether God did or did not want a pluralistic worship; he therefore directed the people along different lines. He thought that certainly the use of force or violence in matters of belief was obviously foolish. Moreover, if there is but one religion which possesses absolute truth, it would ultimately triumph on a basis of its own merit. Were this to be determined by force, then the danger of a victory of the superstitious would be increased as the parable of the tares indicates. Hence he left it an open question with each man free to adapt his own beliefs. Still, he solemnly and strictly forbade that anyone should sink so low as to think that souls perish along with the body and that the world could carry on by chance without the aid of Providence. Therefore, the Utopians believe that sin will be punished and virtue rewarded in the afterlife. They do not consider human anyone who believes otherwise. For he who rejects the sublime nature of his soul is no less than the beast. Such a person they remove from civic responsibilities. For even if he obeys out of fear, for him all the laws and customs seem trivial. Can anyone doubt that he would either elude the public laws of the country by some secret scheme or break them by violence, while he privately served only his own cupidity, since for him there was no fear except the law, and no further hope beyond the body? Thus, no honors are bestowed upon anyone so minded, and no magistracy or public responsibility entrusted to him. He is despised by everyone and considered worthless. Yet they refuse to inflict any punishment on him, since they are convinced a man's beliefs are his own business. Nor do they force him to dissimulation, for deceit they consider equal to atheism. True, they forbid him to voice his opinions publicly, but they not only allow, but even encourage him to make confession of his views in private among the priests and other serious men, so that eventually he might yield to reason.

There are also others who are not molested because their unbelief is supported by reason and they are of no danger to the others. By an error at the opposite extreme, they think that the souls of brutes are eternal, but still not comparable to ours in dignity nor destined to an equal happiness. Almost all the Utopians believe that there is such an immense happiness awaiting men that they regret the sickness but not the death of anyone, except those whom they see die anxiously and unwillingly. For they think that this is an evil sign, as if the despairing and conscience-stricken soul feared death because of some premonition of imminent punishment. Besides they think that his arrival will hardly be pleasing to God since he comes hesitantly and grudgingly. They are horrified at the sight of such a death. After they have commended his soul to the gracious hands of God and prayed that he might mercifully forget all their infirmities, they bury the corpse in the earth.

On the other hand, when one departs this life unhesitatingly and hopefully, no tears are shed, and they follow the funeral with songs, commending the soul to God with great affection. Finally, with more reverence than sorrow, they cremate the body and erect a column in that place with the man's eulogy engraved thereon. After returning home, they recall his virtuous life, but no phase of his life is more frequently or gladly discussed than his happy death. They think this remembrance of his virtuous living is a most efficacious incitement to those who are still living, and a gratifying form of worship to the dead. For they believe that, although invisible to the dim sight of mortals, the dead are among the living when they are talked of, since it would not become the happiness of the departed if they were not free to go where they wished, and it would be ungrateful of them to reject all desire of visiting those with whom they were bound together while they lived in mutual love and charity. They think that in good men freedom, as well as all other qualities, is increased rather than diminished after death. So the dead, they believe, busy themselves among the living and are witnesses to their words and deeds. Therefore, the living approach their daily lives more confidently, trusting in such guidance, and this belief in the presence of their ancestors deters them from secret dishonesty.

They neglect and scorn augury and the other vain divinations of superstition which are prevalent in other nations. But they venerate miracles which defy nature as being the works and witnesses of the Divine Presence. They say that such wonders have frequently occurred there. When in great doubt about affairs of common concern, they petition God by public prayers and often obtain guidance with their confident faith.

They think that the contemplation of nature and the praise it inspires is worship pleasing to God. Still there are many who neglect learning, look for no knowledge of the world nor take any rest in leisure. For they declare that serving others in a goodly way will bring happiness in the time after death. Thus, some serve the sick, others work on road maintenance, gardening, lumbering, or trucking. They work on public projects and as domestic help in private homes, often doing more than the slaves. They readily take upon themselves work that the average citizen would consider beneath his dignity. Because they are constantly at work, they give more leisure time to others. Yet, they do not try to take advantage of this situation, nor do they degrade others for their lives or exalt their own. The more these men act as slaves, the more they are honored by all the rest.

These servants of the people are divided into two groups. The members of one group live as celibates and abstain from eating the meat of warm-blooded animals. By constant vigilance and exhausting labor, they forsake all the pleasures of this life for the sake of the next. Meanwhile, they are stimulated by the hope of obtaining happiness in the near future. The other group is equally fond of labor, but prefers marriage and does not reject its consolations. Its members feel that they owe nature a certain amount of labor in order to populate the fatherland. They do not resist any pleasure which in no way hinders their labor. They enjoy the meat of animals simply because they think that such food makes them stronger for work. The Utopians consider the latter to be the more prudent, but the former to be the more holy. If in preferring the celibate life to matrimony or a harsh life to a placid one, they depended on reasoned argument, the Utopians would laugh at them. But since they confess that they choose this because of religion, the Utopians admire and respect them. They are extremely cautious not to offend the religious scruples of others. They call the men of this kind in their language by the peculiar name of *buthrescas* which in Latin means *dedicated religious*.

The priests are extremely holy and therefore very few. There are no more than thirteen in any city, which is never more than one for each temple. When there is a war, seven of them set forth with the army and seven others replace them temporarily. Upon returning, everyone resumes his former position. Rank is determined by the seniority system and the excess priests serve as assistants to the high priest, who holds the highest position in the hierarchy. They are elected by the people by secret ballot and are consecrated by their own college. They preside over religious affairs, direct the liturgy, and safeguard public morals. It is considered a great disgrace to be brought before them and rebuked for failing to lead an upright life. While it is their task to exhort and to admonish, it is the duty of the prince and other officials to watch and punish those who lead an evil life. The priests, however, exclude from the sacred rites those whom they find to be exceptionally evil. No other punishment carries with it such a dreaded stigma. Unless these evil men immediately repent, their sentence will be determined in a civil court.

The concern of the priests as teachers of children and adolescents is as important as their care of morals and virtues.

They instill in these children from a very tender age those values necessary for the preservation of society. These deeply inbred principles remain with them into manhood and, it is hoped, for the rest of their lives. The welfare of the state is safe only so long as these values are not undermined by perverse ideologies.

Since women are not excluded from the priesthood, the wives of the priests must of necessity be the most select. However, they are rarely elevated to the priesthood, and even then only if they are widows or well on in years. To no other office among the Utopians is greater honor given. Even if any of them commit crimes, they suffer no public judgment, but are left to God alone and to themselves. For the Utopians do not think it is lawful to touch one, no matter how wicked, who was dedicated to God as a holy offering. The Utopians find no difficulty in following this custom since they have so few priests and these are chosen with such care. For rarely do those taken from the cream of the crop, and raised to such a position of honor, fall into a degenerate life. Even if it should happen (human nature being what it is), they are so very few and with no other power that it is not necessary to fear that this occurrence will bring any great harm to the commonwealth. Therefore, only the exceptional are chosen for the priesthood lest the dignity of the order be cheapened. They consider it exceptional to find men capable of living lives beyond the ordinary standards of morality.

People of foreign nations hold them in as much esteem as do the Utopians. It is evident whence this respect originates: While the troops are locked in battle, the priests kneel close at hand, clothed in their sacred vestments. With their palms extended to heaven they pray first for peace, and then for the victory of their own army, with a minimum of bloodshed on both sides. If it should appear that their army is about to overrun the enemy, they attempt to restrain their men from attacking the retreating army. Merely to see and call out to a priest is enough to save an enemy soldier's life and touching their flowing robes preserves all of his remaining possessions from the ravages of war. For this reason they are revered among people everywhere. As often as they have saved their own citizens from the enemy, they have saved the enemy in like manner. It has happened that their own battle line was being overrun and, fearing defeat, they fled with the enemy right on their heels. Only the intervention of the priests prevented a slaughter. After the armies had withdrawn, the conditions of an equitable peace were written up. There never was a people so barbarous that it did not regard the priests' bodies as sacred and inviolable.

The Utopians celebrate the first and last days of every month and of every year, which is divided into months according to the revolution of the moon, just as the cycle of the sun determines the length of the year. They call the first day Cynemern and the last day Trapemern, which in their language means First-Feast and Final-Feast respectively.

Their shrines are quite elaborate and ornate and, since there are so few temples, have a large seating capacity. Inside, however, they are quite dark, due not to the ignorance of the architects, but to the wishes of the priests, who feel that too much light is a distraction during meditation, and that a more subdued atmosphere is more conducive to prayer and worship.

Although they do not possess a universal form of cult, nevertheless there is a certain uniformity in the fact that their variety of beliefs ultimately center in the worship of the Divine Nature. Hence, there is common agreement in what is said and done in their temples. Whatever religious practice is peculiar to a particular sect is limited to its own places of worship and in public worship all is avoided that would offend the beliefs of others. There is no standard image of God in the temple, thus allowing the individual to envision him as best befits his devotion. Mithra is the only title they apply to God and it includes all of his manifestations. In prayer, care is taken to avoid offending the various beliefs of others.

On the Final-Feast they gather the evening before and fast in thanksgiving for having successfully survived the preceding month or year. On the morning of the feast they gather and pray that the succeeding periods will also pass in prosperity. On this occasion also there is a practice of communal and public confession of sins (both of commission and omission) and a plea for forgiveness from parents and husbands. In this way any domestic discord is reconciled before they assemble and they arrive purified before the sacrifices begin. Worshiping with a troubled conscience is looked upon as sacrilegious. Anyone not reconciled with his neighbor will not enter the place of sacrifice In the temple the men are placed on the right side and the women on the left, and they are so arranged that the heads of household can be observed by their inferiors as representatives of authority and discipline in the home. Younger members are not seated as a group but are intermingled with the adults in order to avoid horseplay and in order to inculcate a fearful respect for the divine which is the greatest inducement to virtue.

Immolation of animals is not part of their sacrificial rite as they look upon all living creatures as designed for man's enjoyment, and feel that God does not demand the shedding of blood. The use of incense and candles they consider a better token of worship. As in prayer, they feel themselves lifted up by the odors and lights of the ceremonies.

White garments are worn by the worshipers and the priests are clothed in varicolored vestments. The vestments, though not costly, are wonderfully interwoven with the feathers of different birds which possess a special occult symbolism. These symbols are interpreted by the priests who remind the people of their indebtedness to God, and their duties toward him and their neighbor.

When the priest garbed in this fashion enters the sanctuary, all immediately prostrate themselves in veneration and silence in a manner that strikes the beholder with a feeling of the terrible presence of the Divine. With a signal from the priest they soon rise and sing the praises of God to the accompaniment of musical instruments quite different from our own. Although their music is in some ways similar to our own, it surpasses it in sweetness. In all their music, whether vocal or instrumental, there is a wonderful accommodation to the theme and emotional mood of the occasion.

Finally the priest leads the congregation in a communal prayer that is so prepared that it allows the individual to express his own private needs. The prayers recognize God as the creator of all things and the provider of all mankind. The Utopian is particularly thankful in his prayers for the fact that he has been born in this most happy commonwealth and has had the choice of what he feels is the truest religion. Should, however, God reveal a better place or a superior religion he prays that he may recognize and follow them. If not, it is his petition that others be led to this same manner of life and belief, and that he remain constant in it. He finally prays for a happy death without stipulating when this may occur. Were it God's good pleasure he would prefer to die a difficult death even in the midst of a prosperous life. Following the prayer they again prostrate themselves for a short while and then proceed to dinner. The rest of the day is spent in games and military exercises.

I have now truthfully and to the best of my ability described the nature of that place which I consider to be not only the best but the only area really deserving of the name commonwealth. In other places which boast of the common good, private interests claim priority. In Utopia, where there are no private holdings, all effort is bent toward the public. In all other places, regardless of the prosperity of the country, unless the individual takes care of his own needs, starvation will be his fate. Thus, self-preservation has priority over the common good. Here so long as the public storehouse is replenished, no one ever lacks anything. There is no begrudging the distribution of goods, poverty and begging are unknown, and although possessing nothing, all men are rich. For who is richer than he who lives a happy and tranquil life freed from the anxieties of job holding and the domestic troubles resulting from a nagging spouse and providing for one's progeny? Even eventual retirement from work does not lessen the assurance of sufficiency for all.

I dare anyone to compare the equity in this matter with the so-called justice of other nations. For who can claim that as justice which permits the nobility, the goldsmith, or the money lender by doing little or nothing at all for the common good to lead a life of elegance, while the common laborers scarcely rise above the level of the beast. Yet it is the labor of the latter which sustains the nation. In this respect the condition of the beasts of labor would even seem superior since they are provided for and have no care of the future. The workers in contrast are constantly beset with fruitless labors and the thought of an unprovided old age haunts them to their death. Their daily earnings are insufficient and there is no opportunity to provide for old age.

Is it not an evil and ungrateful state that lavishes gifts on so-called noblemen, goldsmiths, and other pleasure-seeking idlers while at the same time failing to provide for the common laborers who are the very foundation of the nation? After they have spent the best years of their lives in protecting and supporting the nation and are now penniless and beset with infirmities, is it an act of justice that the commonwealth should reward them with the prospect of a miserable death? What aggravates the situation more is that the wealthy in their private feuding and in the laws they promulgate have succeeded in further reducing the income of the poor so that those who deserve the most receive the least.

Therefore, after having considered this matter seriously, it seems to me that all the governments that have flourished since the beginning of time have been nothing but a continual conspiracy of the rich to perpetuate themselves under the guise of statecraft. They contrive and scheme in the first place how to retain their ill-gotten goods and then how to abuse the poor by paying them a bare minimum wage for their labors. This dishonest practice is then put into law. Can this be called good government, when what would have sufficed for all is finally dissipated by their insatiable greed to the point of sharing it among themselves? The Utopians in their abolition of money have also removed the greed associated with it. In so doing they uprooted the cause of theft, pillage, riots, contentions, murders, and betrayals—crimes aggravated rather than terminated by punishment. Would not all other anxieties, including poverty itself, perish with the wiping out of money?

To clarify this further, consider some period when thousands died from famine. I swear that had the warehouses of the rich been thrown open at the end of such a period, enough would have been found to have sustained life during this unfortunate episode. The necessities of life would be present in abundance were it not for the obstacle that money presents to this sort of distribution. Even the rich are aware that they would find themselves in a happier condition, if content with basic needs, and freed of the burden of superfluous wealth. Nor do I not doubt that because of its reasonableness and its compliance with the wisdom and counsel of a knowing Christ, the entire world would follow the practice of the Utopians, were it not for the root of all evil, pride itself. For pride measures prosperity in terms not of its own advantage, but of disadvantage to others. She would not wish to be a goddess did there not remain other wretches to be insolently scorned and ordered about, with whom she might compare herself. She would relinquish her position were the exposition of her riches not a source of torture to others. Yet this servant of hell slithers into the hearts of mankind and there like the bloodsucker prevents men from improving their lot.

So tightly has pride attached itself to mankind that it is removed only with the greatest difficulty. Yet I rejoice in the fact that this type of government has developed among the Utopians, and would gladly see it accepted among all nations. They have joyfully accepted the laws which are the very foundation of their commonwealth, but also, insofar as one can predict, have taken measures to insure their permanence. Having uprooted the other seditious vices, they are free from the internal dissensions which have plagued and brought to ruin the well-defended wealth of so many nations. As long as this domestic tranquility and those life-giving laws remain intact, the efforts of envious neighboring princes, so often repulsed, will come to naught and Utopian rule will remain forever.

When Raphael had finished his story many objections ran through my mind. There were quite a few items in the customs and laws of that people that appeared absurd. Included were not only their ideas on war and their religious rites but particularly their practice (and this is the basis of their social structure) of living a communistic life without a moneyed economy. In eliminating this they have utterly destroyed the nobility, magnificence, and splendor of what in public opinion constitutes the greatest ornament and glory of any nation. However, I knew that by this time he was tired of talking and I questioned whether he would tolerate my voicing an opposite opinion. I also recalled his earlier expressed fear of censure from those who thought that finding fault in any proposal was a sign of wisdom. So taking him by the hand and praising their way of life, and his account of it, I led him to dinner. I did say, however, that there would be another time for deeper thought on these matters and for further discussion. It is my sincere hope that this will be the case. In the meantime I must continue to hold my reservations concerning what he had to say. Yet I must admit that he is trustworthy as well as erudite and experienced. I readily admit that there is much in the Utopian commonwealth that I wish rather than expect to see realized in the cities of our own world.

> *The end of the afternoon discourse of*
> *Raphael Hythloday concerning the*
> *laws and institutions of the small*
> *island of Utopia before known to*
> *but a few, by the most well-*
> *known and most learned man*
> *Mr. Thomas More,*
> *citizen and Sheriff of London*

Selected Latin Writings

Letter to Erasmus of Rotterdam

More's admiration for Erasmus was intellectual and spiritual. As a man of affairs, however, he was also concerned to further Erasmus' material interests, as the first part of the letter indicates. More's reflections on his own problems as the king's ambassador afford valuable insight into the kind of life he led.

London
February 17, 1516

Thomas More To Erasmus:

Greetings,

Since you left, I have received three letters from you. If I told you that I had answered them all, I don't think you would believe me, regardless of how earnestly I lied; particularly since you are aware that I am a lazy correspondent and hardly so scrupulous as to shrink from a small lie as if it were a capital crime. . . .

In regard to you, I would be even more hopeful, were I not so consistently disappointed; and yet why shouldn't I entertain high hopes for you still? The future is not hopeless, even though the past has produced no result; rather, I feel more confident than ever that my previous hopes may be realized.

No man's luck remains always the same, and surely yours is due to change for the better, for you hold great favor with the pope, with kings, with bishops, and with almost every good man in Christendom. One need not remind you of the high esteem in which our bishops hold you—especially the Archbishop of Canterbury—and of the particular grace you have with the king. The fact that you have failed previously to gain the rewards which, in view of your worth and the love shown you by leading men you so richly deserve, is owing in part to your disdain for the methods used by others, and partially to some misfortune, as in the case of the canonry at

Tournai, which Lord Mountjoy had intended to give you. At the moment you do not appear to be against it, as you have sent him all pertinent documents to facilitate your acceptance of it. But, if you remember, when we were at Bruges we discussed this particular subject, and, after examining the pros and cons, you did not seem interested in it; nor was it impossible for Sampson, the Bishop of York's representative, to discern this apparent lack of interest. No doubt you took this view because you were afraid that the position would not be permanent without the authorization of Bishop Guillard, whose consent would not seem likely to a proposal made by a man whose every action he will attempt to hinder; and also because of the requirement that a payment of ten English pounds be made upon receipt of the canonry with the stipulation that an additional two hundred nobles be paid annually to cover the cost of the house. This is the local custom, and failure to follow it will result in the realization of only six nobles a year, and even less if you do not reside there. I suspect, then, that these factors led you to give Sampson and me the impression that you did not want the canonry.

Soon after you left, I journeyed to Tournai, and I found out from Lord Mountjoy and from Sampson that the benefice was given to someone else by the Archbishop of York, who had offered it to him without knowing it had been promised to you. When I heard this, I did not reveal that the proposition was distasteful to you, but instead, prompted them to inform the archbishop that the benefice had already been given to you and that the only possible alternative was to offer you something better. The archbishop replied that this position would not suit you since it is useful only for a resident official and a waste of time for the absentee, and he guaranteed a more profitable offer. So, while I was present and without any protest from me, the benefice was conferred on the archbishop's choice. I have no idea what took place after that. However, I do know this: since you were deprived of that benefice, a better one is forthcoming from the cardinal and I hope he will give it to you soon. He often speaks about you in a kindly manner.

I did not need to ask the archbishop about your pension. He had thought of it prior to my letter and had taken up the matter with Maruffo, his financial adviser, who, as you know, handles these things. They settle accounts together at certain times. The archbishop was staying at Oxford at the time, and when he received my letter he wrote again to his broker and urged him to forward twenty English pounds to you, while promising to repay Maruffo as soon as he was informed that you had received the money. I talked with Maruffo. He told me that he expected you to send him a receipt stating that you had the money. This he would present to the archbishop, enabling him to claim the money, and only after that would he send it on to you. Upon learning of that plan, I feared that any delay in payment to him might have some effect on your payment. "This deceitful plot is unnecessary," I told him. "Either send the money out immediately and charge it to the archbishop's account, or if you dislike giving money with no collateral, I will put up the equivalent." "No," he said, "you needn't worry about it, Erasmus shall have the money at once; as a matter of fact, I have it right now. For he has a draft from me which entitles him to draw up to one thousand ducats whenever he wishes. The amount that he draws from this account will be repaid from his pension." That, my friend, is what he told me. I cannot believe, however, that he gave you a draft of that nature without having the money in his account. Therefore, if the arrangement does not come about in this manner, let me know quickly.

The Archbishop of Canterbury is no longer burdened with the additional office of chancellor; a relief, as you are aware, that he has sought for several years; he has finally attained his life's wish: to live in privacy, with his books and memories of successfully executed responsibilities. The Cardinal of York, by order of the king, has replaced him and exceeded all expectations of his ability as an administrator. This was not an easy accomplishment, in view of the fact that he succeeded an extremely able man at the position.

Our mission, which I'm sure interests you as much as my other activities, was a success, although it lasted much longer than I had expected. At the time of departure, I did not expect to be gone more than two months; however, the mission required six months for completion. We did, however achieve very satisfying results over this last period. Therefore, when I saw that my task was finished and that some problems were arising that might lead to greater delay (a common occurrence in administration), I wrote the cardinal and was granted permission to come home, thanks to the help I received from my friends, particularly Pace, who was still there. . . .

I have never been overjoyed with the office of ambassador. It is not suited for us laymen as it is for you clergy, because you have no wives and children at home—or can find them anywhere in your travels. When we are away for short periods of time, we begin to think of our families. Also, when a priest is sent on a political mission, he is allowed to take with him his entire household, wherever he wishes, and, for the present, the king pays for their support, while here at home he has to provide for their upkeep himself. But when I am sent on a mission, I have to support two households: one here at home and another overseas. The king granted me a generous allowance to support my staff, but nothing was provided for those I left behind; and even though I am, as you are aware, a generous husband, a kindly father, and a merciful master, it has always been impossible to persuade my family to help me by going hungry until I return. Last of all, it is easy for kings, with no personal cost, to pay back the clergy for their efforts by means of church endowments; while no provisions such as these are made available to us, although upon my return, the king singled me out for his annual beneficiary, which is very valuable because of the distinction it affords and the amount of money it entails. However, I haven't accepted it yet and I may never accept it, since this action would require me to vacate my present post in London and take a higher one; or (which I dread even more) to keep my London post and cause friction between myself and the townspeople. If there should be some difference of opinion between them and His Majesty, as is sometimes the case, they would have reason to doubt my loyalty to the office because of my obligation as the king's pensioner.

Certain aspects of the mission did, however, give me great enjoyment; primarily it afforded the opportunity for continuous close association with Tunstall, whose great achievements in letters and strictness of moral life are second to none, while he remains a friendly associate; secondly, my forming a firm acquaintance with Busleiden, whose wealth and generosity serve to make him a splendid host. He took me on a complete tour of his home, which is handsomely decorated and filled with exquisite objects of art; he then showed me his priceless collection of ancient art, which you know is of great interest to me. Lastly he showed me his astoundingly well-filled library and a mind even richer, so that I was thoroughly amazed. I am told that he is soon to be sent on a political mission to the king. The highlight of the trip was my encounter with your own host, Peter Giles, whose learning, sense of humor, modesty, and warm hospitality are such that, God forgive me, I would give a great deal to have his companionship for myself. He gave me your "Apology" and your writings concerning the Psalms, "Beatus Vir," which you dedicated to your good friend Beatus Rhenanus, a man who is truly blessed by this deep and lasting tribute from a dear friend. Dorp has printed his own letter and included it as a preface to your "Apology." I wanted to meet him if the opportunity presented itself. Since I was not able to, I sent my salutations in a personal letter which was not very long because I was pressed for time. I found that greeting him in passing seemed very natural because he is so attractive; he has no equal as a scholar, and, after all, his criticism of the "Folly" provided the occasion for your composing your "Apology."

I am pleased to find that you are making such progress with your works on Jerome and the New Testament. These publications are indeed eagerly awaited by everyone. You may assure yourself, Erasmus, that Linacre thinks highly of you and speaks of you often. I heard this from some acquaintances who were eating with him at the king's table, at which time he spoke earnestly in your favor; the king's general response throughout the conversation seemed to indicate that good fortune might be coming your way. God grant it be so!

Good-bye, then, Erasmus, and give my good wishes to Rhenanus and Lystrius, who are as familiar to me as neighbors from your descriptions and their own letters. My wife asks to be remembered and so does Clement, who is doing so well in Latin and Greek that I expect him to be honored for his learning some day.

Once again good-bye, and this letter will have to satisfy you for several months. In writing it, I am like a selfish person who does not often entertain, but when he does give a banquet, it is so lavish that it lasts forever, so that he can pay all his social debts in one day. For the third time, farewell.

The Bishop of Durham was much pleased with the dedication of your Seneca edition. Note that I am quick to copy your methods; I have written this letter as you wrote yours to me, with the aid of a secretary; I imitate you so much that I wouldn't even bother to write these last few words in my own hand, except that I wanted to assure you that it was from me.

Letter to the University of Oxford

More's concern that the classics, particularly Greek studies, have a central place in the universities motivated this letter. He did not disdain, in paragraphs omitted here, to bring financial and political pressure to bear in order to further his cause.

". . . our most Christian prince," he assures the reader, *"will not allow the liberal arts to perish in the place which his illustrious ancestors established as a famous university. . . ."*

Abingdon
March 29, 1518

Thomas More to the reverend fathers, commissary, proctors and others in the masters' guild of Oxford University, greeting.

There has been some doubt in my mind, learned sirs, about writing you concerning certain matters about which I have made up my mind. My hesitancy in this was due not so much to a fear of exposing my style to such a group of erudite gentlemen, as it was to the danger of appearing to claim superiority. For it would be a presumption on my part—who am of little prudence, less practice, and small learning—to take upon myself the right to advise you, especially since in the field of learning, any one of you is qualified by erudition and wisdom to counsel thousands. Although at first deterred from doing this, I later took courage on reflecting that only an arrogant and foolish stupidity would hinder me, for the wiser and more learned a person is, the less likely is he to rely entirely upon his own knowledge and spurn the advice of others. I was further encouraged by the thought that no one was ever given a poor hearing by just judges (as you are in a very special way) simply because he improvidently offered advice. For advice, even though it lacks prudence, is always deserving of praise and thanks so long as it be truthful and proceed from a friendly heart.

Finally, after due consideration, I decided that I had an obligation to offer your academy what little learning I had with God's help acquired. It was here that my education began and, therefore, out of a sense of duty and loyalty I feel that I cannot pass over in silence that which I believe warrants a hearing.

I considered the real danger in writing you to be that a few would find me audacious. But, on the other hand, my silence would be condemned by many as an act of ingratitude. I have chosen to expose myself to the world's condemnation for audacity rather than invite a single accusation of ingratitude toward your institution, the good name of which I feel obliged to defend to the utmost.

Here is how this whole matter came to pass. While I was in London I frequently heard that a number of your faculty, out of either hatred for Greek letters, a preference for other studies, or, as I believe was in fact the case, a penchant for ridicule and frivolity, had conspired to form a group which they called the Trojans. One of them, more distinguished by age than wisdom, adopted the name Priam; others named themselves after Hector, Paris, and like figures from Trojan antiquity. Intending either a jest or a serious move against the Greek faction, they began ridiculing the study of Greek literature. For this reason it is now reported that one may no longer express his preference for Greek studies, either in private or in public, without being singled out and ridiculed with jeers and taunts by these stupid Trojans, who make sport of everything of which they are ignorant, namely all good literature. That old adage seems to apply most aptly to them: "The Trojans learn only when it is too late."

Since I have heard a great deal about this matter, all of it indicating widespread displeasure, it is especially bitter for me to learn that a few scholars among you could make no better use of your time than to molest the studious efforts of others. However, since I realized things never go so well that such a crowd of men could consist entirely of the wise, temperate, and modest, I began by considering it an affair of little importance. On the other hand, since I have been here in Abingdon in attendance upon our invincible king, I have received word that this foolish behavior has begun to take on the character of insanity. For one of this group of Trojans, whose name I do not know, is a man who in his own estimation is wise, whom his adulators consider a hilarious wit, but who really seems to be insane. This same person, during the Lenten season, in a public sermon, babbled not only against the elegance of Greek and Roman literature but against the liberal arts themselves. The entire sermon was uniformly bad. It is impossible that such a sordid showing could be based upon a single theme. He neither selected his subject matter from a complete passage of Scripture, as was customary in the past, nor did he select it from a few scattered scriptural references, as is now the practice; instead, he chose to base the entire effort on a selection of silly British proverbs. I do not doubt that his foolish sermon had a disturbing effect upon all who were present since even those whose knowledge of the incident has come only by hearsay are deeply distressed. What man among these whose heart was enkindled by even a spark of Christianity would not have grieved at witnessing the debasement of the sublime office of preaching by one whose chief duty it is to safeguard this very office, which has won the entire world for Christ? Who could possibly have designed a more terrible outrage to the preaching of the word than that a man professing to be a preacher should turn a Lenten sermon into a Bacchanalian diatribe during the most holy season of the year, in the presence of a large group of the faithful, from the height of the pulpit, as it were from the throne of Christ, and in full view of the Blessed Sacrament? What must have been the expression on the faces of the congregation, when, having come to hear spiritual wisdom, they perceived this ridiculous monkeylike figure spewing out invectives from the pulpit. They had come piously expecting to hear words of life but left realizing that what they had heard was an attack on literature and what they had seen was the office of preaching disgraced by the stupidity of the preacher. To inveigh against all secular learning could be understood in the case of some pious soul who had withdrawn from the world to pursue the monastic life. Should such a one launch into a tirade in defense of vigils, prayer, fasting, and the path that leads to heaven, one could tolerate the denunciation of the study of literature as an obstacle to the spiritual life. One could tolerate such a person's use of the old clichés about how rustic and illiterate people make their way more directly to heaven. Those hearing him would excuse this because of his simplicity and would benignly understand a sanctimoniousness that, however stupid, was at least honest and sincere. But when they see a man attired in academic gown and ermine ascend the podium and in the midst of an academic gathering dedicated to learning openly debauch almost all literature, they would have to be blind not to see this as an instance of pride, wickedness, and envy of all higher things. Many must have been disturbed by the fact that such a man should desire to preach about Latin, of which he knew so little, or of the liberal arts of which he knew less, or finally, of the Greek language in which he knew not even how to grunt. If the subject had been the seven deadly sins, a theme always conducive to good preaching, one would have thought him not well versed therein. For what is sloth other than the habit of refuting rather than learning something of which one is ignorant? Is it not the worst kind of pride for a speaker to wish that no kind of knowledge be held in esteem except what he has mistakenly convinced himself he possesses? And is not this compounded when he arrogates to himself more praise for his ignorance than for his knowledge, and this not from modesty as is true in some cases?

Now as far as secular learning is concerned, no one denies that salvation can be attained without this or any other kind of education. Yet this education which he calls secular does prepare the soul for virtue. In any case few will doubt that an education in the liberal arts is almost the exclusive motive for many a man's attendance at Oxford. Any good mother can instruct her children at home in the basic and elementary virtues. Furthermore, even should a person wish to come to you to learn theology, he must first prepare himself in other disciplines. A study of human affairs is prerequisite and particularly useful knowledge for theologians. Lacking such study they might be able to preach in a halting fashion to their colleagues, but would certainly make a poor showing before the people. I know of no better source for the requisite skill in this area than the works of poets, orators, and historians.

Furthermore, there are some who derive from knowledge of natural things a way whereby they ascend to the contemplation of spiritual things. They build a path to theology through that philosophy and those liberal arts which this man condemns as secular. It is like despoiling the women of Egypt to honor its queen. How can theology, which this man at least seems to admit as the one science worth pursuing, be studied without a knowledge of Hebrew, Greek, or Latin? Perhaps this fine fellow has convinced himself that there is enough theology written in English or that all theology is contained within the limits of those *quaestiones* which are so arduously debated and for which, I must admit, a little Latin suffices.

Actually, I must deny that theology, that august queen of heaven, can be so confined. For theology dwells and finds her habitation in the sacred writings, and she has traveled through the cells of the Holy Fathers, Augustine, Jerome, Ambrose, Cyprian, Chrysostom, Gregory, Basil, and others like them, who are now held in contempt. In fact for over a thousand years since the death of Christ and until the birth of those quibbling, scholastic *quaestiones* which are tossed about today, this science was based upon their writings. Anyone who claims he can understand the works of the Fathers, without being well versed in each of the languages in which they wrote, will waste his time attempting to impress the learned.

But if this preacher uses as a pretext for cloaking his stupidity the plea that he was not condemning secular learning as such, but only an immoderate interest in it, I fail to see that this interest is such a sin as to compel correction in a public sermon and a denunciation appropriate to a crime that would destroy society. I have not heard that very many have gone so far in this type of study as to pass the bounds of moderation.

Further, this fine fellow, to indicate how far he was removed from moderation, openly attributed heresy to those who were interested in Greek literature. Their teachers he designated as major devils and their pupils he called the same, except that he wittily modified this by using the expression "devilites." This holy man was so filled with wrath that he termed a devil one whom everyone knows the devil himself could not bear to see in the pulpit. He did everything but mention him by name, a fact that was as obvious to all as was the insanity of the speaker.

With all seriousness, learned sirs, it is not my purpose to pose as the sole champion of Greek learning. I realize full well how scholars of your standing appreciate its usefulness. For who is not cognizant of the fact that in the liberal arts and especially in theology, it was the Greeks who discovered or handed on whatever was of value. In the realm of philosophy, with the possible exceptions of Cicero and Seneca, what is there that was not written in Greek or taken directly from the Greeks?

I will not make mention of the New Testament, which was written almost entirely in Greek. Nor need I mention that the most ancient and qualified of the interpreters of the Scriptures were Greeks. I am merely expressing the consensus of all scholars when I say that, in spite of the great quantity of translations from former times and the more recent efforts in this direction, only half of this literature has been translated into Latin. Even though these later translations have been improved upon, they are still no substitute for the original. It was for this reason that the Doctors of the Latin Church, Jerome, Augustine, Bede, and many others set themselves to the task of learning Greek. Even though many of these works were in translation, it was still their wont to read them in the original. We cannot say the same about our present-day scholars. Not only did the Fathers learn Greek themselves, but they recommended its study to those of their successors who wished to be theologians.

For this reason, as I have said, I am not merely advising you as wise men to defend the study of the Greek language but, rather, exhorting you to perform your duty. You should permit no one in your academy to be deterred from the study of Greek, either by public exhortations or private inanities, since the study of this language is demanded by the universal church in all schools. Your own prudence should dictate that not all who among you give themselves over to this study are stupid. As a matter of fact, it is this very study which is partially responsible for the fame of your institution both here and abroad. There appears to be an increase of those whose nominal study of Greek has enhanced the reputation of your institution and promoted the cause of all the liberal arts. It would not be surprising if this enthusiasm should cool somewhat if it is understood that such a serious effort is held in contempt. This is especially important if one considers that at Cambridge, which institution you have always outshone, even those who are not actually studying Greek are led by a common interest in improved studies to contribute to the support of an outstanding Greek scholar.

I think you see my point. Much more could be added by those better informed than am I. I am merely making common cause with what others are saying and doing, not advising you what should be done. You are more aware than I that unless subversive factions can be suppressed at the beginning, a contagion will gradually spread from the worst to the best and it will then become necessary for the good and wise still among you to petition for aid from the outside. . . .

I do not doubt that in your wisdom you will find an easy solution for terminating these disputes and eliminating these horrible factions, and that you will provide that all the liberal arts be freed from ridicule and held in esteem and honor. For such diligence and serious study will do you untold good, and the rewards you will reap from our illustrious prince and the above-mentioned Reverend Fathers almost test the limits of expression.

As I have written this out of a deep affection for you, our own friendship will be firmly cemented. You know that my good will and services will be ever at your disposal, not only as a group but individually. May God keep your famous academy unharmed and may He grant that it flourish more and more in the liberal arts and in virtue.

Thomas More

Abingdon, 29th March, 1518.

An Answer to Martin Luther

This selection from the Responsio ad Lutherum *is a translation of the eighth chapter of the first book. It first appeared in 1523 under the pseudonym Rosseus, and was described as a rebuttal of the insane doctrines of Martin Luther,* refellit insanas Lutheri calumnias. *The occasion of this caustic attack on the German reformer was the publication of Luther's reply to Henry VIII's* Assertio Septem Sacramentorum (*itself an attack on Luther's* De captivitate Babylonica). *Unlike the Appeal to the Nobility of the same period, which attacked the centuries-old abuses of the Church, the Babylonian Captivity caustically attacked the sacramental system and the sacrificial nature of the Mass. Intended for theologians and written in Latin, it opened the eyes of many for the first time to the radical elements in Luther's doctrine. Erasmus declared that it precluded all possibility of peace with the papacy. More, whose knowledge of Luther's doctrines was at this time meager, followed the path of many critics in failing to perceive the real motive of his adversary, which was the cleansing of the Church. Like so many earlier opponents of Luther, Cochleaus and Esmer for example, he stooped to a bitter* ad hominem *course in attempting to expose Luther as the destroyer of ecclesiastical tradition. It is interesting to note that as the religious controversy progressed, the question of the Eucharist rather than that of justification by faith became the fundamental issue that separated Catholic from Protestant. "The king's book" from which More quotes is* Assertio Septem Sacramentorum. (*More had a slight hand in its composition. The work earned Henry, who was soon to break with Rome, the papal title Defensor Fidei, which, ironically, the British monarch has retained ever since.*)

Luther, having unburdened himself of all these charges (like a wind scattering storm clouds), says finally, "Let us look at the subject itself." This, of course, is after he has wasted seven of his twenty-eight pages, one-fourth of his booklet, on matters admittedly beside the point. At this point he now proposes to lay the foundations of the main argument with which he hopes to refute the king's charges.

Here again, however, we have an instance of his empty cleverness, that base slyness that betrays his lack of confidence in himself. He has heard the old adage, "Night is for the weaker forces," so when he feels a battle approaching, he slinks off into the darkness. Fabricating a general answer, he reserves consideration of all that requires a particular reply for that section which purports to deal with such matters. Upon reaching this designated section, we are unable to uncover any evidence that he has fulfilled his promise. Truly, the strongest objections are bypassed in the most offhand manner.

In his general reply, especially, where he makes no attempt to answer so much as a single one of the king's objections, he tries to distract the reader's attention from what he is doing, as if no one would become aware of his wiliness.

Ours, however, will be a different approach. We will drag

the blind, unwilling serpent out of its murky hiding-place into the light. We will quote certain excerpts from the king's book, and then line them up with the answers, so that you can see plainly that Luther has actually faced none of those objections which so highly merit an answer.

THE EUCHARIST

First of all, with regard to the sacrament of the Eucharist, there occur in the Canon of the Mass certain words which are attributed to Christ even though they don't occur in Scripture. Many things were said and done by Christ, as all authorities admit, which are not recorded by the Evangelists. Many sayings of Christ have come down to us by word of mouth from the time of the Apostles. Luther believes this, and does not doubt therefore that Christ said at the Last Supper: "As often as you shall do these things, you shall do them in memory of me."

He considers these words to be so authentically the words of Christ that from them he argues that no one is compelled to receive the Sacrament. Rather, he says, this matter is obviously left up to the free choice of the individual.

We are bound only in this, he says, that as often as we perform certain actions we should perform them in memory of Christ. (In the Evangelists' account of the Lord's Supper, we find only "Do this in commemoration of me," not "As often as you shall do this . . ." These latter words are found in the Mass, and not elsewhere. They are not to be found in the Gospels themselves.) Well, he who believes in and uses certain words only because he finds them in the Canon of the Mass should also accept with like faith the words of the same Canon when it calls the Mass an oblation, a sacrifice.

CONFIRMATION

When Luther quotes certain passages from which it would be reasonable to conclude that Christ instituted the sacrament of Confirmation, he nevertheless withholds belief and says that the Church alone is responsible for its institution. Luther refuses belief because he finds in Scripture no promise of such an institution. Christ, Luther would seem to imply, fulfills only those promises that are recorded in Scripture.

With this kind of thinking, Luther actually would have to deny the institution of the Eucharist if we had only St. John's Gospel to rely on. For in John nothing is said about such an institution. John omits to mention this institution, just as the Synoptics also omit any reference to many other actions of

Christ. "There are many other things that Jesus did," says the Evangelist, "but if they were all written down, not even the world itself would be able to hold the books containing them."

Some of the deeds of Christ were handed down to the faithful by tradition rather than by the written word, and were forever after preserved in the faith of the Church. Why is it not reasonable to believe certain truths only on the authority of the Church, since we accept the Gospels themselves only on that same authority?

If none of the Gospels had ever been written down, there would still remain a Gospel written in the hearts of the faithful, these tablets being much more ancient than all the codices of the Evangelists. The sacraments would remain, and these same sacraments, I am sure, are older than all the books of the Gospels. It is no argument for Luther to say that a man receives a sacrament in vain if its institution is not recorded in the Gospels.

If Luther is willing to accept nothing except what is plainly set down in Scripture, why does he believe in the perpetual virginity of Mary? There is nothing to prove this in Scripture, and Helvidius actually took it upon himself to prove the contrary, relying on no other authority than that of Scripture. The only thing that stands opposed to this belief is the faith of the entire Church—and, of course, that faith of the Church is strongest where the sacraments are concerned. I certainly don't think that anyone who had a spark of faith could be persuaded that Christ, who prayed for Peter lest his faith fail, who established the Church on a firm rock, would permit her to commit herself for centuries to a belief in certain sacraments that were really empty signs.

Even if the institution of the sacraments is found in no written record, the men who lived with Christ could nevertheless testify to the Lord's intention. For He said of them, "You are witnesses who were with me from the beginning." He could have taught them. The Holy Spirit himself could have taught them, of whom Christ said: "When the Paraclete shall come, whom I shall send you, the Spirit of Truth, who proceeds from the Father, He will give testimony of me." And again: "When He has come, whom I shall send you, the Spirit of Truth, who proceeds from the Father, He will give testimony of me." And again: "When He has come, the Spirit of Truth, He will guide you to all truth. For He will not speak of Himself, but whatever He will have heard, He will speak and what is to come, He will tell you."

Can anyone believe, therefore, that the Church herself rashly instituted a false sacrament, and placed her confidence in an empty sign, this Church which has had so many and such great teachers, this Church which the Spirit Himself inspires with the Truth?

MATRIMONY

Luther denies that the sacrament of matrimony was instituted as a sign of grace. How does he know this? Because, as he says, this is nowhere to be found in writing. O mighty Logic, father of so many heresies. From this font, Helvidius himself drank poison. Do you admit no sacrament, Luther, whose institution you cannot find in a book? What book did *He* ever write who instituted all the sacraments? Concerning some of the sacraments, you say, "I believe the Evangelists of Christ." Why then do you not believe the Church which Christ set over the Evangelists, men who were nothing if not members of the Church? Why, if you believe in one reality, do you hesitate to believe in the other? If you admit that a member of a body exists, why do you not believe that the body itself exists?

The Church considers matrimony to be a sacrament. The Church believes that it was instituted by God. This tradition has been handed down to us through the ages, and the same tradition must be passed on to future generations to the end of time. Matrimony is declared to be a sacrament by the Church, that same Church which tells us that the Evangelists wrote the Gospels. For if the Church had not declared the Gospel of St. John's to be his, you, Luther, would not know that it was. For you did not sit beside the writer. How is it that you are unable to accept the Church's word on the divine institution and apostolic succession of the sacraments, when you are willing to do so on the Evangelical authorship of this Gospel?

A few passages have now been heard from among the number written by the king in illustration of the fact that many of Christ's words and actions have descended to us unrecorded by the Evangelists. They have descended by word of mouth from apostolic times, though unmentioned in either Scripture or apostolic writings. The king indicates the role of the Holy Spirit as teacher and governor of the Church in sacramental matters and articles of faith. His demonstration is supported by its logical rigor and witnessed by the sacred writings of the Evangelists and the words of Christ Himself.

Stripped of its jibes, insults, mockery, and wrangling, Luther's reply consists of only two propositions. He finds that truth and certainty reside in the Scriptures alone, and that what remains outside is mere tradition and the province of individual evaluation. Concerning the king's citation of Evangelical and divine authority in support of the existence of unwritten words, instructions, and events, there is only silence, and surely these require a reply. Can Luther's evasion be construed as anything but a confession that he has nothing to say? While this is manifest, a quotation of Luther's own words will make it even more obvious, and clear the miasma in which the rascal has enshrouded himself.

"We will address ourselves now to the very subject itself," he says, "and in the best manner of that Thomistic deity, Aristotle, we will argue from the general to the particular. Generally, then, this Thomistic form of argument is the single, best strength of Henrician wisdom as displayed in his royal little book. According to this form of argument and without scriptural authority or compelling reason, he says: 'It seems to me,' 'I think so,' and, 'I believe so.' This is a fitting occasion for that story my friend Amsdorff used to relate about the argumentative method of the Leipzig theologians. According to this tale, an opponent would refute his respondent's denial of a point by saying: 'It ought to be so.' Denied again, he would say: 'And how can it be otherwise? It must be so.' How cleverly, Thomistically, even Leipzigistically and Henricistically done! Though I had singled out this general Thomistic principle in my *Babylonian Captivity* and there opposed this reliance on ritual, usage, custom, and human authority by an appeal to Sacred Scripture, the lord king can only reply with Thomistic sagacity: 'This must be so; custom has it so, this has long been in usage; I believe the Fathers have written thus; the Church has so ordered, etc.' A thousand books proving that human authority and custom are as nothing in matters of faith would not suffice to prevent a thousand answers by this Thomist king ignoring the evidence of Scripture and saying only, again and again: 'It must be so; custom so has it; the authority of men says so.' Any request for a validation of man's custom and warrant is again met with: 'It must be so; it seems so to me; so I believe!' Is this king's learning by itself superior to that of all men?"

Who could contain their mirth at the sight of a grin emerging on this dull chap's livid and comic face as he sets down that the king could offer nothing save: "This must be so; custom has it so, this has long been in usage; I believe the Fathers have written thus; the Church has so ordered"? Luther's awareness that the king said almost nothing of the sort is common knowledge. The *actual* quotations follow thusly: "Reason proves this; God has transmitted it; the Holy Spirit has taught it; The Gospel says so; Christ himself speaks thus!" Only silence from Luther on all these things!

"It becomes obvious that the single goal of these stubborn blockheads is the establishment of faith in no one but themselves. They demand acceptance of their corrupt intellectual constructions, while I appeal to the impersonal standard of God's word. I do not seek the repeal of human authority and custom, but I do oppose the establishment of compulsory faith in human maxims. What cannot be found in Scripture should not be rigidly imposed for belief. The tolerance that should be accorded those laudable, but extrascriptural, words and deeds should be a free tolerance. In direct contradiction to the desires of the saints, these blockheads construe every traditional word as an article of faith. What greater offense could be given to the Fathers than this transformation of their words and deeds into snares for the destruction of souls?"

We can see the clarity with which Luther presents our demands. What does he require in return? Only that while we, the stubborn blockheads, summon belief in ourselves only, to wit, in the Italian, Spanish, English, and French peoples and in all peoples that are united through Christ's passion in His Church wherever and whenever that may be; he, Luther, simply requires belief in just those scriptural texts which he repeatedly casts into doubt and manifestly twists into heresy. Then, upon reproach, he dares no reply.

We will focus more sharply on this later. Now we will clear up his argument that all extrascriptural matters should be treated freely and by the individual alone. His contention is that free tolerance only should be accorded to those worthwhile sayings and deeds that cannot be found in Scripture. If you are secure in truth, Luther, why don't you answer the arguments advanced by the king? There are many besides those listed above and they will be presented in their proper place. A close reading of both these and your general answer would disclose your complete evasion to anyone. Your feigning, your heedless inattention, and your deaf man's silence make plain your motive in overlooking them: fear of the indefensibility of your position. Having uncovered your fear we will insistently stick these distressing points under your very nose.

To return, then, if as you consistently affirm, all extrascriptural matter is to be maintained only freely and none of it held fast by faith, what is the meaning of this Apostolic admonition: "Stand and hold fast the traditions which you have learned through our word or letter"? The preservation of both word and letter is equally charged by the Apostle. Extrascriptural matter was thus handed down, and on a binding, not a take-it-or-leave-it basis! What do you say to that, Luther? And to this: "Many things were done which are not written in this book," a passage of the Evangelist's? These things which you have remarked as absent from the other scriptural books also, and of which John says that the whole world cannot contain them—aren't they to be regarded as miracles at least? Wouldn't you also find that an ignorance of many of them would jeopardize faith? But could the Evangelists fail to mention the sacraments, so important to the truth and freedom from superstition of the Church? Here you are trapped, for as the king has plainly shown you, the sacrament of the Eucharist was not transmitted in writing by John the Evangelist. Its central importance undercuts the contention that he failed to do so because the others had prerecorded it. Were this a consideration, he would surely have made a lesser omission in its stead. The fact that even essential principles are transmitted by unwritten tradition is therefore indisputable.

In a letter to the Corinthians upon this very sacrament, Paul wrote: "*I* have delivered to you that which I have received from the Lord." Is this delivery made in the form by which he received it—unwritten? Truly, until the writing of the letter, he had used no other form of transmission. He had written neither the Corinthians, nor the Romans, nor any other people. If Paul had chosen the permissible form of direct verbal communication on those occasions when he did write, you would now be doubting those articles of faith based on the Pauline Epistles. Many Epistles by all of the authors are lost, and those extant are subject to bilingual ambiguity and interminable strife over interpretation and meaning. You are such a participant in these very battles that you will never want a chance to deny or affirm whatever you please, you who will allow nothing but scriptural evidence!

What force has this pronouncement of Christ's: "The Holy Spirit, the Paraclete, when He comes, will guide you into all truth"? He doesn't say that the Spirit will "write" to you or whisper in your ear, but he will lead you, will form you interiorly, and with His breath will show your hearts the way to all truth. Was it the Apostles, here addressed by Christ, to whom the way was to be shown? Were they alone told, "I am with you to the consummation of the world"? Who can question the direction of this message to the Church? *Will* not the Holy Spirit show her the way to all truth? *Was* she not told, "Go, preach the Gospel to every creature"? Did they read the Gospel or preach it? And did Christ cast the new law in bronze or strike it on stone tablets, commanding that everything else be considered valueless and cast out?

Can God's own word as set down by the Apostle leave Luther untouched, "I will put my laws in their hearts; I shall inscribe them on their minds"? He makes no mention of stone or wood, for as the old law was stamped by Him upon external stone, so will the new be inscribed with His own finger in the book of the heart; that which existed so briefly upon the hardest material will be made to last forever on the softest. So it has pleased God to show His power. Though the old stone tablets were quickly shattered, the new remain. The word of God will remain forever uneffaced in the heart of man. The heart, the Church of Christ, will forever contain the true Gospel of Christ, written there before any of the Evangelical books. However ingenious the apparent scriptural evidence heretics may bring against the true faith, God has engraved His law in such a way that it is impervious to their guile. The strength of this spring has preserved the faith of Christ against assaults upon both His mother and Himself from their respective enemies, Helvidius and Arius. It has sustained her in turning back deep ranks of heretics which have before employed Luther's own siege weaponry: the denial of Scripture as a proof of the Church's common faith, or an assertion that the two are in contradiction. Whether supported by writing or not, the Church of Christ has never doubted the authenticity of her inspiration by the Holy Spirit. The faith inscribed in our hearts is the best witness against any appearance of contradiction to this. It counsels us that those who subscribe to such interpretations do so out of error, for the Spirit of God cannot contradict Himself and it is certain that Christ would not disappoint His Church on the essentials of her faith.

But if you continue dully to insist upon the written as the only valid form of transmission, and doggedly persist in ignoring the scriptural evidence from the king's book, at least clear up the enigma posed by these facts: the Father is never, at any place in all of Scripture, called "uncreated," the Son is never called "consubstantial," and the Holy Spirit never clearly described as "proceeding from the Father and Son." For truly, the heretics continue to stress the vagueness of all scriptural depictions of the Holy Spirit so strongly that one can easily say, with St. Gregory Nazianzen, that He is *"Theon Agrapton,"* the unwritten God. Would you have, then, each individual man, freely and without spiritual hazard, decide for himself whether or not to believe in the Father as uncreated, the Son as consubstantial, and the Holy Spirit as proceeding from both?

How do you answer the fact that there is a total lack of scriptural evidence regarding the virginity of Mary, as is witnessed by Jerome's laborious proof that none exists in opposition to this doctrine? Though he demonstrated the doctrine in an exemplary manner, he lacked the conclusive scriptural evi-

dence necessary to establish it beyond dispute. His final appeal
is obviously directed to the faith of the Church! Until you
satisfy me by making your stand on this point public, I must
believe that you do wholly accept it, even in your impiety. If
this is true, your position is beyond Scripture and in contradiction to your basic argument!

Even if your impiety won't stop short of casting doubt upon
the Virgin birth, it surely can't extend to impeaching the sacramental character of the Eucharist, almost unique as it is, which
has so far escaped the stain of your sinister touch. But it is likewise incredible that you should retract your basic weapon for
the overthrow of the sacraments, to wit, that without a written
scriptural mandate promising grace or remission of sin there
can be no sacrament.

Now, Luther, even you must be aware of the incongruity
this time. For you are caught between the humiliating disgrace
of a retraction of your central position and a criminal denial
of the sacramental character of the Eucharist. You must abandon one of these points helter-skelter, for the king has you
cornered. He has signed your impure brow with a mark of
wicked folly that is proof against all dissembling, so read his
words, you rascal!

> The Church's belief in the divine institution of the sacra-
> ments, even in the absence of direct scriptural citation, has
> been corroborated by Luther's own cardinal point. Now, let
> us see if the Scriptures in some manner specify this sacrament.
>
> Only Luther abstains from the universal acclamation
> accorded to the validity of the Apostolic ordination at the Last
> Supper. It is clearly written that on this occasion the unique
> power of consecrating the body of Christ was conferred upon
> the priesthood. But Luther says, "It is no sacrament, for there
> was no promise of grace." How can he tell? "Since it is
> unrecorded in Scripture, it was not done by Christ." A familiar
> deduction of his that is undone by the Evangelist's statement
> that, "Many things were done which are not recorded in this
> book."
>
> Luther's common sense forces him to confess the sacra-
> mental character of the Eucharist and this allows us to strike
> even nearer the mark. For he can countenance nothing but
> an unequivocal scriptural promise of grace and there is none
> in connection with this sacrament. No reading of the Last
> Supper texts will ever yield any such promise by any Evange-
> list. The words of the Lord are there for anyone to read: "This
> is my Blood of the New Testament, which will be shed for you
> and for many unto the remission of sins." They indicate the
> redemption which His suffering and crucifixion extend to man.
> But neither celebrant nor communicant receives a promise of

grace or forgiveness by His injunction: "Do this in commemoration of me." Nor does Paul later make any such promise to worthy communicants when he warns the unworthy that they eat and drink judgment unto themselves. And even if parts of St. John 6 can be construed as affording participants in the Eucharistic feast such a promise of grace, it will afford Luther nothing, for he refuses to admit that this chapter makes any mention of the sacrament whatsoever.

Thus Luther is unable to provide for himself the gloriously promised scriptural assurance of grace that his work has led us to expect as the foundation of every sacrament. He is, on the contrary, forced to rely upon the extrascriptural tradition and faith of the Church, and this with respect to almost the only sacrament which he has retained!

Doesn't this have a familiar ring, Luther, or is your besotted condition such that you are unable even to hear? Why didn't these points find any place in the reply of which you are so proud? Can't we discover the reason in your need to disguise the king's demolition of your central thesis and his consequent deflation of your attack against the sacraments? The statement that "there is no sacrament whose promise of grace is not found in the evident testimony of Scripture," has formed the cornerstone of your *Babylon*, and you have rashly broadened this base by including the contention that there can be no article of faith that is not explicitly manifest in Scripture. But the prince now compels you to make a crucial decision: You must either sacrifice to this exalted principle of yours your faith in the sacramental character of the Eucharist, or, to keep faith with this one of our few remaining sacraments, you must abandon your principle and flee to the extrascriptural haven that is the common faith of our so-called Papist Church!

Latin Epigrams

Perhaps the finest description of the Latin poems of More is to be found in a letter appraising them written by the humanist Beatus Rhenanus (Beat Bild) to his friend Willibald Pirckheimer. After listing the true qualities of a good epigram, wit combined with brevity, lightheartedness and termination with a pointed message, he writes: "Certainly all of these properties are to be found in the Epigrams *of More, particularly in those composed by himself. In the others from the Greek, of course, the originality belongs to the ancients. Yet even here More deserves great credit as a translator. There is no doubt that translating requires greater skill since unlike the author, unencumbered and free to use whatever comes to him, the translator must constantly keep in mind the subject he has chosen to translate. In such a situation his ability is more severely taxed than when he writes something of his own. In both of these areas Thomas More is outstanding for he composes with great taste and he translates felicitously. How sweetly and smoothly flow his verses. Nothing is forced, harsh, awkward, or obscure. He writes the purest and most limpid Latin. In addition everything is joined with a happy wit so that I have never read anything with greater pleasure. I can believe that the Muses have endowed this man with all their gifts of humor, elegance, and wit. How gracefully he makes fun of Sabinus for bringing up someone else's children. With what wit does he not ridicule Lalus, who goes to such extremes in his desire to appear French. Yet, his witticisms are by no means mordant but are rather honest, sweet, mild rather than bitter. He provokes laughter, but never with malice, he ridicules but without abuse."*

The Epigrammata, *or Latin poems, first appeared in an edition of the* Utopia *published in March of 1518 by Froben in Basel; a second edition appeared in December of that year and a third and emended edition in 1520.*

The coronation ode with which the Epigrammata *open reveals More's willingness to flatter the new king; it should be noted, however, that the young Henry's devotion to learning was a source of hope for humanists.*

TO HENRY VIII ILLUSTRIOUS KING OF BRITAIN AND HIS
MOST HAPPY QUEEN CATHARINE ON THE
OCCASION OF HIS CORONATION

If there ever was a day in England,
If there ever was a day for bandwagons,
This is that glorious red-letter day.
Bring out your beakers and flagons.

This day sees the end of our slavery,
This day sees the end of our grief.
Today we inaugurate freedom.
All hail to our new royal chief.

Here's a king to rule *all* nations,
Instead of ours alone.
Let there be song and laughter
From the Isle of St. Martin's to Scone.

Today the clouds are scattered.
The sun was never more bright.
Crowds are gathering everywhere
To acclaim the people's delight.

All London is celebrating.
Children dance in the street.
We'll toast our noble king today
With enough wine to float the fleet.

Our nobles, long nonentities,
Our nobles now lift their heads.
Celebrate the future!
The old dreary past is dead.

Our merchants, long crushed by taxes,
Once again set out to sea.
Our laws, too long inactive,
Regain validity.

Farewell, old penury days,
When citizens lived in ditches.
Now the kingdom's poorest
Can share in the country's riches.

Now profits escape the government's
Tax-gatherers' clutching hands.
No longer are Englishmen clamped in jail
For possessing houses and lands.

Men no longer speak in whispers
For fear of the secret police.
Informers all go jobless.
The king has cooked their geese.

Now men and women meet openly.
There's no more reason to lurk.
The drinkers crowd the taverns,
And the pious pray in the kirk.

Dense crowds await his Majesty

Wherever he drives in his coach.
People gather from everywhere
When informed of his approach.

Everyone seeks a vantage point
To see him as he passes.
Gentlefolk of the highest station,
And the commonest of the masses.

Of the nobles in our country,
There's no one like our king.
The noblest of our nation
He surpasses in everything.

The hand of our noble Henry
Is as skilled as his heart is brave,
To settle knightly arguments
With leveled spear or glaive.

A fiery power is in his eye.
There's beauty in his face.
Admirable in strength is he,
The ornament of our race.

Never was man more perfect
In knightly or elegant arts,
Since Achilles dragged Sir Hector
Around Troy's walls with his cart.

If mind and heart were visible,
How perfect our king would appear,
Excelling even the noblest
In our hemisphere.

The beautiful calmness of his face
Reveals a lofty mind,
One capable of bearing
Fortunes of every kind.

How great his care to honor
Only worthiness.
How far removed his bearing
From pride or brazenness.

One knows at once that such a king

Repudiates deceit.
His very countenance itself
Is antithetic to conceit.

On the other hand, how just he is,
How wonderfully skilled in ruling.
His every administrative act
Bespeaks his princely schooling.

Fears, harms, dangers, griefs
Will now vanish from our nation.
Peace, ease, joy and laughter
Will be our daily ration.

Unlimited power has a tendency
To breed corruption in men,
But God has given our noble prince
Immunity from this sin.

He is quick to trap the criminal
And to punish all the traitors,
Curbing disruptive pamphleteers
And all their liberal paters.

He's extending to all our businessmen
A much-needed helping hand
Clamping down on the maniacs
Desirous of ruining our land.

He now gives good men honors
And lets them help to rule
In offices which once were held
By the shiny egg-pated fool.

Our prince has taken proper steps
To restore some force to law,
Which has long become a mockery
And an underworld guffaw.

No idolator of predecessors,
He's repealed our bad legislation
Which proves he doesn't put his love
Of party over the nation.

Of course it's no surprise to us

To see him abolish abuses,
This man was dipped in Pierian Springs
By nine Castilian muses.

In the past, our many heads of state
Could misrule with impunity.
Our present prince respects the law,
Desires no immunities.

Our reigning lord despises
To use his office for gain,
And is therefore respected
Throughout the royal domain.

O prince, terror to enemies
But protection to our nation—
Our love for you will know no bounds
Short of deification.

And thus with power unlimited
You'll deter our many foes.
The Scots, the French will think twice
Before firing their crossbows.

And certainly our noble lord
Will rid us of civil strife.
The Leftist now is stifled
Like a tightly gagged fishwife.

You yourself are sacred to us,
So no anger against you can arise.
With new dangers to our nation,
Our love merely magnifies.

You are the nation's darling.
No one could be dearer.
You're the nearest to all our hearts.
No one could be nearer.

All the virtues of your ancestors
Are found again in you.
Wisdom, strength, intelligence
Are your royal retinue.

No wonder then that England

And all her people rejoice.
No wonder they sing your praises,
Your virtues, with one voice.

Of course to all these reasons
For rejoicing we must add a queen,
The happiest choice for a king's mate
In the history of this demesne.

You can be sure your people are happy
To see her share your throne.
You can be sure they take great pride
To have her as their own.

This is a queen who could outdo
The devotion of any bride.
Whose love is vastly greater
Than Dido's the suicide.

Her countenance has the beauty
Of goodness personified.
To serve as maids before her throne
The best are unqualified.

This lady, Sire, for love of you
Has waited many years,
Turning down in the meantime.
Scores of cavaliers.

One alone she thought of,
And that was you, my lord.
You alone she worshiped,
You alone adored.

She is truly regal,
Having descended from many a king.
No maiden could be worthier
Of a royal wedding ring.

There could be no worthier
To share your royal life.
Just as no other man
Could be worthy of such a wife.

England, therefore, brings today

Praise from grateful hearts—
On this your coronation day.
And we poets on our part

Can only wish you many years
Of wearing your royal crown—
And may your progeny never cease to reign
In good old London Town.

TO AN ENGLISHMAN AFFECTING FRENCH

My friend and companion, Lalus,
Was born in England, and brought up on our island.
Nevertheless, although a mighty sea,
Language, and customs separate us from the continent,
Lalus still is scornful of all things English.
He admires, in fact, and wants only what is French.
He struts about in French dress,
He is fond of little imported capes.
He is happy with his belt, his purse, his sword—
Only if they are also foreign.
And again with regard to his hat, his beret, his cap,
And well as with regard to his shoes, and his underwear,
And actually his clothes in general,
He is happy only if he looks like a fop from head to toe.
Why, he even has a servant, a Frenchman,
And France herself, I think, if it tried,
Could not treat this servant more in its own fashion.
For he pays the servant nothing—like a Frenchman;
Clothes him in worn-out rags—in the French manner;
Feeds him little and that poorly—as the French do;
Works him hard—like a Frenchman.
At social gatherings, on the street,
Or in the marketplace—publicly—
He quarrels with his servant
In the very best fashion *français*.
What! Have I said that he does all this in the French way?
I should rather say in a half-French way.
For, unless I'm greatly mistaken
He can parley français only as a parrot does.
Nevertheless, he swells with pride
If he can get off three whole words in French.
And if there is anything he can't say in his favorite foreign
          tongue
He tries at least to say it with a foreign accent:

That is, with an open palate,
With a shrill sort of effeminate sound,
Like women chattering, lisping prettily,
As though his mouth were full of beans,
Pronouncing with emphasis those very letters
Which the foolish French avoid
As the cock avoids the fox, or the sailor the cliffs.
And so it is with this kind of accent
That he speaks Latin, English,
Italian, Spanish, and German—
Every language, in fact, except French—
For French is the one language he pronounces
With a definite English accent.
Of all the fools! to scorn one's native land
And feign and counterfeit the follies of the French!
Such a man, I think has become insane
From drinking the River Gallus.
Since he is trying to change from English to French,
May the gods change him from a cock to a capon.

TO CANDIDE, ON WHAT SORT OF WIFE TO CHOOSE
(IAMBIC VERSES IN BRACHYCATALECTIC DIMETERS)

Time has caught up with you, Candide.
It warns you at last
Your here-and-there loves
Are a thing of the past.
No more will you chase
From bed to bed
The most uncertain Cyprian,
As often caught as fled.
Marriage in mind, you look for
A virgin whom you may fetter
With rites, with loving concord,
To yourself. Thus your people
—Than whom, none better—
May find sweet increase.
Your father has already
Done as much, through you;
What your predecessors
Could provide and do
You, for your posterity,
Are indebted to
Perform in turn.
Yet, Candide, if you are wise

You will not strain
To over-scrutinize
Her dazzling prospects
Or her dowry's size.
Frail is the love
Money has procured
Out of a dull
Dishonoring lust
For money and property.
The man who would love
For money's sake
Is but loved for the difference
Money can make.
Such weak love flees
Once the money's exchanged;
It dies newborn
Of the very disease
That gives it life.
Besides, the money that was
The avid miser's original aim
Fails to provide him
The promised satisfaction.
Worse, willy-nilly,
There he is,
In the view of society,
Wed to a wife
He does not love.
What about beauty? Doesn't it
Diminish with illness,
Decline with the years, really,
Like small flowers in hot sun?
When it does, love secured
By cheeks where the color flows,
Love made fast
By ties so slight,
Is let loose and vanishes.
True is love,
Well-poised and well-aware,
When entered upon for cause,
Taking thought, with intelligence;
When brought into being
Under the brave auspices
Of honor for evident virtue
(Which, certain and permanent,
Does not diminish with illness
Nor decline with the years.)

So then, friend, first
Since you seek a wife
Look at the people
Who gave her life.
The girl will reflect
In her ways, the excellence
That graces her mother
Whose habits she imbibed
As a small, tender child.
Next, look for sound sweetness
In the nature of your bride.
May serenity reside
In the girl's speech;
May savagery be absent
From her mouth.
May there be
In her countenance shy decency
And in her discourse
No shameless impudence.
More, may she be reposeful
Nor willingly entangle men
In leaping lusts.
May she not be fickle of heart
Nor having a roving eye.
May she be neither
A babbler, given to constant
Gabble over trifles,
Nor a tight-lipped close-mouthed clod
Perpetually dumb.
Finally, may she be
Either educated, versed
In the humanities,
Or educable, apt
At absorbing learning.
Happy the girl
Who is able to draw
Out of the best of the books of earlier days
The principles of holy living.
They will invigorate her.
She will not swell up pompous
With pride in prosperity;
In times of trouble she will not be
Grief-stricken, prostrated
By misery.
She will be merry beside you;
She will not become,

No matter what betide you,
A reproachful sorrower.
Well taught herself, she
Will teach well; your children
—And, later, grandchildren—
Will drink in learning with their milk.
As for you, you will be glad
To leave the men to themselves
After work, and to find rest
In your clever wife's company.
She too will enjoy that time;
Perhaps while her agile fingers
Pluck true chords from the strings,
She may sing, and so delightfully
(In a voice, Procne,
No less sweet
Than that of your young sister)
Apollo will hide
To hear her songs.
She will fashion
Joy for you
Out of charm and wisdom,
Marking days and nights
With sweetness of phrase
And dulcet speech
Unbroken by harshness
From her delightful,
Always gentle mouth.
Freely she will soothe you
Should high spirits make you light
With thoughtless merriment;
Subtly she will sustain you
If anxious grief depresses you,
Her power to aid you strengthened
By well-informed eloquence
And a discriminating knowledge
Of important matters.
Such a girl I think certainly
The poet Orpheus
Married. He would never
Have taken the trouble
To work to recover
Out of the depths of hell
A stupid wife.
Such, we believe, was
Nato's famous daughter

Who aimed no less high
Than to equal
Her father in song.
Thus I imagine Tully's daughter,
Than whom none
Ever was dearer to a father,
Than whom
No one of her time
Was more learned.
Such a one surely was she
Who bore the two Gracchi.
She bore them and with great art
Taught them, and was
No less gifted for their good
As teacher than as parent.
Well, let's recapitulate.
Our hero hopes to find
A maiden to mate.
He hopes for one, only one,
Yet such a one
As will have him prefer
His one to many;
He will find all in her.
Perhaps he may choose the girl
Everyone finds excellent;
All Britain acclaims her,
Borne blithe as a bird
On wings of fame;
All sing, all have heard
Of this girl's glory
(Nor does her unique story
Imply the kind of fame
Cassandra's nation gave
Cassandra's name.)
What is there to say,
Candide, but yes,
To the thought of the girl
These lines portray?
Do not permit yourself
To feel a need for great beauty
Or to be won over
By Lucre.
These two thoughts
Are true:
She has beauty enough
Who pleases you;

No man owns more
Than one who owns enough,
And who owns enough?
The man who thinks he does.
May the wife who is mine
Not love me friend, if I
Have lied to you in any line.
To complaints
That some girl may lack
Beauty as her birthright
I say, "And if she were
Blacker than coal,
She might well be
More beautiful than a swan to me
As far as I, with my birthright, can see."
To complaints that some girl
Lacks wealth (that slippery stuff)
As her birthright, I say, "And if she
Were poorer than Iro,
Ithaca's least beggar, she'd be
Richer than Ithaca's King Croesus to me
Should that be as my birthright lets me see."

Translated by Marie Ponsot

ABOUT SOME SAILORS WHO DURING A STORM THREW THE MONK TO WHOM THEY HAD CONFESSED INTO THE SEA

When in a roaring storm the heaving sea rose high,
And the waves' anger raged against the struggling ship,
Uneasy conscience descended upon the frightened sailors.
"Our ill-spent lives," they shouted, "have brought these dangers
    down on us."
Whereupon, since there was a monk aboard,
They dumped their sins into his ear forthwith.
Then, however, observing that the sea had not calmed down,
But was threatening instead more than ever to swamp the ship,
One of them cried out: "No wonder we're barely afloat.
All this time we've been weighted down by our cargo of sin.
Why not throw overboard this monk who carries the guilt of
    us all,
And let him take our sins away with him?"
All the sailors, agreeing, laid hold of the monk and heaved
    him into the sea.
With that, the ship, they say, floated light as a cork.

From this story—yes, this story—learn one lesson:
Sin is so weighty a load, even a ship cannot bear it.

Translated by Marie Ponsot

CANDIDUS, A PASTOR

You've been chosen pastor, dear Candidus,
Of an especially large congregation.
I send you and your flock, therefore,
My most hearty congratulation.

Unless partiality affect my judgment,
They've never had such a priest,
A man whose spirit no worldliness
Ever swayed in the least.

Moreover, I find character like yours
Today extremely rare;
Priests of old alone possessed
Such virtues beyond compare.

It remains but to offer your parish
This very homely suggestion;
Do what you flee and flee what you do.
All else is out of the question.

BISHOP POSTHUMUS

You're a bishop now, dear Posthumus,
And it's only proper to say,
It's well that church authority
Is allotted in such a way
That men like you are given the rule
Of dioceses today.

I rejoice that an office so great
Has been given the likes of you—
That honors no longer are vainly conferred
As they have been hitherto:
Thoughtlessly and by impulse,
As if just any dolt would do.

In fact, my friend, in the recent past,

As if by a kind of curse,
The Church has appointed less than the best,
As I've often said in my verse.
But in your case it goes further by far:
No one could imagine worse.

Translated by Marie Ponsot

WHAT FORM OF GOVERNMENT IS BEST

You ask which governs better, a king or a senate.
Neither, if (as is frequently the case) both are bad.
But if both are good, then I think that the senate is better,
Since the greater good lies in having numerous good men.
It is much easier for a monarch to be bad.
A senate may occupy a position between good and evil,
But hardly ever do you have a king who is not either one or
        the other.
An evil senator can be offset by those who are better than he,
But a king can be ruled by no one.
A senator is elected by the people to rule,
While the king attains his office by being born.
In the one case, blind chance is supreme;
In the other, there is room for reason.
The one feels that he was created a senator by the people;
The other feels that the people were created
For the purpose of being subject to his rule.

A king in the first years of his reign tends to be mild,
But over a long period of time, his selfishness will wear his
        people down.
I am not impressed by the famous proverb
Which recommends that one endure the well-fed fly
Lest a hungry one take its place.
It is a mistake to believe that a selfish king can be satisfied.
Such a leech will never leave the flesh until it is drained.

You say that a serious disagreement impedes a senate's
        decisions,
While the king has no one to disagree with.
But that is the worse evil of the two,
For when there is a difference of opinion—
But what started all this inquiry anyway?
Is there anywhere a people upon whom you yourself
By your own decision can impose either a king or a senate?

If that does lie within your power, you are already a king.
Stop considering to whom you may give power.
The prior question is, "Why give it at all?"

FUSCUS THE DRINKER

"Must I go blind? What can I do?" asked Fuscus.
"Give up drinking," said his doctor.
"Take my advice since you ask it."
Fuscus, however, would rather let his eyes
Dissolve in a cask deliciously
Than save them to dissolve in a casket.

Translated by Marie Ponsot

AN ILLUSTRIOUS BISHOP REFERRED TO
EARLIER AS POSTHUMUS

Most reverend Father, you often quote
St. Paul: "The letter kills."
Into every sort of doctrinal speech
The dictum you instill.

Your life, of course, does demonstrate
What a killer it is, that alphabet.
You've avoided it like a curse:
You're the least lettered bishop yet.

Translated by Marie Ponsot

THE PASTOR WHO ANNOUNCED A FAST DAY
AFTER IT HAD PASSED

When our pastor was announcing on Sunday
The events of the coming week,
He laid great stress on the importance
Of preparing by fast and penance
For the feast of the great and holy
Apostle and martyr, St. Andrew,
Whose festival, as it happened,
Had been celebrated the day before.

TO SABINUS

Look here, Sabinus, the four children whom your wife has
                borne up to now
Do not in the least resemble you, and you yourself do not
                consider them yours.
But, in preference to the four, you take to your heart,
The only one who is anything like to you.
You call the four illegitimate,
You keep them at a distance, you disown them.
You fasten upon this youngest alone to be your heir,
And, like an ape, you carry him in your arms
All over the town for everyone to admire.
And yet authoritative scholars whose happy task
It is to examine carefully whatever nature brings forth,
Authoritative scholars, I say, tell us
That whatever image dominates the mother's mind when the
                child is begotten,
Secretly in some mysterious way imposes
Accurate and indelible traces of itself upon the seed.
These marks penetrate deeply and grow with the embryo,
And thus the child reflects the image inbred in it from the
                mother's mind.
When your wife had the four children
She was quite unconcerned about you who were miles away.
That is why she bore children who do not in the least resemble
                you.
But this son, of all your children,
Looks like you for when he was conceived,
His mother was deeply concerned for you, and had you
                completely in mind.
She was worried for fear that you, Sabinus,
Might inconveniently arrive too soon upon the scene.

HESPERUS AT CONFESSION

When the priest was questioning Hesperus
In confession (as he's bound to do),
He carefully sought to discover
If he believed in the Bugaboo.

"To ask me," answered Hesperus,
"About evil spirits is odd!

I have quite enough trouble believing
In the existence of God."

Letter to Martin Dorp

The Letter to Dorp is found in More's Lucubrationes, *Basel,
1563, pp. 365–438, and in the Leyden edition of Erasmus'*
Epistolae, *1703, Vol. III, Pt. ii, Col. 1892. Martin van Dorp
was born at Naaldwyd in Holland in 1485 and educated at the
Collège du Lis in Louvain. In 1515 he received his doctorate
in theology and was appointed president of the Collège du Saint-
Esprit. He died in 1525 and was buried at the Charterhouse
in Louvain. More wrote the epitaph for his tomb. The basic
theme of the letter is a concern for a reliable translation of
the Bible and the qualifications of the true theologian, who,
it is not surprising to discover, is not a scholastic but a humanist.*

Bruges
October 21, 1515

Greeting—

If I were at liberty to come and see you as I would like
to, my dear Dorp, we would be able to carry on a more
intimate and appropriate discussion of the subjects about which
I will inappropriately write. Then I would also be able to enjoy, at least for a while, your actual company, as sweet a
pleasure as I could experience. Erasmus has stirred up within
my heart an extraordinary desire to see you, to become acquainted with you and to acquire your friendship. He is extremely fond of us both and I am sure that we too are fond
of him. . . .

But to get to the reason for my present compulsion to write
to you while I have been staying here, I have by chance come
upon some who seem to be men of letters, at least in my
opinion. I have spoken with them and in our conversation men-

tioned Erasmus' name and yours also. They knew of Erasmus from his writings and his reputation but they knew you for other reasons. They told me things that were not only unpleasant but also unbelievable. They said that you are being quite unfriendly to Erasmus, and that this was obvious in your letters to him. They promised to bring me those letters the next day because they realized that it was difficult for me to accept their word. The next day they came back and they brought me three letters, one addressed by you to Erasmus. This letter, as his answer seems to indicate, he had not received; but, like myself, he had read a copy of it which someone had given him. In this letter you attack the *Praise of Folly* and you offer the suggestion that he write a "Praise of Wisdom." You give little approval to his plan to emend the text of the New Testament using the Greek manuscripts and you exhort him to constrict it within such narrow limits that you virtually oppose the entire plan. The second letter consisted of a short apology wherein he explained that he was still traveling and weary of his journey but that he intended to write to you in greater detail when he reached Basel. And finally there was a third letter in which you answered this letter from Erasmus.

I read this letter while these men were still with me. There was nothing in it to insinuate to me that you have any hostile feelings toward Erasmus. . . . Nevertheless, there was some indication that you were confused more than I had thought possible. Since I desired to eradicate this idea from their minds rather than to substantiate it, I said that I read nothing in the letter which might not come from the heart of a friend. One of them objected: "I am not criticizing what he wrote but the fact that he did write. Because he wrote, I am of the opinion that he acted with hostility." If the *Folly* offends any person so much, I have never heard of it (not even at Louvain, although I have been there frequently and for long periods of time since the *Folly* was published), excepting for one or two bitter old men reliving their childhood, mocked and derided by even the children about them. With the exception of these, all seem to have acclaimed the work, both here at Bruges and also at Louvain; indeed it is so acclaimed that people even memorize parts of it.

But as I began to say: If the *Folly* offends a person so much that he deemed it necessary to challenge Erasmus to write a retraction, then since Dorp was called to the side of Erasmus not long ago—and on his own evidence, all by himself—why did he write a letter? If he thought that he should present some admonition, then why did he not present it personally to Erasmus? Why did he not give his orders face to face (to quote from Terence) concerning what was to be done instead of withdrawing and shouting them in the street, while Erasmus was so far away that he was the last person to know and then heard from others what he should have been the first if not the only one to hear? "You must consider," said one of the men, "the sincerity of his action in this affair. First, he pretends publicly to defend a man against whom no one places any indictment. Next everyone widely reads the reasons for his defense, although I doubt that anyone, except the one who ought to, hears his objections." When he had finished, other remarks were made, which I do not need to list here. My replies and my manner in dismissing them were of such a nature as to convince them that I would not listen to any attack upon yourself, and that I was on almost as good terms with you as with Erasmus, and that I could not possibly be on better terms with him. As for your preferring to discuss the matter with him in writing rather than in conversation, whatever your intention I am sure that you did not act out of ill will; and he too has no doubts about this, for he knows very well how you feel about him.

As for your second letter, which is now widely circulated with unfortunate results, I find it easy to believe that it was made public by accident rather than through any deliberate move on your part. I find myself taking this point of view mostly because I found several statements in this letter which I am sure you would have edited if you had wanted to publish it; for they are not the kind of thing that you would write nor would they be written to him. You would not have addressed such caustic statements to such an important friend, nor would you have addressed yourself in such an informal manner to such a learned man as he. On the other hand, I am sure that you would have been more benevolent in writing as your temperate character leads me to believe and that also you would have been more meticulous in your expression, for you are a scholar. In addition, as regards the jests and jeers with which your letter abounds, I am sure that you would have used them much less frequently, or at least, my dear Dorp, more appropriately. I do not consider of great importance the fact that you attack the *Folly,* that you mock the poets and that you deride all grammarians. Nor do I make much of your disapproval of the annotations on Holy Scripture or of your opinion that a thorough knowledge of the Greek literature is irrelevant, for all of these objections are views which each man may hold without offending another. They have also been discussed by you thus far in such a manner that anyone who reads your objections will surely be able to supply retorts to several of them. By no means do I think that you have opposed any of these points to excess. Indeed, even I see the absence of several points that I wish you had made in your letter against Erasmus. They would have given him the opportunity of buttressing his argument with more ammunition against you.

But I assure you that I am deeply disturbed because in your letter you seem to attack Erasmus in a manner which is not worthy of either of you. You treat him at times as if you hate him; at others as if you were mockingly contemptuous of him; at others, instead of admonishing him, you chastise him like a stern critic or strict censor; and still again you twist the meaning of his words as if you wished, in a moment of excitement, to turn the attitudes of the theologians and even the universities against him. I do not wish my letter to be understood as an attack on you, for it is my firm conviction that you have done none of this out of ill will toward him. Although I am in need of defense myself, I will act as defender for one whom, I realize, all surely consider a man far too outstanding to be classed with themselves. And indeed in reality he is. Because I loved you and was concerned for your reputation, I wanted to warn you about those things which men who do not fully understand your temperate character and complete sincerity are citing as proof that your actions are full of greed for your reputation and that you are serving your own honor by making sneak attacks on that of another. Just as in Vergil, my dear Dorp, where Aeneas was enveloped in a cloud and thus mingled with the Carthaginians and saw the tapestries which depicted himself and his exploits, so I wish that you, as an invisible observer, could see the facial expressions of those who read this last letter of yours. I am sure that you would hold me in higher esteem for my frank advice on making corrections than you would those who criticize behind your back the very points that they cringingly praise in your presence. By making corrections you can make all understand— as I do now—that you did not send this letter, but that it escaped from you.

Nevertheless, I am surprised to think that it would occur to anyone to curry favor by praising such matters in your presence; and, as I started to say, I wish that you could see from your window the grimaces, the tone of voice, and the emotions which the reader exhibits on seeing such statements. Several times in the letter to Erasmus you severely criticize our theologians, Erasmus, and your own poor grammarians, as if you were the occupant of the throne among the highest of theologians and were consigning him a place among the lowly grammarians. You claim your place among the theologians and this is only just, but you take not only a place, but the first place. Even so he should not be thrust from the throne of theologians down to the benches of the grammarians; though I am sure that Erasmus would not mock the grammarians as you do, more frequently than wittily. As a matter of fact, he perhaps merits that title before all others. His modesty, however, is so great that he will not admit it, because he knows that the term "grammarian" is synonymous with learning. . . .

But to return to your letter: It contains another remark of almost identical character, "If ever you see the Decretals, Erasmus. . . ." As if it were quite impossible for him to see the Decretal letters, which you imply that you have seen. Furthermore, you confront him with these dissertations: "The water was disturbed by a heron"; and "everything is thrown into confusion by the ignorant when they enter the ring of argumentation." Again, you say: "Erasmus, if you do not understand either art, you are unable to tell the difference between a dialectician and a sophist." And still later: "Unless it be that in your eyes sophists are all those men who get the better of you in an argument, that is, all dialecticians." Is it really your conviction, Dorp, that everything is thrown into confusion by Erasmus when he becomes engaged in an argument? That he is ignorant of the nature of dialectics or that he does not understand exactly what a sophist is? And that he is the only one that cannot comprehend what almost all schoolboys know? I am certain that even you will admit that he is very specially gifted when it comes to rhetoric and, if you admit this, I do not see any conceivable way of depriving him of dialectics. Not the least of the philosophers were correct when they maintained that dialectics and rhetoric were no more distinct than one's fist and the palm of his hand, because dialectics binds together more tightly the same thing that rhetoric freely elucidates. Just as the former strikes with the point of the blade, in this way too the latter by its sheer force completely levels and destroys. But let us suppose that dialectics and rhetoric have nothing in common. Simply because he does not take his argument into the schools, because he does not debate before groups of schoolboys, and because he ignores those petty problems, as you will do later, you think that he has never bothered to acquaint himself with them. In fact, it is your opinion that he is inferior to all dialecticians in argumentation.

Note how vehemently I disagree with you. Think of a man who has some education and is moderately endowed with talent (I mean one with far less talent than Erasmus). I do not think

that such a person will take second place in argument to all
dialecticians, if both parties in the discussion are acquainted
with the subject. Natural talent will compensate for deficiency
in formal schooling. In fact, the principles of dialectics are
produced by one's natural intelligence; in other words, they
are methods of reasoning that have proved their usefulness in
investigating. It is my belief that not even one person would
doubt Erasmus' ability to cope with those petty problems, if
he wanted to (and I do not mean in those rowdy debates
where reason is subordinated to shouting and men reach the
point of spitting at one another because their self-control and
sense of shame are forgotten). Such a man would cope with
these problems, either in serious writing or in an earnest discussion, so as to be not merely adequate, but equal or even
superior to the best. Erasmus, whose learning and ability command universal admiration, is far from being inferior in argumentation to every single dialectician; this includes even schoolboys. . . .

I cannot understand why, when dialectics is mentioned, you
connected the scholars of Louvain and Paris since they are so at
odds with one another. In fact, they do not even agree on the
name of the subject. One group calls itself the Realists, while
the others call themselves Nominalists. But, on the other hand,
both groups deal with Aristotle, and constantly disagree about
him. How can one choose between interpretations, when the
scholars of Louvain and Paris differ, and even contradict one
another? If such squabbles are within the scope of dialectics
(though they have nothing to do with Aristotle), then it is not
Aristotelian logic, as you put it, but some other brand that both
sides are propounding. However, if such controversial matters
are outside the scope of dialectics (and certainly they are outside its scope if they are outside his scope, assuming that he
gave a full treatment of dialectics) it would be absurd to carry
on this dispute so vehemently for so many years, on irrelevant
matters, with the purpose of learning dialectics.

Actually, Dorp, I have come to believe that most of the
opinions debated in this lengthy and bitter struggle, which resembles a battle for home and hearth, have little to do with
logic and contribute little to its mastery. For example, in the
study of grammar, it is enough to learn the rules for speaking
Latin and to understand what others have written in that
language. It is not necessary to inquire into all the details of
grammar and to grow old while fussing about letters and syl-
lables. It is the same with dialectics. I should think it enough to
be taught the nature of words, the force of propositions, and
finally the rules of syllogisms, and then at once to apply dia-

lectics as an instrument to the other branches of learning. Aristotle obviously kept this idea in mind, for his entire treatment of dialectics consists of those ten superb categories, either of things or names, a treatise on propositions, and lastly the rules for the different kinds of syllogisms: those leading to a necessary conclusion, those that persuade with probability, and those that involve clever fallacies. To this material, Porphyry added, by way of introduction, the five universal predicables, whether you prefer to call them things or words. Moreover, neither of them proposed the kinds of problem that hinder rather than encourage minds still untrained and needing further formation. Porphyry was even explicit in avoiding them. But now a maze of foolish aberrations has been introduced. These were set aside by the ancients, but their introduction now will spell the destruction of liberal arts, and pollute the pure tradition of the ancients and everything else with their filth. As regards grammar (and I do not want to consider Alexander and the others like him who teach grammar in some way even though they may teach it imperfectly) there is one Albert who, in professing to expound grammar, provided us with a sort of logic or metaphysics which was really neither of the two. It was, moreover, a substitution of sheer nightmares and rampant imagination for grammar. Nevertheless, this farcical nonsense was admitted into the academies, and approved by so many that as a result only those who could be called Albertist were considered worth their salt in the field of grammar.

When ignorant teachers pass on an opinion, it becomes strengthened in the course of the years and after a while can pervert even the soundest of minds. It does not surprise me, therefore, that a new kind of nonsense, worse than that of the sophists, has gradually replaced dialectics. With its mask of brilliant wit, this nonsense has great appeal for its hearers. When I made recent mention of these matters, a certain dialectician, who is considered to be most learned, said this (and I shall quote him verbatim, lest I be unable to reproduce his eloquence): "Aristotle had only a rough style; today schoolboys have a solid basis in the *Little Logicals*." I am sure that if Aristotle should rise up from his grave and argue with them, they would easily silence him not with mere sophistry, but with his own logic.

As for this book, the *Little Logicals*—as far as I can see it is so called for the very small amount of logic that it contains—it is worth looking at. It contains so-called suppositions, ampliations, restrictions, appellations, and passages that contain little rules, which are not merely misleading, but often untrue, such as the distinction between these two and similar statements:

"A lion than an animal is braver" and "A lion is braver than an animal"—as if they did not have identical meanings. In fact, both statements are so silly that they have virtually no meaning whatsoever, though, if they have any meanings, these meanings are identical. The same distinction is made between: "Wine I've drunk twice" and "Twice I've drunk wine." They claim that it is a very real difference, but in reality there is none at all. If a person eats raw meat after it has been roasted and even burned, then they would insist that if he were to say: "Raw meat I have eaten" he would be speaking the truth, but not if he were to say: "I have eaten raw meat." And if someone were to rob me of part of my money, I would be a liar if I were to say: "He has robbed me of my money." But just so that I would not completely lack a way to frame my accusation in court, I may say: "Of my money, he has robbed me." And it is also possible that in some fictitious case a person might say truthfully: "The pope I have whipped," while in the same case it would be false to say: "I have whipped the pope." This situation arises when the person who is now pope has as a boy been beaten by me. In fact, those old men who teach young boys such things deserve a beating every time that they open their mouths to teach. They also maintain that the statement, "Every man is a father who has a son," is false unless every single man were to have a son; for to them it is the same as saying: "Every man has a father and every man has a son. . . ."

Is this the kind of dialectics that Aristotle teaches? Is it the kind that Jerome praises, or that Augustine approves, or that the mad Orestes (to quote Persius) would swear to be a madman's? It really surprises me that sharp-witted men should understand those statements in a way that no one else in the world understands them. Words do not belong to a particular profession. They are not private property, to be borrowed by anyone who wants them for his own private use. Speech is, to be sure, a common possession, but they spoil some of the words that they have gotten from cobblers. They have taken them from the common people, and they misuse what is common. But it is their objection that their rule of logic demands a certain interpretation. Will this damned rule, designed in some corner by men who hardly know how to speak, impose new laws of speech on the world? Grammar teaches correct speech. It does not devise extraordinary rules of language but advises those who are unskilled in the ways of speech how to observe the world's ordinary customs of speech. A dialectics that is sound acts no differently. Surely this syllogism: "Every animal runs; every man is an animal," therefore, "Every man runs" is not a syllogism because it is correctly set up in accordance with the rule of dialectics and is formed into a *barbara* syllogism, but because reason, which made a rule for that purpose, tells us that the conclusion follows from the premises. Otherwise, if reason were to make the rule in another way, in any other way, it would swerve from the nature of things. It is the same with the proposition: "The whore will be a virgin." Let them not say that this proposition is to be understood as: "The whore that is, or that will be" because the rule demands it thus. But let them first produce a reason for such a rule from the meaning of the words. For if that interpretation is to be given, then it must be evident from the thing itself or from the normal meaning of the words.

Many who have spoken Latin for some time now have the talent and the learning and are in my opinion equal to those when it comes to a knowledge of correct speech. But why is it that not one of them was able to see the truth in this proposition: "The whore will be a virgin," or could distinguish between these two propositions: "Money I do not have," and "I do not have any money." Although no one would deny that a change in the position of the words often renders a change in the meaning, "Drink before eating," does not mean the same as "Eat before drinking." But when there is such an alteration in meaning it is my contention that men are unanimous in their agreement, under the influence of reason. The precepts of dialecticians are not so demanding as they are persuading, for it is their duty to follow our custom in the use of language and to force us to move in any direction, with reasons that are true. On the other hand, sophists lead us to a spot where we are surprised to find ourselves. They accomplish this through their deceptive use of words. The cleverness by which men show that they are victorious in an argument and the ingenuity by which they decide in their own favor is both stupid and a foolish use of cleverness and ingenuity; for we do not understand their way of using words, which is contrary to universal acceptance. While this does not even deserve to be called sophism, nevertheless it is not considered sophistic nonsense, but numbered among the most secret treasures of dialectics. It is not learned by schoolboys as something to be forgotten but rather welcomed by venerable men to the inner sanctum of theology. Some use these sophisms as the basis for obscure theological problems, drawing from them such absurd propositions that no one else could produce such a plethora of ridiculous nonsense. It is, however, much more to my liking that madmen of this kind should recover their sanity rather than that I should come under the influence of such fools. But why do I speak of these matters to you, Dorp? I have no doubt that such childish nonsense irks you as much as it does me. You could change and perhaps you will be able to, with the help of those who are like you. This can only happen if you refuse to give in to the nonsense of those who should much rather be following than regulating your judgment.

But again about your letter. I want to make the point that the words of Erasmus did not give you reason to say, as you do, that he chastised the theologians of Louvain for their ignorance. Your statement about the other theologians is even farther from the truth. Erasmus said that he refused to have anything to do with those theologians, if there exist such, and obviously there do, who have learned nothing but sophistic prattles. He was not referring to all theologians because earlier in the same letter he had stated that there were many who had distinguished themselves. About this statement of his, you remark: "I think that he was referring to the theologians of Louvain." Why do you think so, Dorp? Would it be difficult to find anywhere men of that stripe, or rather stuffing? You certainly have a fine opinion of the theologians of Louvain if you think that they alone, and all of them, fit such a description, but that is neither the opinion nor the gist of the statement of Erasmus. Later in the letter you take his meaning to include all theologians throughout the world, not merely theologians of Louvain, but Erasmus referred neither to all theologians nor to those of Louvain. Then, as if you were unconscious of what either of you had been saying, you do not merely stoop to such language but break out like one whose mind is in a whirl: "Do we not see the lowest form of laborers, even the meanest slaves, endowed with brilliant minds? Why then are such epithets hurled against all theologians: stupid, ignorant, obnoxious, brainless? To insult anyone does not demand any skill. It is neither a gentlemanly thing to do, nor the mark of a good man, if we ponder the stern statement of our Saviour: 'Whoever says to his brother, "Raca," shall be liable to the Sanhedrin; and whoever says, "Thou fool," shall be liable to the fire of Gehenna.'" Jerome has a comment on this passage: "If we are to render account for an idle word, how much more so for an insulting one. The man who says, 'Thou fool,' to a believer in God, is guilty of impiety toward religion."

These words of yours, Dorp, exhibit both piety and sternness, and are truly worthy of a serious theologian. If only you had spoken them in the proper context! They are too pointed to perish out of necessity. If you had hurled them from a pulpit down upon a crowd they would not fail to hit anyone and it would be obvious whom they had struck. But I am sorry to see that Erasmus is the sole object of your denunciation; for he is the one man who deserves no part of your denunciation. Your quotation from the Gospel: "Whoever says to his brother, 'Thou fool,' shall be liable to the fire of Gehenna," in no way pertains to him. Without naming names, he merely wants to say that amid the large number of human beings there are one or two fools. On the other hand, ten hells would not be enough for him that says: "The number of fools is infinite." With regard to your question, "What is the meaning of these epithets hurled against all theologians?" that is the question that I am asking you, Dorp, because the remarks that he directed toward only a few, you alone have directed toward all. It surprises me very much that you have taken the initiative in doing this. Just as "to insult anyone," as you say, "does not demand any skill," so too does it not demand any skill to distort, as you do, fine words by misquoting them. Words that are rather well written against those who deserve them, you have attempted to turn against those who do not deserve them and thus imply that they were not well written after all. You can see how easy it is to do that in any situation. . . .

Selected English Writings

Introduction

Four hundred years after Thomas More's death in 1535, the church for which he gave his life finally chose to bestow its canonical approval on his martyrdom by officially numbering him among the sanctified. Thus what unofficial hagiography had preached for four centuries came to be accepted as respectable fact: Thomas More was a saint, an authentic Christian martyr. But, as anyone with even a nodding acquaintance with the ways of hagiographers knows, those chroniclers, biographers, and editors who devote themselves to recording and, inevitably, to embellishing the facts of a saint's life, have frequently rendered their historical hero all but inaccessible. Hagiographers sometimes produce literature, as in *The Little Flowers of St. Francis;* more often they produce pious anecdote. In either case the historian interested in coming close to the facts of a man's life finds most hagiographers a downright menace.

All of this is a prelude to pointing out that the "campaign biography" of Thomas More which appeared in 1935, the year of the canonization, is in fact a sophisticated, scholarly, twentieth-century version of the legend of a saint. R. W. Chambers, whose *Thomas More* is undoubtedly the single most influential work on More, may have been, although not a Roman Catholic himself, among the last of the hagiographers. That Chambers' work is literature compounds the problem: One wishes to believe what the evidence contradicts.

But more to the point in a discussion of More's English prose, the same Mr. Chambers had, before 1935, written a remarkable essay defining the prose tradition that culminated in the birth and growth of modern English. The essay, "On The Continuity of English Prose," which formed part of Chambers' Introduction to the Early English Text Society's edition of Harpsfield's sixteenth-century life of More, attempted with great persuasiveness and erudition to demonstrate that More's English prose is solidly and self-consciously in the tradition of medieval English spiritual and devotional treatises. Of the possible influences of sixteenth-century humanism on

151

More's writing, there is scarcely a murmur, and then the murmur is usually one of disapproval. More is, in short, according to Chambers, the wellspring of modern English prose, and from the thirteenth-century *Ancren Riwle* to the seventeenth-century King James Bible, the tide of English is strengthened and reenforced by the English writings of Thomas More.

A generation of readers has been persuaded by Chambers' influential essay to regard Thomas More as not only the heir to medieval spirituality and stylistics, but also as the "great restorer of English prose." Both propositions are open to serious qualification. Leaving aside the ticklish question of the influence of medieval devotional treatises upon More's piety and prose, and avoiding the semantic problems raised by that grandiloquent phrase "restorer of English prose," we are left with a view of More as essentially a latter-day medieval man whose English prose style results from the saturation of his mind by such works as the *Ancren Riwle* and *The Cloud of Unknowing.* This view, to be maintained, must slight or even ignore the humanist influences on the prose of More's *The History of King Richard III,* composed both in Latin and in English early in his literary career (around 1513) over a period of several years, and polished and revised as only a work of literary art would be. Those given to large resounding generalizations about More's English prose style would do better, consequently, to come to terms with More's *Richard III* and the models and influences which helped to shape it, rather than with the later, hastily written controversial English works.

The beautifully written *Dialogue of Comfort,* on the other hand, composed in the Tower while awaiting what More expected to be a horribly painful death, does suggest strong affinity with medieval prototypes, as does the earlier treatise *The Four Last Things.* The point is this: One emphasizes either the "medieval" or the "humanist" dimension of Thomas More at one's peril. The price one pays for such distortion is the reduction of the richly complex man who was Thomas More to an oversimplified—and usually partisan—symbol. To put the matter bluntly, Chambers' Thomas More is both something less and something more than the historical More. Chambers' More is, in short, a partially drawn figure.

When Mr. Chambers, for example, informs us that the main line of English prose extends from Juliana of Norwich, Richard Rolle, and Walter Hilton through the English works of Thomas More, we are able to recognize and place such works of More's as *The Four Last Things* and *The Dialogue of Comfort,* but we are also led to ask about the influence of sixteenth-century humanism upon so important a work as *The History of*

King Richard III, which was, after all, written simultaneously in both Latin and English, which betrays more marks of Latin than of medieval English influence, and which, finally, owes more to classical models such as Thucydides, Sallust, and Tacitus, than it does to medieval historiography. And, similarly, when Chambers concludes that "Thomas More ranks with William Langland before him, and Edmund Burke after him, among the greatest of our Reforming Conservatives," and when the same biographer interprets the *Utopia* as an anti-progressive, reactionary document, the skeptical reader may be permitted to raise an eyebrow. How is one to recognize in such a portrait the Thomas More who was the lifelong friend of Erasmus, and the writer of such "progressive," "reform" works as the letters to Dorp, to the University of Oxford, and to a certain monk? Where is the witty author of the epigrams, some of which were bawdy and others of which were politically subversive? Where is the humanist who laughed over the anti-scholastic, antimedieval humanist hoax, *Epistolae Obscurorum Virorum?* One is forced, rather sadly, to conclude that Chambers' beautifully written and widely influential biography of More, is, in the final analysis, a sophisticated polemic against modernism and liberalism. Regardless of what one may think about the world views those vague terms connote, one must admit that R. W. Chambers' *Thomas More* seems more intent upon manipulating More as a weapon in a modern ideological struggle than upon illuminating, so far as possible, the elusive, many-sided mystery of the great sixteenth-century humanist. One does not have to go quite so far as did one writer who recently described Chambers' biography as a "radically false portrait" in order to experience some uneasiness in the presence of the Thomas More who emerges from Chambers' eloquent pages.

Chambers' work is symptomatic of that larger problem which has dogged More studies for the last four centuries. A modern editor-anthologist of More's writings, has, consequently, not only special obligations which must be met, but also special pitfalls which must be avoided. He must scrupulously attempt to avoid what Matthew Arnold called "the spirit of party" in dealing with one who, like More, has so frequently been victimized by precisely that same "spirit of party."

Any selection from More's voluminous writings will inevitably reflect the values of the one doing the selecting. Such selections, in any case, represent but a portion of that larger feast which More's prolific pen has made available. The Yale Thomas More Project, which is in the process of providing scholarly, critical editions, and also popular editions for a wider public, is, fortunately, about to close one of the great gaps in our knowledge of Thomas More. (His works in their entirety have been available, we must remember, only to those few scholars who have had access to the rare sixteenth-century editions of his works.) Judging by the first two volumes to be published by Yale, Richard Sylvester's beautiful edition of *Richard III*, and the *Utopia*, edited by Surtz and Hexter, both complete with brilliant introductions, full critical apparatus, notes, glossary, and index, one feels that the writings of Thomas More are about to receive the kind of attention they so richly deserve.

In 1936 an extremely important essay by the late Marie Delcourt was published in the annual publication *Renaissance et Humanisme*. Entitled "Recherches sur Thomas More," Delcourt's essay demonstrated, somewhat tendentiously at times, the schizoid quality of More scholarship and biography for the past four hundred years. She traces the genesis of the dual view of More to what she calls the two More traditions, the English and the Latin. More's Latin works, taken as a whole, present their author as an urbane, witty humanist who devoted his pen to ridiculing the existing intellectual and ecclesiastical establishment. The English works, on the other hand, by and large are the products of an otherworldly ascetic, a vigorous and at times violent champion of the Counter-Reformation. When we recall that More's English works were collected by his Roman Catholic nephew and published in a beautiful folio volume in 1557, with the clear intention, stated in the editor's preface, of aiding the Catholic restoration under Mary Tudor, we have a clear proof of the way in which his coreligionists looked upon his vernacular writings. When we further realize that the first five biographies of More written by Catholic Englishmen (William Roper, Nicholas Harpsfield, Thomas Stapleton, the unknown Ro. Ba., and Cresacre More, the martyr's great-grandson) were saint's lives written in the heated atmosphere of sixteenth-century polemics, then we begin to understand how onesided the so-called English More tradition has been.

It is important that we recall these facts as we prepare to plunge into the selections from More's English writings. That they are in English provides half the explanation of the subject matter, tone, and emphases we encounter in these works. It is not too much of an oversimplification to say that Thomas More wrote things in Latin which he would never have written, Reformation or no Reformation, in English. The Latin works, with their satirical thrusts, the playful, patronizing attacks, the harsh denunciations of abuses, were directed to an elite readership not likely to misunderstand More's dialectics. The vernacular writings, on the other hand, were intended for a wider, less learned, less sophisticated audience, and were, consequently, less free-wheeling, more prudent.

The other half of the explanation of the discrepancy between the Latin and English writings is closely related to the first: The Protestant Reformation had intervened between the production of most of the Latin works and the later controversial works in English. In 1528 More's humanist friend Cuthbert Tunstall, Bishop of London, alarmed by the influx of heretical books into England, invited More to take upon himself the burdensome task of combatting, in English, the writings of the reformers. Referring to More as one able to emulate Demosthenes in English as well as in Latin, Tunstall advised More to write "in our own language such books as may show to simple and unlearned men the cunning malice of the heretics."

To men like Erasmus and More the demand for theological and ecclesiastical reform was one thing, schism quite another. When More saw what he considered seditious attacks by heretics upon the religio-political hegemony of Rome, he reacted with a ferocity that was, unfortunately, generally characteristic of the men on both sides of the theological aisle. Thomas More became one of the most vigorous defenders of what Emmanuel Mounier used to refer to as "the late, departed Christendom," as distinct from Christianity. And herein lies the tragedy of More's life, a tragedy imposed upon him and shared by his own times. The reform from within advocated by the early humanists—Colet, Erasmus, More—had now become an impossible cause to espouse for those remaining loyal to Rome. The very idea of reform, preempted by the rebels, was now suspect in orthodox eyes, and, by the same token, those who, like More, defended the Roman Church against the heretics conceded nothing, defended all. In such a polemical, heated atmosphere, More found himself defending tenets and practices in terms which would probably have repelled the man who wrote the preface to his translations from Lucian, the epigrams, the *Utopia*, the letter to Martin Dorp, and the letter to a monk. In times of crisis, criticism of one's own is a luxury denied: Loyal opposition is a peacetime occupation. In a frequently cited passage, More wrote what has often been looked upon as a qualified retraction of his earlier writings:

... If any man would now translate *Moria* [Erasmus' *Praise of Folly*] into English, or some works either that I have myself

written ere this, albeit there be no harm therein, folk yet being
(as they be) given to the harm of what . . . is good, I would not
only my darling's [Erasmus'] books but my own also help to
burn them both with my own hands, rather than folk should
(through their own fault) take any harm of them, seeing that
I see them likely in these days so to do.

There we have set down in graphically clear terms the concerns
which go far toward explaining the peculiar tone and emphases
of the controversial English works as distinct from the Latin
works: Those things he and Erasmus penned in Latin were,
first of all, written in earlier, more halcyon days, and, in the
second place, they were written in a tongue, Latin, which
automatically excluded the unlearned, that is, those most
likely to misunderstand.

I stress this point as an essential part of an introduction to
More's English writings in order to help the reader to understand the pressures and needs which give to much of More's
English writings their peculiar texture and quality. The man
who described himself in his own epitaph as a molester of
murderers and heretics, the man who referred to the great
leader of the Reformation as "Luther the drunken," and "lousy
Luther," the man who justified (reluctantly to be sure) the
burning of unrepentant heretics—this is hardly the same man
who in 1523 advised Henry VIII to tone down the exuberance
and absolutism of his allegiance to the papacy, the man who
ridiculed monkish superstition and ignorance, who dialectically
examined the possibility of religious tolerance in his *Utopia*.
Times had changed, and one tangible result of the change can
be charted in the pages of Thomas More's books.

The entrance of Thomas More into the theological arena,
incidentally, can also be regarded as an interesting vindication
of the humanists' claim to omnicompetence on the basis of their
literary and philological skills. It was this kind of claim, often
made arrogantly, which aroused much of the hostility these
men encountered from the entrenched establishment. More,
although a learned, widely read man, was not, after all, a
theologian. Tunstall, himself a humanist luminary, in choosing
such a man as More to defend the old faith, was clearly concerned, as his letter to More indicates, to enlist More's literary
skill, his "eloquence," against the reformers.

Not all of More's English works, of course, deal with theological controversy or the spiritual life, although in sheer quantity most of the English works do fall into this category. A
modern editor, as a consequence, faced with the difficult task
of making selections from Thomas More's voluminous English
writings, must attempt to strike a balance between the twin
demands of presenting, on the one hand, a truly representative

cross section of those writings, and, on the other, of choosing those texts which may possess immediacy and relevance for the modern reader. The second alternative is, obviously, the more attractive, but in the interests of bringing the historical, the "essential" More slightly closer to that same modern reader, one cannot avoid considering certain texts which may possess fewer resonances and less significance for a contemporary audience. Mere historicism, however, has not been the principle of selection in compiling these extracts. In what follows, an attempt has been made, in short, to present an accurate sketch of More's English writings. A further attempt has been made, in selecting the materials in this anthology, to render the portrait of Thomas More, writer of sixteenth-century English prose, not only authentic, but, one hopes, interesting and meaningful to whoever may stroll through the pages which follow.

A word on the text seems called for. In all cases the 1557 black letter folio edition of the English works compiled by William Rastell has served as the basis for the present text, unless otherwise noted. As for the attempts to modernize More's language, an explanation, or possibly more accurately, a brief for the defense, may be in order.

In an anthology of this sort, which aims both at making More's works accessible to a wide general readership and also at retaining as much of the authentic flavor of the original as possible, compromise is the inevitable lot of the editor. Spelling and punctuation have, for the most part, been modernized. (Those interested in morphological purity and absolute textual integrity—both legitimate concerns of the scholar—will, of course, resort to the original sixteenth-century editions.) More's word order and syntactical casualness (or if you like, chaos) have, on the whole, been left intact. To tamper with More's syntax—and frequently this is a strong temptation— for the sake of clarity is to open a Pandora's box of problems. The reader, it is hoped, will quickly learn to relax and float with the idiomatic tides and currents of More's English. Again, in the interests of arriving at a maximum of textual integrity with a minimum of obstacles to intelligibility, archaic and obsolete terms have usually been retained and have been glossed at the bottom of each page.

The result of all of this is, inevitably, a synthetic, editorial construct. I can only plead guilty—with an explanation. My sole aim has been to make the mind of a great man, insofar as he expressed that mind in his writings, at least minimally available to as wide a contempory audience as possible.

JAMES J. GREENE

A Merry Jest: How a Sergeant would Learn to play the Friar

Almost none of More's poetry was written in English. Aside from the relatively dismal state of poetry in the vernacular in the first decade of the sixteenth century and the radical changes which were affecting the English language and rendering obsolete older techniques of versification, More was undoubtedly interested, as a man of letters, in recognition by the literary elite of Europe, namely the international community of humanists. Since their common linguistic bond was Latin, More obviously expended his more serious literary energies upon his Latin verse.

The following piece, possibly composed some time around 1503, can be looked upon as a late variation of a medieval fabliau, a genre which, aside from Chaucer, seems to have attracted few writers in England. More's sense of the comic—which did not preclude the farcical—his reverent irreverence for figures of prestige and authority, are evident in this frothy anecdote.

> Wise men alway
> Affirm and say
> That best is for a man
> Diligently
> For to apply
> The business that he can;°
> And in no wise
> To enterprise
> Another faculty,°
> For he that will
> And can° no skill
> Is never like to the.°
> He that hath laft°
> The hosier's craft

business . . . can the craft or profession he knows   **faculty** business, craft   **the** (pronounced "thee," unaspirated *th*), thrive   **laft** left

158

And falleth to making shone,°
The smith that shall
To painting fall,
His thrift is well nigh done.
A black draper
With white paper
To go to writing school;
An old butler
Become a cutler
I wene° shall prove a fool.
And an old trot
That can,° God wot,°
Nothing but kiss the cup,
With her physic
Will keep one sick
Till she have soused him up.
A man of law
That never saw
The ways to buy and sell,
Weening° to rise
By merchandise,
I pray God speed him well.
A merchant eke°
That will go seek
By all the means he may
To fall in suit
Till he dispute
His money clean away.
Pleading the law
For every straw
Shall prove a thrifty man,
With bate° and strife,
But by my life
I cannot tell you whan.
When a hatter will go smatter
In philosophy;
Or a peddler
Wax a meddler
In theology;
All that ensue
Such craftes new
They drive so far acast°
That evermore

shone shoes   wene think   can knows   wot knows   Weening thinking
eke also   bate debate, contention   All that ensue . . . far acast all that
results from such new crafts is that they go so far astray

They do therefore
Beshrew themselves° at last.

This thing was tried
And verified
Here by a sergeant late,
That thriftily° was,
Or° he could pass,
Rapped about the pate,
While that he would
See how he could
In God's name play the frere.
Now if you will
Know how it fill°
Take heed and ye shall hear.

It happened so
Not long ago
A thrifty man there died.
An hundred pound
Of nobles round
That had he laid aside.
His son he wolde°
Should have this gold
For to begin with all.
But to suffice
His child, well thrice
That money was too small.
Yet or this day
I have heard say
That many a man certesse°
Hath with good cast°
Been rich at last
That hath begun with less.
But this young man
So well began
His money to employ,
That certainly
His policy to see it was a joy.
For lest some blast
Might overcast
His ship, or by mischance
Men with some wile
Might him beguile

Beshrew themselves ruin themselves   **thriftily** soundly   **Or** before   **fill**
befell, came to pass   **wolde** willed   **certesse** in truth   **cast** planning

And minish his substance;
For to put out
All manner doubt,
He made a good purvey,°
For every whit°
By his own wit
And took another way.
First fair and wele°
Thereof much dele,°
He dight° it in a pot.
But then him thought
That way was nought,
And there he left it not.
So was he fain°
From thence again
To put it in a cup.
And by and by
Covetously
He supped it fair up.
In his own breast
He thought it best
His money to enclose.
Then wist he well
Whatever fell
He could it never lose.
He borrowed then
Of other men
Money and merchandise.
Never paid it
Up he laid it
In like manner wise.
Yet on the gear°
That he would wear
He rought° not what he spent,
So it were nice°
As for the price
Could him not miscontent.
With lusty sport
And with resort
Of jolly company,
In mirth and play
Full many a day
He lived merrily.

purvey play   **whit** circumstance   **wele** well   **dele** a large portion of it
dight placed   **fain** willing, anxious   **gear** apparel   **rought** reckoned,
cared   **nice** carefully made, handsome

And men had sworn
Some man is born
To have a lucky hour.
And so was he;
For such degree°
He got and such honor
That, without doubt,
When he went out
A sergeant well and fair
Was ready straight
On him to wait
As soon as on the mayor.
But he doubtless
Of his meekness
Hated such pomp and pride,
And would not go
Accompanied so
But drew himself aside.
To Saint Katherine
Straight as a line
He got him at a tide;°
For devotion
Or promotion°
There would he needs abide.
There spent he fast
Till all was past,
And to him came there many
To ask their debt,
But none could get
The value of a penny.
With visage stout
He bare it out,
Even unto the hard hedge°
A month or twain,
Till he was fain°
To lay his gown to pledge.
Then was he there
In greater fear
Than ere that he came thither,
And would as fain
Depart again,
But that he wist not whither.°
Then after this

---

degree advancement, position, status **tide** time **promotion** out of a
fear of being spied upon **hard hedge** the very limit **fain** willing **that
. . . whither** that he knew not where to go

To a friend of his
He went and there abode,
Where as he lay
So sick alway,
He might not come abroad.

It happened than
A merchant man
That he owed money to,
Of an officere
Then gan enquere
What him was best to do.
And he answerde
"Be not afeared,
Take an action therefore;
I you behest°
I shall him rest
And then care for no more."
"I fear," quod he,
"It will not be,
For he will not come out."
The sergeant said,
"Be not afraid,
It shall be brought about.
In many a game
Like to the same
Have I been well in ure,°
And for your sake
Let me be bake
But if I do this cure."°

Thus part they both,
And forth then goeth,
A pace this officere,
And for a day
All his array
He changed with a frere.
So was he dight°
That no man might
Him for a friar deny.
He dipped and ducked°
He spoke and looked
So religiously.

behest promise **Have I been well in ure** I have had much experience
But . . . cure unless I fulfill this charge or duty **dight** arrayed **dipped and ducked** bowed and curtsied

Yet in a glass
Or° he would pass,
He toted° and he peered;
His heart for pride
Leaped in his side
To see how well he freered.

Then forth a pace
Unto the place
He goeth in God's name,
To do this deed;
But now take heed,
For here beginneth the game.

He drew him nigh
And softily
Straight at the door he knocked.
And a damsel
That heard him well
There came and it unlocked.
The friar said,
"Godspeed, fair maid;
Here lodgeth such a man,
It is told me."
"Well sir," quod she,
"And if he do, what than?"
Quod he, "Mistress,
No harm doubtless;
It longeth for our order°
To hurt no man,
But as we can
Every wight to forder.°
With him truly
Fain speak would I."
"Sir," quod she, "by my fay,°
He is so sike°
Ye be not like°
To speak with him today."
Quod he, "Fair may,°
Yet I you pray
This much at my desire
Vouchsafe to do
As go him to

Or before   **toted** gazed   **longeth . . . order** it is the business of our order
to hurt no man   **Every wight to forder** every man to further   **fay** faith
sike sick   **like** likely   **may** maid

And say an Austin° friar
Would with him speak
And matters break
For his avail° certain."
Quod she, "I will;
Stand ye here still
Till I come down again."
Up is she go
And told him so
As she was bade to say.
He mistrusting
No manner thing°
Said, "Maiden, go thy way,
And fetch him hither
That we together
May talk." Adown she goeth,
Up she him brought,
No harm she thought,
But it made some folk wroth.°

This officere,
This feigned frere,
When he was come aloft
He dipped than
And greeted this man
Religiously and oft.
And he again,
Right glad and fain,
Took him there by the hand.
The friar then said,
"Ye be dismayed
With trouble, I understand."
"Indeed," quod he,
"It hath with me
Been better than it is."
"Sir," quod the frere,
"Be of good cheer,
Yet shall it after this.
For Christes sake
Look that you take
No thought within your breast.
God may turn all,
And so he shall,
I trust, unto the best.

Austin Augustinian **matters . . . avail** and discuss matters that will benefit him **mistrusting . . . thing** suspecting nothing **wroth** angry

But I would now
Commune with you
In council, if you please,
Or ellis nat°
Of matters that
Shall set your heart at ease."

Down went the maid.
The merchant said,
"Now say on, gentle frere,
Of this tiding
That ye may bring
I long full sore to hear."

When there was none
But they alone,
The friar, with evil grace,
Said, "I arrest thee,
Come on with me,"
And out he took his mace.
"Thou shall obey,
Come on thy way,
I have thee in my clutch;
Thou goest not hence
For all the pence
The mayor hath in his pouch."
This merchant there,
For wrath and fear,
He waxing well nigh wood,°
Said, "Whoreson, thief,
With a mischief,
Who hath taught thee thy good."
And with his fist
Upon the list°
He gave him such a blow
That backward down,
Almost in swoon
The friar is overthrow.
Yet was this man
Well fearder than°
Lest he the friar had slain,
Till with good raps
And heavy claps
He dawde° him up again.

Or ellis nat *or otherwise not*   wood *mad*   list *ear*   Well fearder than
more fearful then   dawde *roused*

The friar took heart
And up he start,
And well he laid about,°
And so there goeth
Between them both
Many a lusty clout.
They rent and tear
Each other's hair,
And clave° together fast,
Till with lugging
And with tugging
They fell down both at last.
Then on the ground
Together round,
With many a sadde° stroke,
They roll and rumble,
They turn and tumble
As pigs do in a poke.

So long above
They heave and shove
Together, that at last
The maid and wife,
To break the strife,
Hied them upward fast.
And when they spy
The captains lie
Both waltering° on the place,
The friar's hood
They pulled a good
Adown about his face.
While he was blind
The wench behind
Lent him laid on the floor°
Many a joule°
About the noule°
With a great batildore.°
The wife came yet
And with her feet
She helped to keep him down,
And with her rock°
Many a knock

---

well he laid about with his fists   **clave** clung   **sadde** heavy   **waltering** rolling   **Lent him . . . floor** dealt him while he was stretched out on the floor   **joule** blow   **noule** head   **batildore** a bat used to beat clothes in washing   **rock** distaff

She gave him on the crown.
They laid his mace
About his face,
That he was wood for pain.
The friar frappe°
Got many a swap,
Till he was full nigh slain.
Up they him lift,
And with ill thrift
Headlong along the stair
Down they him threw,
And said, "Adieu,
Commend us to the mayor."

The friar arose,
But I suppose
Amazed was his head.
He shook his ears,
And from great fears
He thought him well afled.
Quod he, "Now lost
Is all this cost;
We be never the nere.°
Ill may he the°
That caused me
To make myself a frere."

Now masters all
Here now I shall
End there as I began:
In any wise
I would advise
And counsel every man
His own craft use,
All new refuse,
And lightly let them gone.
Play not the frere,
Now make good cheer,
And welcome everyone.

frappe may mean struck, or it may mean bound   **nere** nearer   **the** thrive
(pronounced "thee")

The History of King Richard III

More's History of King Richard III, *composed over several years in both English and Latin sometime around 1513 (according to More's nephew and publisher, Rastell), is, for its time, a remarkable piece of historical writing. Departing radically from the dreary chronological cataloging of events typical of chronicle writing, More's* Richard, *although unfinished, represents an attempt to impose unity, form, and meaning upon the writing of history. The unity, of course, derives mainly from More's depiction of the monolithically villainous character of Richard, the last of the Yorkist kings. The* History *is actually a work of historical biography, or, more accurately, a piece of Tudor propaganda. Henry VII, the founder of the Tudor dynasty and father of the then reigning king, was the same Henry who had defeated Richard III in 1485 at Bosworth Field. Any damage done to the memory and reputation of Henry's predecessor and foe necessarily resulted in bolstering up the shaky Tudor claim to the throne of England.*

One of More's chief sources for this work was undoubtedly the oral accounts he had heard from Cardinal Morton, a Lancastrian prelate wronged by Richard and a man in whose home More had received some of his early education. (It was once erroneously held, despite abundant evidence to the contrary, that Morton had written this work. Modern scholarship, however, has established More's authorship beyond dispute.) More's other sources for his history are shrouded in obscurity. His models, however, were clearly the historians of antiquity— Sallust, Suetonius, Thucydides—writers who embellished their work with the flowers and tropes of rhetoric and who inserted imaginatively conceived set speeches into their narrative, practices followed by More in his Richard.

As was the custom, More's History *was incorporated into successive chronicles (by Harding, Hall, Grafton), and in this way came to the attention of Shakespeare, whose* Richard III *hews closely to More's portrait.*

RICHARD'S CHARACTER

Richard, Duke of York, a nobleman and a mighty, began, not by war but by law, to challenge° the crown, putting his claim into the Parliament, where his cause was either for right or favor° so far forth advanced that King Henry's blood° (albeit he had a goodly prince) utterly rejected, the crown was by authority of Parliament entailed unto the Duke of York and his issue male in remainder, immediately after the death of King Henry. But the duke not enduring so long to tarry, but intending under pretext of dissension and debate arising in the realm to prevent° his time and to take upon him the rule in King Harry's life, was with many nobles of the realm at Wakefield slain, leaving three sons, Edward, George, and Richard.

All three, as they were great states of birth, so were they great and stately of stomach,° greedy and ambitious of authority, and impatient of partners. Edward, revenging his father's death, deprived King Henry and attained the crown. George, Duke of Clarence, was a goodly noble prince, and at all points fortunate, if either his own ambition had not set him against his brother, or the envy of his enemies, his brother against him. For were it by the queen and the lords of her blood who highly maligned the king's kindred (as women commonly, not of malice but of nature, hate them whom their husbands love), or were it a proud appetite of the duke himself intending to be king, at the least wise° heinous treason was there laid to his charge, and finally, were he faulty were he faultless, attainted was he by Parliament and judged to the death, and thereupon hastily drowned in a butt of Malmsey.° Whose death King Edward (albeit he commanded it), when he wist it was done, piteously bewailed and sorrowfully repented.

Richard, the third son, of whom we now treat, was in wit° and courage equal with either of them, in body and prowess° far under them both, little of stature, ill-featured of limbs, crook-backed, his left shoulder much higher than his right, hard favored of visage, and such as is in states called warlike, in other men otherwise. He was malicious, wrathful, envious, and from before his birth, ever froward.° It is for truth reported

challenge claim   for right or favor either on its merits or as a result of partisanship   blood offspring   prevent anticipate, act before   stomach manner, disposition   at the least wise in any case   butt of Malmsey a barrel of wine   wit intelligence, mental acuity   prowess may also connote moral probity   froward perverse

that the duchess, his mother, had so much ado in her travail that she could not be delivered of him uncut, and that he came into the world with the feet forward, as men be born outward, and (as the fame runneth) also not untoothed, whether men of hatred report above the truth, or else that nature changed her course in his beginning, which in the course of his life many things unnaturally committed.

None evil captain was he in the war, as to which his disposition was more metely° than for peace. Sundry victories had he, and sometime overthrown, but never in default as for his own person, either of hardiness or politic order.° Free° was he called of dispense, and somewhat above his power liberal; with large gifts he got him unsteadfast friendship, for which he was fain to pillage and spoil in other places, and get him steadfast hatred. He was close and secret, a deep dissimuler,° lowly° of countenance, arrogant of heart, outwardly companionable where he inwardly hated, not letting° to kiss whom he thought to kill; dispiteous° and cruel, not for evil will always, but oftener for ambition, and either for the surety or increase of his estate. Friend and foe was much what indifferent,° where his advantage grew; he spared no man's death whose life withstood his purpose. He slew with his own hands King Henry VI, being prisoner in the Tower, as men constantly say, and that without commandment or knowledge of the king, who would undoubtedly, if he had intended that thing, have appointed that butcherly office to some other than his own born brother. Some wise men also ween that, his drift covertly conveyed, [Richard] lacked not in helping forth his brother of Clarence to his death, which he [Richard] resisted openly, howbeit somewhat (as men deemed) more faintly than one who was mindful of his wealth. And they that thus deem think that he long time in King Edward's life forethought to be king in case that the king, his brother (whose life he looked that evil diet should shorten), should happen to decease (as indeed he did) while his children were young. And they deem that for this intent he was glad of his brother's death, the Duke of Clarence, whose life must needs have hindered him so intending, whether the same Duke of Clarence had kept him true to his nephew the young king or enterprised to be king himself. But of all this point is there no certainty, and whoso divineth upon conjectures may as well

metely suitable   **but never . . . order** his defeats never resulted from either lack of personal courage or failure of strategy   **Free** generous **dissimuler** dissembler   **lowly** humble   **letting** hesitating   **dispiteous** lacking mercy   **Friend . . . indifferent** he was indifferent to friend and foe

shoot too far as too short. Howbeit this have I by credible information learned, that the self° night in which King Edward died, one Mistlebrook, long ere morning, came in great haste to the house of one Pottyer dwelling in Redcross Street Without Cripplegate. And when he was with hasty rapping quickly let in, he showed unto Pottyer that King Edward was departed. "By my trouthe,° man," quod Pottyer, "then will my master the Duke of Gloucester be king." What cause he had so to think, hard it is to say, whether he being toward him° anything knew that he such thing purposed, or otherwise had any inkling thereof, for he was not likely to speak it of naught.

But now to return to the course of this history, were it that the Duke of Gloucester had of old foreminded° this conclusion, or was now at first thereunto moved and put in hope by the occasion of the tender age of the young princes, his nephews (as opportunity and likelihood of speed° putteth a man in courage° of that he never intended), certain is it that he contrived their destruction, with the usurpation of the regal dignity upon himself. And for as much as he well wist° and helped to maintain a long-continued grudge and heart burning° between the queen's kindred and the king's blood, either party envying [the] other's authority, he now thought that their division should be (as it was indeed) a fortherly° beginning to the pursuit of his intent, and a sure ground for the foundation of all his building, if he might first under the pretext of revenging of old displeasure abuse the anger and ignorance of the one party, to the destruction of the other, and then win to his purpose as many as he could. And those that could not be won might be lost ere they looked therefore. For of one thing was he certain, that if his intent were perceived, he should soon have made peace between the both parties with his own blood.

KING EDWARD'S DEATHBED ORATION

King Edward in his life, albeit that this dissension between his friends somewhat irked him, yet in his good health he somewhat the less regarded it, because he thought whatsoever business should fall between them, himself should always be able to rule both the parties. But in his last sickness, when he perceived his natural strength so sore enfeebled that he despaired all recovery, then he, considering the youth of his children, albeit he nothing less mistrusted then that that hap-

---

self same   **trouthe** faith   **toward him** close to him   **foreminded** planned
speed success   **putteth . . . courage** gives a man the courage   **wist** knew
heart burning dissension   **fortherly** favorable

pened,° yet well foreseeing that many harms might grow by their debate, while the youth of his children should lack discretion of themselves and good counsel of their friends, of which either party should counsel for their own commodity° and rather by pleasant advice to win themselves favor than by profitable advertisement° to do the children good, he called some of them before him that were at variance. . . . When these lords, with divers others of both the parties, were come in presence, the king lifting up himself and underset with pillows, as it is reported, in this wise said unto them:

"My Lords, my dear kinsmen and allies, in what plight I lie, you see and I feel. By which the less while I look to live with you the more deeply am I moved to care in what case I leave you, for such as I leave you, such be my children like to find you. Which if they should (that God forbid) find you at variance, might hap to fall themselves at war ere their discretion would serve to set you at peace. Ye see their youth, of which I reckon the only surety to rest in your concord. For it sufficeth not that all [of] you love them, if each of you hate other. If they were men, your faithfulness happily would suffice. But childhood must be maintained by men's authority, and slipper° youth underpropped with elder's counsel, which neither they can have but° ye give, nor ye give it if ye agree not. For where each laboreth to break what the other maketh, and for hatred of each other's person impugneth each other's counsel, there must it needs be long ere any good conclusion go forward. And also while either party laboreth to be chief, flattery shall have more place than plain and faithful advice, of which must needs ensue the evil bringing up of the prince, whose mind in tender youth infect,° shall readily fall to mischief and riot, and draw down with him this noble realm to ruin, but if° grace turn him to wisdom; which if God send, then they who by evil means before pleased him best shall after fall farthest out of favor, so that ever at length evil drifts come to nought, and good plain ways prosper. Great variance hath there long been between you, not always for great causes. Sometimes a thing right well intended, our misconstruction turneth unto worse, or a small displeasure done us, either our own affection or evil tongues agreveth.° But this wote° I well, ye never had so great cause of hatred as ye have of love. That we be all men, that we be Christian men, this shall I leave for preachers to tell you—and yet I wote never whether any preacher's words ought more to

---

albeit . . . happened although at that time he had no suspicion of what did in fact later happen   **commodity** advantage   **advertisement** instruction   **slipper** unstable   **but** unless   **whose . . . infect** whose mind having been infected   **but if** unless   **agreveth** aggravates   **wote** know

move you than his that is by and by going to the place that they all preach of. But this shall I desire you to remember, that the one part of you is of my blood, the other of mine allies, and each of you with other, either of kindred or affinity, which spiritual kindred of affinity (if the sacraments of Christ's Church bear that weight with us that would God they did) should no less move us to charity than the respect of fleshly consanguinity. Our Lord forbid that you love together the worse for the self cause that you ought to love the better. And yet that happeneth. And nowhere find we so deadly debate as among them which by nature and law most ought to agree together.

"Such a pestilent serpent is ambition and desire of vainglory and sovereignty, which among states where he once entreth creepeth forth so far, till with division and variance he turneth all to mischief. First longing to be next [to] the best, afterward equal with the best, and at last chief and above the best. Of which immoderate appetite of worship, and thereby of debate and dissension, what loss, what sorrow, what trouble hath within these few years grown in this realm, I pray God as well forget as we well remember. Which things, if I could as well have foreseen as I have with my more pain than pleasure proved,° by God's blessed Lady (that was ever his oath) I would never have won the courtesy of men's knees, with the loss of so many heads. But since things past cannot be again called, much ought we the more beware by what occasion we have taken so great hurt afore, that we eftsoons° fall not in that occasion again. Now be those griefs past, and all is (God be thanked) quiet, and likely right well to prosper in wealthful peace under your cousins, my children, if God send them life and you live. Of which two things, the less loss were they by whom though God did his pleasure, yet should the realm always find kings and peradventure as good kings. But if you among yourself in a child's reign fall at debate, many a good man shall perish and happily° he too, and ye too, ere this land find peace again.

"Wherefore in these last words that ever I look to speak with you: I exhort you and require you all, for the love that you have ever borne to me, for the love that I have ever borne to you, for the love that Our Lord beareth to us all, from this time forward, all griefs forgotten, each of you love other. Which I verily trust you will, if ye any thing earthly regard, either God or your king, affinity or kindred, this realm, your own country, or your own surety."

And therewithal the king no longer enduring to sit up, laid

proved experienced   **eftsoons** quickly, immediately afterward   **happily** by chance

him down on his right side, his face toward them. And none was there present who could refrain from weeping. But the lords recomforting him with as good words as they could, and answering for the time as they thought to stand with his pleasure, there in his presence (as by their words appeared) each forgave other, and joined their hands together, when (as it after appeared by their deeds) their hearts were far asunder.

THE DEBATE OVER SANCTUARY

[The queen, Edward's widow, has fled with one of the princes to the safety of a church, invoking for protection the ancient law of sanctuary.]

When the king [Edward V] approached near to the city, Edmond Sha, goldsmith, then mayor, with William White and John Mathew, sheriffs, and all the other aldermen in scarlet, with five hundred horse of the citizens in violet, received him reverently at Harnesey, and riding from thence, accompanied him into the city, which he entered the fourth day of May, the first and last year of his reign. But the Duke of Gloucester bare him in open sight so reverently to the prince, with all semblance of lowliness, that from the great obloquy in which he was so late before, he was suddenly fallen in so great trust, that at the council next assembled he was made the only man chosen and thought most meet to be protector of the king and his realm, so that (were it destiny or were it folly) the lamb was betaken to the wolf to keep. . . .

Now although the protector so sore thirsted for the finishing of that [which] he had begun, who thought every day a year till it were achieved, yet durst he no further attempt as long as he had but half his prey in his hand, well witting° that if he deposed the one brother, all the realm would fall to the other if he either remained in sanctuary or should happily be shortly conveyed to his further liberty. Wherefore incontinent° at the next meeting of the lords at the council, he proposed unto them that it was a heinous deed of the queen [widow of the late Edward IV, mother of the presently reigning young king, Edward V, and sister-in-law to the protector, Richard Duke of Gloucester] and proceeding of great malice toward the king's counselors that she should keep in sanctuary the king's brother from him, whose special pleasure and comfort were to have his brother with him. And that by her done to none other intent but to bring all the lords in obloquy and murmur of the people.

witting knowing   **incontinent** immediately

As though they were not to be trusted with the king's brother that by the assent of the nobles of the land were appointed as the king's nearest friends, to the tuition° of his own royal person:

"The prosperity whereof standeth (quod he) not all in keeping from enemies or ill viand,° but partly also in recreation and moderate pleasure, which he cannot in this tender youth take in the company of ancient persons, but in the familiar conversation° of those that be neither far under nor far above his age, and none the less of estate convenient° to accompany his noble majesty. Wherefore with whom rather than with his own brother? And if any man think this consideration light (which I think no man thinketh that loveth the king), let him consider sometimes without small things greater cannot stand. And verily it redoundeth greatly to the dishonor both of the king's highness and of all us that be about his grace to have it run in every man's mouth, not in this realm only, but also in other lands (as evil words walk far), that the king's brother should be fain to keep sanctuary. For every man will ween that no man will so do for nought. And such evil opinion once fastened in men's hearts, hard it is to wrest out, and may grow to more grief than any man here can divine.

"Wherefore me thinketh it were not worst to send unto the queen for the redress of this matter some honorable trusty man, such as both tendereth the king's weal,° and the honor of his council, and is also in favor and credence with her. For all which considerations, none seemeth me more meetly than our reverent father here present, my Lord Cardinal,° who may in this matter do most good of any man, if it please him to take the pain. Which I doubt not of his goodness he will not refuse for the king's sake and ours, and wealth° of the young duke himself, the king's most honorable brother, and after my sovereign lord himself my most dear nephew, considering that thereby shall be ceased the slanderous rumor and obloquy now going and the hurts avoided that thereof might ensue, and much rest and quiet grow to all the realm. And if she be percase° so obstinate, and so precisely set upon her own will that neither his wise and faithful advertisement can move her, nor any man's reason content her, then shall we by mine advice, by the king's authority, fetch him out of that prison, and bring him to his noble presence, in whose continual company he shall be so well cherished and so honorably entreated, that all

tuition protection **viand** food **conversation** society, company **convenient** suitable **tendereth . . . weal** has tender feelings about the king's well-being **my Lord Cardinal** Thomas Cardinal Bourchier, Archbishop of Canterbury **wealth** well-being **percase** perchance

the world shall to our honor and her reproach perceive that it was only malice, frowardness,° or folly that caused her to keep him there. This is my mind in this matter for this time, except any of your lordships anything perceive to the contrary. For never shall I by God's grace so wed myself to mine own will but that I shall be ready to change it upon your better advice."

When the protector had said,° all the council affirmed that the motion was good and reasonable, and to the king and the duke his brother honorable, and a thing that should cease great murmur in the realm, if the mother might be by good means induced to deliver him. Which thing the Archbishop of York, whom they all agreed also to be thereto most convenient, took upon him to move her, and therein to do his uttermost devoir.° Howbeit if she could be in no wise entreated with her good will to deliver him, then thought he and such other as were of the spiritualty° present that it were not in any wise to be attempted to take him out against her will. For it would be a thing that should turn to the great grudge° of all men, and high displeasure of God, if the privilege of that holy place should now be broken. Which had so many years been kept, which both kings and popes so good had granted, so many had confirmed, and which holy ground was more than five hundred years ago by Saint Peter's own person in spirit, accompanied with great multitude of angels, by night so specially hallowed and dedicated to God (for the proof whereof they have yet in the Abbey Saint Peter's cope to show), that from that time hitherward was there never so undevout a king that durst that sacred place violate, or so holy a bishop that durst it presume to consecrate.

"And therefore," quod the Archbishop of York, "God forbid that any man should for anything earthly enterprise to break the immunity and liberty of that sacred sanctuary that hath been the safeguard of so many a good man's life. And I trust," quod he, "with God's grace we shall not need it. But for any manner need, I would not we should do it. I trust that she shall be with reason contented, and all thing in good manner obtained. And if it happen that I bring it not so to pass, yet shall I toward it so far forth do my best that ye shall all well perceive that no lack of my devoir, but the mother's dread and womanish fear shall be the let."°

"Womanish fear, nay womanish frowardness," quod the Duke of Buckingham, "for I dare take it upon my soul she well knoweth she needeth no such thing to fear, either for her son or for herself. For as for her, here is no man that will be at war

frowardness obstinacy   **said** spoken   **devoir** duty   **spiritualty** clergy
grudge ill will, resentment   **let** obstacle, hindrance

with women. Would God some of the men of her kin were women too, and then should all be soon in rest. Howbeit there is none of her kin the less loved for that they be her kin, but for their own evil deserving. And nonetheless if we loved neither her nor her kin, yet were there no cause to think that we should hate the king's noble brother, to whose grace we ourself be of kin. Whose honor if she as much desired as our dishonor, and as much regard took to his wealth, as to her own will, she would be as loath to suffer him from the king, as any of us be. For if she have any wit° (as would God she had as good will as she hath shrewd wit), she reckoneth herself no wiser than she thinketh some that be here, of whose faithful mind she nothing doubteth, but verily believeth and knoweth that they would be as sorry of his harm as herself, and yet would have him from her if she bide there. And we [are] all (I think) content that both be with her, if she come thence and bide in such place where they may with their honor be.

"Now then if she refuse in the deliverance of him to follow the counsel of them whose wisdom she knoweth, whose truth she well trusteth, it is ethe to perceive that frowardness letteth her° and not fear. But go to suppose° that she fear (as who may let her to fear her own shadow), the more she feareth to deliver him, the more ought we fear to leave him in her hands. For if she cast such fond° doubts that she fear his hurt, then will she fear that he shall be fetched thence. For she will soon think that if men were set (which God forbid) upon so great a mischief, the sanctuary would little let° them. Which good men might, as me thinketh, without sin somewhat less regard than they do.

"Now then if she doubt lest he might be fetched from her, is it not likely enough that she shall send him somewhere out of the realm? Verily, I look for none other. And I doubt not but she now as sore mindeth it as we the let thereof.° And if she might happen to bring that to pass (as it were no great maistry,° we letting her alone), all the world would say that we were a wise sort of counselors about a king, who let his brother be cast away under our noses. And therefore I ensure you faithfully for my mind, I will rather maugrye her mind,° fetch him away than leave him there, till her frowardness or fond fear convey him away. And yet will I break no sanctuary

---

wit reasonableness, intelligence   **ethe . . . letteth her** easy to see that willful perversity is what is stopping her   **go to suppose** even if we suppose   **fond** foolish   **let** stop, hinder   **she now . . . let thereof** she is planning to do it just as surely as we are planning to prevent it   **maistry** accomplishment   **maugrye her mind** in spite of her intention; a variant form of maugre and magry

therefore. For verily since the privileges of that place and other like have been of long continued, I am not he that would be about to break them. And in good faith if they were now to begin, I would not be he that should be about to make them. Yet will I not say nay, but that it is a deed of pity that such men as the sea, or their evil debtors have brought in poverty, should have some place of liberty to keep their bodies out of the danger of their cruel creditors. And also if the crown happen (as it hath done) to come in question, while either part taketh [the] other as traitors, I will well there be some places of refuge for both.

"But as for thieves, of which these places be full, and who never fall from the craft after they once fall thereto, it is pity the sanctuary should serve them. And much more manne-quellers° whom God bade to take from the altar and kill them, if their murder were willful. And where it is otherwise there need we not the sanctuaries that God appointed in the old law. For if either necessity, his own defense, or misfortune draw him to that deed, a pardon serveth, which either the law granteth of course, or the king of pity may.

"Then look me now how few sanctuary men there be, whom any favorable necessity compelled to go thither. And then see on the other side what a sort there be commonly therein, of them whom willful unthriftiness° hath brought to nought. What a rabble of thieves, murderers, and malicious heinous traitors, and that in two places specially. The one at the elbow of the city, the other in the very bowels. I dare well avow it, weigh the good that they [i.e., the two notorious London sanctuaries he has just mentioned] do with the hurt that cometh of them, and ye shall find it much better to lack both than have both. And this I say, although they were not abused as they now be, and so long have been, that I fear me ever they will be while men be afraid to set their hands to the amendment, as though God and Saint Peter were the patrons of ungracious living.

"Now unthrifts° riot and run in debt, upon the boldness of these places. Yea, and rich men run thither with poor men's goods; there they build, there they spend and bid their creditors go whistle them. Men's wives run thither with their husband's plate, and say they dare not abide with their husbands for beating. Thieves bring thither their stolen goods, and there live thereon. There devise they new robberies; nightly they steal out, they rob and reave° and kill, and come in again as though those places gave them not only a safeguard for the harm they have done, but a license also to do more. Howbeit,

mannequellers murderers   **unthriftiness** wastefulness   **unthrifts** prodi-gals, wastrels   **reave** pillage much of this mischief, if wise men would set their hands to, it might be amended, with great thank of God and no breach of the privilege. The residue, since so long ago I wote ne'er what pope and what prince, more piteous than politic hath granted it and other men since of a certain religious fear have not broken it, let us take a pain therewith and let it in God's name stand in force, as far forth as reason will. Which is not fully so far forth as may serve to let us of the fetching forth of this nobleman to his honor and wealth, out of that place in which he neither is nor can be a sanctuary man.

"A sanctuary serveth always to defend the body of that man who standeth in danger abroad, not of great hurt only, but also of lawful hurt. For against unlawful harms never pope nor king intended to privilege any one place. For that privilege hath every place. Knoweth any man any place wherein it is lawful [for] one man to do another wrong? That no man unlawfully take hurt, that liberty, the king, the law, and very nature forbiddeth in every place, and maketh to that regard for every man every place a sanctuary. But where a man is by lawful means in peril, there needeth he the tuition of some special privilege, which is the only ground and cause of all sanctuaries. From which necessity this noble prince is far, whose love to his king, nature and kindred proveth, whose innocence to all the world his tender youth proveth. And so sanctuary as for him, neither none he needeth, nor also none can have. Men come not to sanctuary as they come to baptism, to require it by their godfathers. He must ask it himself who must have it. And reason,° since no man hath cause to have it but [he] whose conscience° of his own fault maketh him fain need to require it, what will then hath yonder babe? Which if he had discretion to require° it, if need were, I dare say would now be right angry with them who keep him there. And I would think, without any scruple of conscience, without any breach of privilege, to be somewhat more homely° with them that be there sanctuary men indeed. For if one go to sanctuary with another man's goods, why should not the king, leaving his body at liberty, satisfy the part of his goods even within the sanctuary? For neither king nor pope can give any place such a privilege that it shall discharge a man of his debts, being able to pay."

And with that, divers of the clergy who were present, whether they said it for his pleasure or as they thought, agreed plainly that by the law of God and of the church the goods of a sanctuary man should be delivered in payment of his debts, and stolen

---

And reason and this is reasonable   **conscience** knowledge   **require** ask for   **homely** plain-dealing, rough

goods to the owner, and only liberty reserved him to get his living with the labor of his hands.

"Verily," quod the duke, "I think you say very truth. And what if a man's wife will take sanctuary because she list to run from her husband. I would wene° if she can allege none other cause, he may lawfully, without any displeasure to Saint Peter, take her out of Saint Peter's Church by the arm. And if nobody may be taken out of sanctuary who sayeth he will bide there, then if a child will take sanctuary because he feareth to go to school, his master must let him alone. And as simple as that example is, yet is there less reason in our case than in that. For therein though it be a childish fear, yet is there at the leastwise some fear. And herein is there none at all. And verily I have often heard of sanctuary men, but I never heard erste° of sanctuary children. And therefore, as for the conclusion of my mind: whoso may have deserved to need it, if they think it for their surety, let them keep it. But he can be no sanctuary man that neither hath wisdom to desire it nor malice to deserve it, whose life or liberty can by no lawful process stand in jeopardy. And he that taketh one out of sanctuary to do him good, I say plainly that he breaketh no sanctuary."

When the duke had done, the temporal men whole, and good part of the spiritual also, thinking none hurt earthly meant toward the young babe, condescended° in effect that if he were not delivered, he should be fetched. Howbeit they thought it all best, in the avoiding of all manner of rumor, that the lord cardinal should first assay to get him with her good will. And thereupon all the council came unto the Star Chamber at Westminster. And the lord cardinal, leaving the protector with the council in the Star Chamber, departed into the sanctuary to the queen, with divers other lords with him, were it for the respect of his honor or that she should by presence of so many perceive that this errand was not one man's mind, or were it for that the protector intended not in this matter to trust any one man alone; or else that if she finally were determined to keep him, some of that company had happily° secret instruction incontinent, magry his mind,° to take him [the young prince in sanctuary] and to leave her no respite to convey him, which she was likely to mind° after this matter broken to her, if her time would in any wise serve her.

---

wene think   **erste** before this   **condescended** agreed   **happily** perhaps **incontinent, magry his mind** at once, in spite of his attitude or opinion. "His" here presumably refers to the cardinal, who has already expressed himself as against taking anyone from sanctuary by force. Richard Sylvester, editor of the Yale edition of More's *History*, emends the text to read "her," that is, the queen's.   **mind** intend, plan

RICHARD MOVES TOWARD THE THRONE: THE LEGAL MURDER
OF HASTINGS

. . . On the Friday, the thirteenth day of June, many lords assembled in the Tower, and there sat in council, devising° the honorable solemnity of the king's [Edward V's] coronation, of which the time appointed then so near approached that the pageants and subtleties were in making day and night at Westminster, and much victual killed therefore, that afterward was cast away. These lords so sitting together commoning° of this matter, the protector° came in among them, first about nine of the clock, saluting them courteously and excusing himself that he had been from them so long, saying merely that he had been asleep that day. And after a little talking with them, he said unto the Bishop of Ely,° "My lord, you have very good strawberries at your garden in Holbern; I require you let us have a mess of them."

"Gladly, my lord," quod he, "would God I had some better thing as ready to your pleasure as that." And therewith in all the haste he sent his servant for a mess of strawberries. The protector set the lords fast in commoning,° and thereupon praying them to spare him for a little while, departed thence.

And soon after one hour, between ten and eleven, he returned into the chamber among them, all changed with a wonderful sour angry countenance, knitting the brows, frowning and frothing and gnawing on his lips, and so sat him down in his place, all the lords much dismayed and sore marveling of this manner of sudden change, and what thing should him ail. Then when he had sitten still a while, thus he began: "What were they worthy to have that compass and imagine the destruction of me, being so near of blood unto the king, and protector of his royal person and his realm?" At this question all the lords sat sore astonished, musing much by whom this question should be meant, of which every man wist himself clear. Then the lord chamberlain, as he who for the love between them thought he might be boldest with him, answered and said that they were worthy to be punished as heinous traitors, whatsoever they were. And all the others affirmed the same.

---

devising discussing, planning **commoning** talking, discussing **protector** Richard, Duke of Gloucester, later to become King Richard III **Bishop of Ely** John Morton, later cardinal, who ended up a bitter antagonist of Richard's. It was in Morton's home that More received some of his education as a youth, and it was there also, no doubt, that he imbibed a good deal of anti-Richard sentiment. It used to be conjectured that the cardinal was the actual author of *Richard III*, or at least the Latin version, a theory long since exploded by modern scholarship.

"That is," quod he, "yonder sorceress, my brother's wife, and others with her," meaning the queen. At these words many of the other lords were greatly abashed who favored her. But the Lord Hastings was in his mind better content that it was moved by her° than by any other whom he loved better, albeit his heart somewhat grudged that he was not afore made of counsel in this matter, as he was of the taking of her kindred and of their putting to death, which were by his assent before devised° to be beheaded at Pomfret this selfsame day, in which he was not aware that it was by others devised that himself should the same day be beheaded at London.

Then said the protector, "Ye shall all see in what wise that sorceress and that other witch of her counsel, Shore's wife, with their affinity° have by their sorcery and witchcraft wasted my body." And therewith he plucked up his doublet sleeve to his elbow upon his left arm, where he showed a werish,° withered arm and small, as it was never other. And thereupon every man's mind sore misgave them, well perceiving that this matter was but a quarrel. For well they wist that the queen was too wise to go about any such folly. And also if she would, yet would she of all folk least make Shore's wife of counsel,° whom of all women she most hated, as that concubine whom the king her husband had most loved. And also no man was there present but well knew that his arm was ever such since his birth. Nonetheless, the lord chamberlain (who from the death of King Edward kept Shore's wife, on whom he somewhat doted in the king's life, saving,° as it is said, he that while forbare her,° of reverence toward his king, or else of a certain kind of fidelity to his friend) answered and said, "Certainly, my lord, if they have so heinously done, they be worthy heinous punishment."

"What!" quod the protector, "thou servest me, I wene, with 'ifs' and with 'ands.'° I tell thee they have so done, and that I will make good on thy body, traitor!" And therewith, as in a great anger, he clapped his fist upon the board a great rap. At which token given, one cried "Treason!" without the chamber. Therewith a door clapped, and in come there rushing men in harness, as many as the chamber might hold. And anon the protector said to the Lord Hastings, "I arrest thee, traitor."

"What, me, my lord," quod he. "Yea, thee, traitor," quod

that it was moved by her that the hostility was directed against her   **devised** intended, plotted   **affinity** partisans, allies   **werish** withered   **make . . . of counsel** take Shore's wife into her counsel   **saving** with the exception that   **forbare her** did not share her company   **ands** "and" in sixteenth-century usage (sometimes spelled *an*) was often used as a synonym for the conjunction *if*

the protector. And another let fly at the Lord Stanley, who shrank at the stroke and fell under the table, or else his head had been cleft to the teeth, for as shortly° as he shrank, yet ran the blood about his ears.

Then were they all quickly bestowed in divers chambers, except the lord chamberlain,° whom the protector bade speed and shrive him apace.° "For by Saint Paul," quod he, "I will not to dinner till I see thy head off." It booted him not° to ask why, but heavily° he took a priest at adventure,° and made a short shrift, for a longer would not be suffered, the protector made so much haste to dinner, which he might not go to till this were done for saving of his oath. So was he brought forth into the green beside the chapel within the tower, and his head laid down upon a long log of timber, and there stricken off. And afterward his body with the head entered at Windsor, beside the body of King Edward, whose both souls Our Lord pardon.°

A marvelous case is it to hear, either the warnings of that he should have avoided, or the tokens of that he could not avoid.

SHORE'S WIFE

Now then by and by, as it were for anger, not for covetousness, the protector sent into the house of Shore's wife (for her husband dwelled not with her), and spoiled° her of all that ever she had, above the value of two or three thousand marks, and sent her body to prison. And when he had a while laid unto her for the manner sake° that she went about to bewitch him, and that she was of counsel with the lord chamberlain to destroy him; in conclusion when no color could fasten upon these matters,° then he laid heinously to her charge that thing which herself could not deny, that all the world wist was true, and that nonetheless every man laughed at to hear it then so

shortly quickly   the lord chamberlain Lord Hastings and the lord chamberlain are one and the same   apace at once   It booted him not it was useless for him   heavily sorrowfully   at adventure at random   pardon Hastings had been an intimate associate of the late king, Edward IV, and was, consequently, devoted to Edward's two sons: the young king, Edward V, and his brother, at this time being held by their mother for safekeeping in sanctuary. Such ties made Hastings a clear and present threat to Richard, who, according to More, was plotting to remove the late king's two sons, and thereby pave for himself an unobstructed path to the throne of England. The two young princes were, it must be remembered, Richard's nephews   spoiled robbed   laid . . . manner sake lodged a charge against her for the sake of appearances   no color . . . these matters these charges proved to be without foundation

suddenly, so highly, taken: that she was nought of her body.° And for this cause (as a goodly continent prince, clean and faultless of himself, sent out of heaven into this vicious world for the amendment of men's manners) he caused the Bishop of London to put her to open penance, going before the cross in procession upon a Sunday with a taper in her hand.

In which she went in countenance and pace demure so womanly, and albeit she were out of all array, save her kirtle° only, yet went she so fair and lovely, namely° while the won-dering of the people cast a comely red in her cheeks (of which she before had most miss°) that her great shame won her much praise among those who were more amorous of her body than curious° of her soul. And many good folk also who hated her living, and glad were to see sin corrected, yet pitied they more her penance than rejoiced therein, when they considered that the protector procured it more of a corrupt intent than any virtuous affection.

This woman was born in London, worshipfully friended, honestly brought up, and very well married, saving somewhat too soon; her husband an honest citizen, young and goodly and of good substance. But forasmuch as they were coupled ere she were well ripe, she not very fervently loved [him] for whom she never longed. Which was happily the thing that the more easily made her incline unto the king's appetite when he required her. Howbeit, the respect of his royalty, the hope of gay apparel, ease, pleasure, and other wealth was able soon to pierce a soft, tender heart. But when the king had abused her, anon her husband (as he was an honest man and one who could his good,° not presuming to touch a king's concubine) left her up to him altogether.

When the king died, the lord chamberlain took her. Which in the king's days, albeit he was sore enamored upon her, yet he forbare her, either for reverence, or for a certain friendly faithfulness. Proper she was and fair; nothing in her body that you would have changed, but if you would have wished her somewhat higher.° Thus say they who knew her in her youth. Albeit some that now see her (for yet she liveth) deem her never to have been well visaged. Whose judgment seemeth me somewhat like as though men should guess the beauty of one long before departed by her scalp taken out of the charnel house. For now is she old, lean, withered, and dried up, nothing left but rivelled° skin and hard bone. And yet, being even such,

---

nought . . . body she had used her body for immoral purposes   **kirtle** skirt   **namely** especially   **most miss** had most lacked   **curious** solicitous **one . . . good** one who knew what would be to his advantage   **higher** taller   **rivelled** shriveled

whoso well advise° her visage might guess and devise which parts how filled would make it a fair face.

Yet delighted not men so much in her beauty as in her pleasant behavior. For a proper wit had she, and could both read well and write, merry in company, ready and quick of answer, neither mute nor full of babble, sometimes taunting without displeasure and not without disport.° The king would say that he had three concubines, which in three divers properties diversely excelled. One the merriest, another the wiliest, the third the holiest harlot in his realm, as one whom no man could get out of the church lightly to any place, but it were to his bed. The other two were somewhat greater personages, and nevertheless of their humility content to be nameless, and to forbear the praise of those properties. But the merriest was this Shore's wife, in whom the king therefore took special pleasure. For many he had, but her he loved, whose favor, to say truth (for sin it were to belie the devil), she never abused to any man's hurt, but to many a man's comfort and relief. Where the king took displeasure, she would mitigate and appease his mind; where men were out of favor she would bring them in his grace. For many that had highly offended, she obtained pardon. Of great forfeitures she got men remission. And finally in many weighty suits she stood many men in great stead, either for none, or very small rewards, and those rather gay than rich. Either for that she was content with the deed self well done, or for that she delighted to be sued unto, and to show what she was able to do with the king, or for that wanton women and wealthy be not always covetous.

I doubt not some shall think this woman too slight a thing to be written of and set among the remembrances of great matters, which they shall specially think who happily shall esteem her only by what they now see her. But me seemeth° the chance so much the more worthy to be remembered in how much she is now in the more beggarly condition, unfriended and worn out of acquaintance, after good substance, after as great favor with the prince, after as great suit and seeking to with all those who those days had business to speed, as many other men were in their times, which be now famous only by the infamy of their ill deeds. Her doings were not much less, albeit they be much less remembered, because they were not so evil. For men use,° if they have an evil turn, to write it in marble, and whoso doth us a good turn, we write it in dust, which is not worst proved by her. For at this day

advise study, consider   disport entertainment   me seemeth it seems to me   men use men are accustomed she beggeth of many at this day living, who at this day had begged if she had not been.

Now then . . . it was by the protector and his council concluded that this Doctor Shaw should in a sermon at Paul's Cross signify to the people that neither King Edward [IV] himself nor the Duke of Clarence [the protector's two brothers] were lawfully begotten, nor were the very° children of the Duke of York [the protector's father], but gotten unlawfully by other persons by the adultery of the duchess, their mother [and also the protector's own mother]. And that also Dame Elizabeth Lucy was verily the wife of King Edward, and so the prince and all his children bastards who were gotten upon the queen.

According to this device,° Doctor Shaw the Sunday after at Paul's Cross, in a great audience (as always assembled great number to his preaching), he took for his theme, *Spuria vitulamina non agent radices altas.* That is to say, bastard slips never take deep root. Thereupon when he had showed the great grace that God giveth and secretly infoundeth° in right generation after the laws of matrimony, then declared he that commonly those children lacked that grace, and for the punishment of their parents were for the more part unhappy, who were gotten in bastardy and especially in adultery. Of which, though some by the ignorance of the world, and the truth hid from knowledge, inherited for the season° other men's lands; yet God always so provideth that it continueth not in their blood long, but the truth coming to light, the rightful inheritors be restored and the bastard slip pulled up ere it can be rooted deep.

And when he had laid for the proof and confirmation of this sentence certain examples taken out of the Old Testament and other ancient histories, then began he to descend into the praise of the Lord Richard, late Duke of York, calling him father to the lord protector, and declared the title of his heirs unto the crown, to whom it was after the death of King Henry VI entailed by authority of Parliament. Then showed he that his very right heir of his body lawfully begotten was the lord protector only. For he declared then that King Edward was never lawfully married unto the queen, but was before God, husband unto Dame Elizabeth Lucy, and so his children bas-

very true, legitimate   **device** scheme   **infoundeth** infuses   **for the season** for a time

tards. And besides that, neither King Edward himself nor the Duke of Clarence among those who were secret in the household° were reckoned very surely for the children of the noble duke, as those that by their favors° more resembled other known men than him. From whose virtuous conditions he said also that King Edward was far off. But the lord protector, he said, that very noble prince, the special pattern of knightly prowess, as well in all princely behavior as in the lineaments and favor of his visage, represented the very face of the noble duke, his father. This is, quod he, the father's own figure, this is his own countenance, the very print of his visage, the sure undoubted image, the plain express likeness of that noble duke.

Now was it before devised that in the speaking of these words the protector should have come in among the people toward the sermon, to the end that those words, meeting with his presence, might have been taken among the hearers as though the Holy Ghost had put them in the preacher's mouth and should have moved the people even there to cry, "King Richard! King Richard!" that it might have been after said that he was specially chosen by God, and, in [a] manner, by miracle. But this device quailed,° either by the protector's negligence or the preacher's overmuch diligence. For while the protector found by the way tarrying,° lest he should prevent° those words, and the doctor fearing that he should come ere his sermon could come to those words, hastened his matter thereto. He was come to them, and past them, and entered into other matters ere the protector came. Whom when he [Doctor Shaw] beheld coming, he suddenly left the matter with which he was in hand, and without any deduction° thereunto, out of all order and out of all frame,° began to repeat those words again: This is the very noble prince, the special pattern of knightly prowess, who as well in all princely behavior as in the lineaments and favor of his visage representeth the very face of the noble Duke of York, his father. This is the father's own figure, this his own countenance, the very print of his visage, the sure, undoubted image, the plain, express likeness of the noble duke, whose remembrance can never die while he liveth. While these words were in speaking, the protector, accompanied with the Duke of Buckingham, went through the people into the place where the doctors commonly stand in the upper story, where he stood to hearken [to] the sermon. But the people were so far from crying, "King Richard! King

those who . . . household those who were privy to the household secrets **favors** features **quailed** failed **found . . . tarrying** managed to delay, "stalled" **prevent** arrive before **deduction** introduction, transition **out of all frame** out of its proper place

Richard!" that they stood as they had been turned into stones, for wonder of this shameful sermon. After which once ended, the preacher got him home and never after durst look out for shame, but kept him out of sight like an owl.

And when he once asked one who had been his old friend what the people talked of him, although his own conscience well showed him that they talked no good, yet when the other answered him that there was in every man's mouth spoken of him much shame, it so struck him to the heart that within [a] few days after he withered and consumed away.°

THE CROWN IS OFFERED TO RICHARD

[*Richard's crony, the Duke of Buckingham, has just offered him the crown.*]

When the protector had heard the proposition, he looked very strangely thereat and answered that although he partly knew the things by them alleged to be true, yet such entire love he bare unto King Edward and his children that so much more regarded his honor in other realms about than the crown of any one, of which he was never desirous, that he could not find in his heart in this point to incline to their desire. For in all other nations where the truth were not well known, it should peradventure be thought that it were his own ambitious mind and device to depose the prince and take himself the crown. With which infamy he would not have his honor stained for any crown. In which he had ever perceived much more

---

° Not the least of the many ironies in More's life is the fact that he himself was victimized by the kind of politically inspired sermon described here. While he was a prisoner in the Tower, and some weeks before his trial and execution, instructions went out from the government to the clergy ordering them on several successive Sundays to preach against both Sir Thomas More and Bishop John Fisher, who was also awaiting trial on the charge of treason. One of these sermons was published and has survived. This is the sermon attacking the two men as traitors, preached by Simon Matthew, the Bishop of London, a man who, because of a speech defect, had given up the habit of using his cathedral pulpit, until, that is, the government ordered him to mount the steps and denounce the ex-Chancellor. Matthew's sermon, in addition to providing corroborative evidence that More's legal guilt had been predetermined and that his trial was, consequently, a mockery, also illustrates, along with Doctor Shaw's pathetic sermon, the quality, the extent, and the effects of the union of crown and crozier in the turbulent political life of medieval and Renaissance Europe. This alliance of Church and State, so characteristic of historical Christendom, prevailed before, during, and after the events we have come to call the Reformation. This union was, incidentally, a fact of politico-religious life which, generally speaking, Thomas More himself both understood and approved.

labor and pain than pleasure to him that so would so use it, as he that would not were not worthy to have it.

Notwithstanding, he not only pardoned them the motion that they made him, but also thanked them for the love and hearty favor they bare him, praying them for his sake to give and bear the same to the prince, under whom he was and would be content to live, and with his labor and counsel as far as should like the king to use him, he would do his uttermost devoir to set the realm in good state. Which was already in this little while of his protectorship (the praise given to God) well begun, in that the malice of such as were before occasion of the contrary and of new intended to be, were now, partly by good policy, partly more by God's special providence than man's provision repressed.

Upon this answer given, the Duke [of Buckingham], by the protector's license, a little rouned,° as well with other noblemen about him as with the mayor and recorder of London. And after that, upon like pardon desired and obtained, he showed aloud unto the protector for a final conclusion, that the realm was appointed° King Edward's line should not any longer reign upon them, both for that they had so far gone that it was now no surety to retreat, as for that they thought it for the weal universal° to take that way, although they had not yet begun it. Wherefore, if it would like his grace to take the crown upon him, they would humbly beseech him thereunto. If he would give them a resolute answer to the contrary, which they would be loath to hear, then must they needs seek and should not fail to find some other nobleman that would.

These words much moved the protector, who else, as every man may wit, would never of likelihood have inclined thereunto. But when he saw there was none other way, but that either he must take it or else he and his both go from it, he said unto the lords and commons: "Since we perceive well that all the realm is so set, whereof we be very sorry that they will not suffer in any wise King Edward's line to govern them, whom no man earthly can govern against their wills, and we well also perceive that no man is there to whom the crown can by so just title appertain as to ourself, as very right heir lawfully begotten of the body of our most dear father, Richard, late Duke of York, to which title is now joined your election, the nobles and commons of this realm, which we of all titles possible take for most effectual; we be content and agree favorably to incline to your petition and request, and according to the same here

a little rouned walked around and held whispered conferences　**appointed** agreed　**weal universal** common good

we take upon us the royal estate, preeminence and kingdom of the two noble realms, England and France, the one from this day forward by us and our heirs to rule, govern, and defend, the other by God's grace and your good help to get again and subdue, and establish forever in due obedience unto this realm of England, the advancement whereof we never ask of God longer to live than we intend to procure." With this there was a great shout, crying, "King Richard! King Richard!" And then the lords went up to the king (for so was he from that time called) and the people departed, talking diversely of the matter, every man as his fantasy gave him.

But much they talked and marveled of the manner of this dealing, that the matter was on both parts made so strange, as though neither had ever communed with other thereof before, when that themselves well wist there was no man so dull that heard them but he perceived well enough that all the matter was made between them.° Howbeit, some excused that again, and said all must be done in good order though. And men must sometimes for the manner sake not be knowing what they know.° For at the consecration of a bishop, every man woteth well by the paying for his bulls that he purposeth to be one, though he pay for nothing else.° And yet must he be twice asked whether he will be bishop or no, and he must twice say nay, and at the third time take it as compelled thereunto by his own will. And in a stage play all the people know right well that he who playeth the sultan is percase° a sowter.° Yet if one should can so little good° to show out of season° what acquaintance he hath with him and call him by his own name while he standeth in his majesty, one of his tormentors might happen to break his head, and worthily,° for marring the play.

And so they said that these matters be king's games, as it were stage plays, and for the more part played upon scaffolds, in which poor men be but lookers on. And they who wise be will meddle no farther. For they that sometimes step up and play with them, when they cannot play their parts, they disorder the play and do themselves no good.

---

all the matter ... them the whole affair had been arranged between them ahead of time　**for the manner sake ... know** for the sake of appearances and ceremony they must pretend to be ignorant of what in fact they really know　**every man woteth ... nothing else** everyone knows that since he has already paid for the papal bulls making him a bishop, he very much wants to be one, even though that is the only money he has paid out. This ironic gibe seems to be directed at the practice of simony, whereby men paid money to both church and state for ecclesiastical offices　**percase** perhaps　**sowter** shoemaker　**yet if ... little good** if a man knows so little about how to act　**out of season** at an inappropriate time　**worthily** deservedly

THE MURDER OF THE YOUNG PRINCES

Now fell there mischiefs thick. And as the thing evil gotten
is never well kept, through all the time of his [Richard's] reign
never ceased there cruel death and slaughter, till his own destruction ended it. But as he finished his time with the best
death and the most righteous, that is to wit, his own, so began
he with the most piteous and wicked, I mean the lamentable
murder of his innocent nephews, the young king and his tender
brother. Whose death and final misfortune hath nevertheless
so far come in question that some remain yet in doubt whether
they were in his days destroyed or not. Not for that only° that
Perkin Warbeck,° by many folks' malice and more folks' folly,
so long space abusing the world, was as well with princes as
the poorer people reputed and taken for the younger of those
two, but for that also that all things were in late days so covertly
demeaned, one thing pretended and another meant, that there
was nothing so plain and openly proved but that yet for the
common custom of close and covert dealing, men had it ever
inwardly suspect, as many well-counterfeited jewels make the
true mistrusted. Howbeit, concerning that opinion, with the
occasions moving either party we shall have place more at large
to entreat, if we hereafter happen to write the time of the late
noble prince of famous memory, King Henry VII, or percase
that history of Perkin in any compendious process° by itself.

But in the meantime, for this present matter, I shall rehearse
you the dolorous end of those babes, not after every way that
I have heard, but after that way that I have so heard by such
men and by such means as me thinketh it were hard but it
should be true.°

King Richard, after his coronation, taking his way to
Gloucester to visit in his new honor the town of which he bare
the name of his old, devised as he rode to fulfill that thing which
he before had intended. And forasmuch as his mind gave him
that, his nephews living, men would not reckon that he could
have right to the realm, he thought, therefore, without delay
to rid them, as though the killing of his kinsmen could amend
his cause and make him a kindly° king. Whereupon he sent
one, John Green, whom he especially trusted, unto Sir Robert
Brackenbury, Constable of the Tower, with a letter and cre-

---

not for that only not only because   **Perkin Warbeck** after enlisting wide
support, including several European monarchs, led an uprising and
was eventually executed in 1499 by Henry VII   **compendious process** concise treatment or story   **hard . . . true** it is difficult to believe that it is
not true   **kindly** natural, here in the sense of fitting, proper

dence° also, that the same Sir Robert should in any wise put the two children to death. This John Green did his errand unto Brackenbury, kneeling before Our Lady in the Tower, who plainly answered that he would never put them to death, to die therefore.° With which answer John Green returning recounted the same to King Richard at Warwick yet in his way. Wherewith he took such displeasure and thought, that the same night he said unto a secret page of his, "Ah, whom shall a man trust? Those that I have brought up myself, those that I had went° would most surely serve me—even those fail me and at my commandment will do nothing for me."

"Sir," quod his page, "there lieth one on your pallet without whom, I dare well say, to do your Grace pleasure, the thing were right hard that he would refuse," meaning by this Sir James Tyrell, who was a man of right goodly personage° and for nature's gifts worthy to have served a much better prince, if he had well served God and by grace obtained as much truth and good will as he had strength and wit. The man had a high° heart, and sore longed upward, not rising yet so fast as he had hoped, being hindered and kept under by the means of Sir Richard Ratcliff and Sir William Catesby, who, longing for no more partners of the prince's favor, and namely° not for him, whose pride they wist would bear no peer, kept him by secret drifts out of all secret trust. Which thing this page well had marked and known.

Wherefore, this occasion offered,° of very special friendship he took his time to put him forward and by such wise do him good that all the enemies he had, except the devil, could never have done him so much hurt. For upon this page's words King Richard arose (for this communication had he sitting at the draught,° a convenient carpet° for such a counsel), and came out into the chamber, on which he found in bed Sir James and Sir Thomas Tyrell, of person like and brethren of blood, but nothing of kin in conditions.° Then said the king merrily to them, "What, sirs, be ye in bed so soon," and calling up Sir James, broke to him secretly his mind in this mischievous matter. In which he found him nothing strange.° Wherefore on the morrow he sent him to Brackenbury with a letter, by which he was commanded to deliver Sir James all the keys of the Tower for one night, to the end he might there accomplish the

credence credentials   **to die therefore** even if he should die for refusing to do so   **went** thought   **personage** person, appearance   **high** haughty, proud   **namely** especially   **this occasion offered** a Latinate, ablative absolute construction meaning this occasion having presented itself   **draught** privy   **convenient carpet** suitable meeting place   **conditions** qualities   **found . . . strange** found him not unsympathetic, favorably inclined

king's pleasure, in such thing as he had given him commandment. After which delivered and the keys received, Sir James appointed the night next ensuing to destroy them, devising before and preparing the means.

The prince, as soon as the protector left that name and took himself as king, had it showed unto him that he should not reign, but his uncle should have the crown. At which word, the prince, sore abashed, began to sigh and said: "Alas! I would my uncle would let me have my life yet, though I lose my kingdom." Then he who told him the tale used him with good words, and put him in the best comfort he could. But forthwith was the prince and his brother both shut up, and all other removed from them, only one called Black Will, or William Slaughter excepted, set to serve them and see them sure.° After which time the prince never tied his points° nor aught wrought of himself, but with that young babe his brother lingered in thought and heaviness till this traitorous death delivered them of that wretchedness. For Sir James Tyrell devised that they should be murdered in their beds. To the execution whereof he appointed Miles Forest, one of the four who kept them, a fellow fleshed in murder before time. To him he joined one John Dighton, his own horsekeeper, a big, broad, square, strong knave.

Then all the others being removed from them, this Miles Forest and John Dighton, about midnight (the silly° children lying in their beds), came into the chamber and suddenly lapped° them up among the clothes, so bewrapped them and entangled them, keeping down by force the featherbed and pillows hard unto their mouths that within a while, smothered and stifled, their breath failing, they gave up to God their innocent souls into the joys of heaven, leaving to the tormentors their bodies dead in the bed.

Which after that the wretches perceived, first by the struggling with the pains of death, and after long lying still, to be thoroughly dead, they laid their bodies naked out upon the bed, and fetched Sir James to see them. Who upon the sight of them caused those murderers to bury them at the stair foot, meetly deep in the ground, under a great heap of stones. Then rode Sir James in great haste to King Richard and showed him all the manner of the murder, who gave him great thanks, and, as some say, there made him knight. But he allowed not, as I have heard, the burying in so vile a corner, saying that he

---

see . . . sure serve as their guard or keeper   **points** strings or laces by which stockings were tied to the doublet   **silly** innocent   **lapped** wrapped

would have them buried in a better place because they were a king's sons. Lo the honorable courage of a king! Whereupon they say that a priest of Sir Robert Brackenbury's took up the bodies again and secretly entered° them in such place as by the occasion of his death who only° knew it could never since come to light. Very truth is it and well known that at such time as Sir James Tyrell was in the Tower for treason committed against the most famous prince, King Henry VII, both Dighton and he were examined and confessed the murder in manner above written, but whither the bodies were removed they could nothing tell.

And thus, as I have learned of them that much knew and little cause had to lie, were these two noble princes, these innocent, tender children, born of most royal blood, brought up in great wealth, likely long to live to reign and rule in the realm by traitorous tyranny taken, deprived of their estate, shortly shut up in prison and privily slain and murdered, their bodies cast God wot where by the cruel ambition of their unnatural uncle and his dispiteous° tormentors. Which things on every part well pondered: God never gave this world a more notable example, neither in what unsurety standeth this worldly weal, or what mischief worketh the proud enterprise of a high heart, or finally what wretched end ensueth such dispiteous cruelty.

For first, to begin with the ministers, Miles Forest at Saint Martin's piecemeal rotted away. Dighton indeed yet walketh on alive, in good possibility to be hanged ere he die. But Sir James Tyrell died at Tower Hill, beheaded for treason. King Richard himself, as ye shall hereafter hear, slain in the field, hacked and hewed of his enemies' hands, harried° on horseback dead, his hair in despite torn and tugged like a cur dog. And the mischief that he took, within less than three years of the mischief that he did, and yet all the meantime spent in much pain and trouble outward, much fear, anguish, and sorrow within. For I have heard by credible report of such as were secret with his chamberers that after this abominable deed done, he never had quiet in his mind; he never thought himself sure. Where he went abroad, his eyes whirled about, his body privily fenced,° his hand ever on his dagger, his countenance and manner like one always ready to strike again, he took ill rest at nights, lay long waking and musing, sore wearied with care and watch, rather slumbered than slept, troubled with fearful dreams, suddenly sometimes start up, leap out of his bed and run about the chamber, so was his restless heart continually

entered interred   **only** alone   **dispiteous** merciless   **harried** dragged
about   **privily fenced**   secretly guarded

tossed and tumbled with the tedious impression and stormy remembrance of his abominable deed. Now had he outward no long time in rest. For hereupon soon after began the conspiracy or rather good confederation between the Duke of Buckingham and many other gentlemen against him.

The Dialogue Concerning Heresies

In March, 1528, Cuthbert Tunstall, the Bishop of London and an old friend of More's, granted him permission to own and read the heretical writings of the reformers. Praising More for his famous eloquence in Latin and in English, the prelate laid upon More's shoulders the onerous burden of combatting in the vernacular the English works of the Protestant reformers. The immediate result of More's new career as the champion of theological orthodoxy, The Dialogue Concerning Heresies, *published in 1528, is a work which, in the form of a dialogue between a witty, Lutheran-oriented messenger and a persona named Thomas More, attempts to answer the charges and attacks of the Lutheran reformers on a variety of subjects. The work is liberally sprinkled with More's wit and with what he calls "merry tales," a practice which offended some of his more solemn opponents.*

An interesting sidelight on this phase of More's career, one which provides an insight into the man's integrity, is provided by the clergy's offer to More of a large sum of money—four or five thousand pounds, a considerable amount in those days —as a reward for his literary labors on behalf of the Church. William Roper, More's son-in-law, records More's response:

> Not so, my lords, quoth he, I had liefer see it all cast into the Thames, than I, or any of mine, should have thereof the worth of one penny. For though your offer, my lords, be indeed very friendly and honorable, yet set I so much by my pleasure, and so little by my profit, that I would not, in good faith, for so much, and much more too, have lost the rest of so many nights' sleep as was spent upon the same. And yet wish would I, for all that, upon condition that all heresies were suppressed, that all my books were burned and my labor utterly lost.

THE MIRACLE OF LIFE

"If men should tell you that they saw before an image of the crucifix a dead man raised to life, ye would much marvel thereof, and so might ye well. Yet could I tell you somewhat that I have seen myself that methinketh as great marvel, but I have no lust to tell you because that ye be so circumspect and wary in belief of any miracles that ye would not believe it for me, but mistrust me for it."

"Nay, sir," quod he [the messenger], "in good faith, if a thing seemed me never so far unlikely, yet if ye would earnestly say that yourself have seen it, I neither would nor could mistrust it."

"Very well," quod I, "then ye make me the bolder to tell you. And yet will I tell you nothing, but that I would, if need were, find you good witness to prove it."

"It shall not need, sir," quod he, "but I beseech you let me hear it."

"Forsooth," quod I, "because we speak of a man raised from death to life. There was in the parish of Saint Stephen's in Walbrook in London, where I dwelled before I came to Chelsea, a man and a woman which are yet quick and quething,° and young were they both. The eldest I am sure passeth not twenty-four. It happened [to] them, as doth among young folk, the one to cast the mind to the other. And after many lets,° for the maiden's mother was much against it, at last they came together and were married in Saint Stephen's Church, which is not greatly famous for any miracles, but yet yearly on Saint Stephen's Day it is somewhat sought unto and visited with folks' devotion. But now, short tale to make, this young woman, as manner is in brides ye wote well, was at night brought to bed with honest° women. And then after that went the bridegroom to bed, and everybody went their ways and left them twain there alone. And the same night, yet abide, let me not lie, now in faith, to say the truth, I am not very sure of the time, but surely as it appeared afterward, it was of likelihood the same night, or some other time soon after, except it happened a little afore."

"No force° for the time," quod he.

"Truth," quod I, "and as for the matter, all the parish will testify for truth the woman was known for so honest. But for

---

quick and quething alive and talking   **lets** obstacles   **honest** virtuous, chaste   **no force** it doesn't matter

the conclusion, the seed of them twain turned in the woman's body first into blood, and after into shape of man child, and then waxed quick and she great therewith. And was within the year delivered of a fair boy, and forsooth it was not then—for I saw it myself—passing the length of a foot. And I am sure he is grown now an inch longer than I."

"How long is it ago," quod he?

"By my faith," quod I, "about twenty-one years."

"Tuch," quod he, "this is a worthy miracle!"

"In good faith," quod I, "never wist° I that any man could tell that he had any other beginning. And me thinketh that this is as great a miracle as the raising of a dead man."

"If it seem so," quod he, "to you, then have you a marvelous seeming, for I ween° it seemeth so to no man else."

"No," quod I, "can ye tell what is the cause? None other sure but that the acquaintance and daily beholding taketh away the wondering, as we nothing wonder at the ebbing and flowing of the sea, or the Thames because we daily see it. But he that had never seen it nor heard thereof would, at the first sight, wonder sore thereat, to see that great water come wallowing up against the wind, keeping a common course to and fro, no cause perceived that driveth him. If a man born blind had suddenly his sight, what wonder would he make to see the sun, the moon, and the stars; whereas one that hath seen them sixteen years together marveleth not so much of them all as he would wonder at the first sight of a peacock's tail. And very cause can I see none why we should of reason more marvel of the reviving of a dead man than of the breeding, bringing forth, and growing of a child unto the state of a man. No more marvelous is a cuckoo than a cock, though the one be seen but in summer and the other all the year. And, I am sure, if ye saw dead men as commonly called back to life again by miracle as ye see men brought forth by nature, ye would reckon it less marvel to bring the soul again into the body, keeping yet still his shape, and his organs not much perished, than of a little seed to make all that gear° new, and make a new soul thereto."

THE VERACITY OF WITNESSES: MEN VS. WOMEN

"Now where ye require° how many witnesses should be requisite and suffice to make you think yourself in reason to have good cause to believe so strange a thing, methinketh

---

wist knew   **ween** think   **gear** equipment, matter   **require** ask

that right few were sufficient of them that would say they saw a great good thing done by the power and goodness of God, except it be hard for us to believe either that God is so mighty that he may do it, or so good that he would do it.

"But because ye would wit° of me how many records were requisite, that thing standeth not so much in number as in weight. Some twain be more credible than some ten. And albeit that I see not greatly why I should mistrust anyone that seemeth honest and telleth a good tale of God in which there appeareth no special cause of lying, yet, if any witness will serve you, then would I wit of you how many yourself would agree. For I now put case° that there came ten divers honest men of good substance out of ten divers parts of the realm, each of them with an offering at one pilgrimage, as for example at Our Lady of Ipswich, each one of them affirming upon their oath a miracle done upon themselves, in some great sudden help, well appearing to pass the power of craft or nature, would ye not believe that among them all at the leastwise twain of those ten said true?"

"No, by Our Lady," quod he, "not and° there were ten and twenty."

"Why so?" quod I.

"Mary," quod he, "for were they never so many, having none other witness but each man telling his tale for himself, they be but single all, and less than single. For every miracle hath but one record, and yet he not credible in his own cause. And so never a miracle well proved."

"Well," said I, "I like well your wisdom that ye be so circumspect that ye will nothing believe without good, sufficient and full proof.

"I put you then," quod I, "another case, that ten young women, not very specially known for good, but taken out at adventure, dwelling all in one town, would report and tell that a friar of good fame,° hearing their confessions at a pardon, would have given them all in a penance to let him lie with them. On your faith, would ye not believe that among so many some of them said true?"

"Yes, that I would," quod he, "by the Mary mass believe they said true all ten, and durst well swear for them and° they were but two."

"Why so," quod I, "they be as single witness as the other of whom I told you before. For none of them can tell what was said to another, and yet they be unsworn also, and therewith be they but women, which be more light and less to be regarded, dwelling all in one town also, and thereby might the more easily conspire a false tale."

"They be," quod he, "witness good enough for such a matter; the thing is so likely of itself that a friar will be womanish,° look the holy whoreson never so saintly."

"Ye deny not," quod I, "but God may as easily do a good turn by miracle as any man may do an evil by nature."

"That is true," quod he, "and he list.°"

"Well," quod I, "see now what a good way ye be in, that are of your own good godly mind more ready to believe two simple women that a man will do nought° than ten or twenty men that God will do good."

REASON, AS WELL AS FAITH, IS NEEDED FOR THE INTERPRETATION OF SCRIPTURE

Now in the study of Scripture, in devising upon the sentence,° in considering what ye read, in pondering the purpose of divers comments, in comparing together divers texts that seem contrary and be not, albeit I deny not but that grace and God's especial help is the great thing therein, yet useth he for an instrument man's reason thereto. God helpeth us to eat also but yet not without our mouth. Now as the hand is the more nimble by the use of some feats; and the legs and feet more swift and sure by custom of going and running; and the whole body the more wieldy and lusty by some kind of exercise; so is it no doubt but that reason is by study, labor, and exercise of logic, philosophy, and other liberal arts corroborate and quickened,° and that judgment both in them and also in orators, laws and stories, much ripened. And albeit poets be with many men taken but for painted words, yet do they much help the judgment and make a man among other things well furnished of one special thing, without which all learning is half lame.

"What is that?" quod he.

"Mary," quod I, "a good mother wit. And, therefore, are in mine opinion these Lutherans in a mad mind that would now have all learning, save Scripture only, clean cast away. Which things, if the time will serve, be, as me thinketh, to be taken and had, and with reason brought, as I said before, into the service of divinity. And as holy Saint Jerome saith, the Hebrews well despoil the Egyptians when Christ's learned men take out of the pagan writers the riches and learning and wisdom that

womanish the context suggests that the word here means having a desire or passion for women   **and he list** if it pleases him   **nought** wrong, evil **devising . . . sentence** construing the meaning   **corroborate and quickened** strengthened and vivified

God gave unto them, and employ the same in the service of divinity about the profit of God's chosen children of Israel, the Church of Christ, which he hath of the hard, stony pagans made the children of Abraham."

ON TRANSLATING SCRIPTURE INTO THE VERNACULAR

It is dangerous to translate the text of Scripture out of one tongue into another, as holy Saint Jerome testifieth, for as much as in translation it is hard always to keep the same sentence whole—it was, I say, for these causes at a council held at Oxford provided upon great pain that *no man should from thenceforth translate into the English tongue,* or any other language *of his own authority,* by way of book, lybel,° or treatise; nor no man openly or secretly *any such book,* lybel, or treatise read, newly made in the time of the said John Wycliffe, or since (or that should be made any time after) *till the same translation were by the diocesan, or,* if need should require, *by a provincial council, approved. . . .*

. . . Good folk [are] in fear to suffer the Scripture in our English tongue. Not for the reading and receiving, but for the busy chamming° thereof, and for much meddling with such parts thereof as least will agree with their capacities. For undoubtedly, as ye spoke of our mother Eve, inordinate appetite of knowledge is a means to drive any man out of Paradise. And inordinate is the appetite when men unlearned, though they read it in their language, will be busy to ensearch and dispute the great secret mysteries of Scripture, which, though they hear, they be not able to perceive. This thing is plainly forbidden us that be not appointed nor instructed thereto. And therefore holy Saint Gregory Nazianzenus, that great, solemn doctor, sore toucheth and reproveth all such bold, busy meddlers in the Scripture, and showeth that it is in Exodus, by Moses ascending up upon the hill where he spoke with God, and the people tarrying beneath, signified that the people be forbidden to presume to meddle with the high mysteries of Holy Scripture, but ought to be content to tarry beneath, and meddle none higher than is meet for them. But receiving from the height of the hill by Moses that that is delivered them— that is, to wit, the laws and precepts that they must keep, and the points they must believe, look well thereupon, and often, and meddle well therewith—not to dispute it, but to fulfill it.

And as for the high secret mysteries of God and hard texts of his Holy Scripture, let us know that we be so unable to

lybel little book, tract or pamphlet   **chamming** chewing

ascend up so high on that hill that it shall become us to say to the preachers appointed thereto, as the people said unto Moses, "Hear you God, and let us hear you." And surely the blessed holy doctor Saint Jerome greatly complaineth and rebuketh that lewd,° homely° manner that the common lay people, men and women, were in his days so bold in the meddling, disputing, and expounding of Holy Scripture. And [he] showeth plainly that they shall have evil proof° therein that will reckon themselves to understand it by themselves without a reader. For it is a thing that requireth good help, and long time, and a whole mind given greatly thereto. And surely—since, as the holy Apostle Saint Paul, in divers of his epistles, saith, God hath by his Holy Spirit so instituted and ordained his Church that he will have some readers, and some hearers, some teachers, and some learners—we do plainly pervert and turn upside down the right order of Christ's Church when the one part meddleth with the other's office.

Plato the great philosopher specially forbiddeth such as be not admitted thereunto, nor men meet therefore to meddle much and busy themselves in reasoning and disputing upon the temporal laws of the city, which would not be reasoned upon but by folk meet therefor, and in place convenient.° For else they that cannot very well attain to perceive them begin to mislike, dispraise, and contemn them. Whereof so followeth the breach of the laws and disorder of the people. For, till a law be changed by authority, it rather ought to be observed than contemned; or else the example of one law boldly broken and set at naught waxeth a precedent for the remnant to be used like. And commonly, the best laws shall worst like° much of the common people, which most long—if they might be heard and followed—to live all at liberty under none at all. Now if Plato, so wise a man, so thought good in temporal laws —things of men's making—how much is it less meet for every man boldly to meddle with the exposition of Holy Scripture, so devised and endited° by the high wisdom of God that it far exceedeth in many places the capacity and perceiving of man.

It was also provided by the emperor, in the law civil, that the common people should never be so bold to keep dispicions° upon the faith or Holy Scripture, nor that any such thing should be used among them or before them. And therefore, as I said before, the special fear in this matter is lest we would be so busy in chamming of the Scripture ourselves (which ye say

lewd ignorant   homely crude   have evil proof fall into error   convenient appropriate   like please   devised and endited planned and composed   keep dispicions hold discussions

we were able enough to do) which undoubtedly the wisest and the best learned and he that therein hath by many years bestowed his whole mind is yet unable to do. And then far more unable must he needs be that boldly will, upon the first reading because he knoweth the words, take upon him, therefore, to teach other men the sentence,° with peril of his own soul, and other men's too, by the bringing men into mad ways, sects, and heresies, such as heretics have of old brought up and the Church hath condemned. And thus in these matters, if the common people might be bold to cham it, as ye say, and to dispute it, then should ye have the more blind the more bold, the more ignorant the more busy, the less wit the more inquisitive, the more fool the more talkative of great doubts and high questions of Holy Scripture and of God's great and secret mysteries, and this, not soberly of any good affection, but presumptuously and irreverently at meat and at meal. And there, when the wine were in and the wit out, would they take upon them with foolish words and blasphemy to handle Holy Scripture in more homely° manner than a song of Robin Hood. And some would, as I said, solemnly take upon them, like as they were ordinary readers, to interpret the text at their pleasure, and therewith fall themselves and draw down others with them into seditious sects and heresies whereby the Scripture of God should lose his honor and reverence and be, by such irreverent and unsitting° demeanor, among much people quite and clean abused unto the contrary of that holy purpose that God ordained it for. Whereas if we would no further meddle therewith, but well and devoutly read it, and, in that that is plain and evident as God's commandments and his holy counsels, endeavor ourselves to follow with help of his grace asked thereunto; and in his great and marvelous miracles consider his godhead; and in his lowly birth, his godly life, and his bitter passion, exercise ourselves in such meditations, prayer, and virtues as the matter shall minister us occasion, acknowledging our own ignorance where we find a doubt, and therein leaning to the faith of the Church, wrestle with no such text as might bring us in a doubt and werestye° of any of those articles wherein every good Christian man is clear. By this manner of reading can no man nor woman take hurt in Holy Scripture.

Now then, the things on the other side that unlearned people can never by themselves attain, as in the Psalms and the prophets and divers parts of the gospel, where the words be sometimes spoken as in the person of the prophet himself, sometimes as in the person of God, sometimes of some other, as angels,

sentence meaning **homely** rough, careless **unsitting** unsuitable **werestye** perplexity

devils, or men, and sometimes of our Savior Christ (not always of one fashion, but sometimes as God, sometimes as man, sometimes as head of this mystical body, his Church militant here in earth, sometimes as head of his Church triumphant in heaven, sometimes as in the person of his sensual parts of his own body, otherwhile in the person of some particular part of his body mystical), and these things with many others, often times interchanged and suddenly sundry things of divers matters diversely mingled together—all these things, which is not possible for unlearned men to attain unto, it were more than madness for them to meddle withal, but leave all these things to them whose whole study is beset thereupon, and to the preachers appointed thereunto, who may show them such things in time and place convenient with° reverence and authority, the sermon so tempered as may be meet and convenient° always for the present audience. Whereunto it appeareth that our Savior himself and his apostles after him had ever special respect.

And therefore, as I say forsooth,° I can in no wise agree with you that it were meet for men unlearned to be busy with the chamming of Holy Scripture, but to have it chammed unto them. For that is the preacher's part, and theirs that after long study are admitted to read and expound it. And to this intent weigh all the words,° as far as I perceive, of all holy doctors that anything have written in this matter.

But never meant they, as I suppose, the forbidding of the Bible to be read in any vulgar tongue. Nor I never yet heard any reason laid why it were not convenient to have the Bible translated into the English tongue. But all those reasons, seemed they never so gay and glorious at the first sight, yet when they were well examined they might in effect, for aught that I can see, as well be laid against the holy writers that wrote the Scripture in the Hebrew tongue, and against the blessed evangelists that wrote the Scripture in Greek, and against all those in likewise that translated it out of every of those tongues into Latin, as to their charge that would well and faithfully translate it out of Latin into our English tongue. For as for that our tongue is called barbarous is but a fantasy, for so is, as every learned man knoweth, every strange language to other. And if they would call it barren of words, there is no doubt but it is plenteous enough to express our minds in anything whereof one man hath used to speak with another. Now as touching the difficulty which a translator findeth in expressing well and lively the sentence of his author (which is hard always to do so surely, but that he shall sometimes minish° either of the sentence° or of the grace that it beareth in the former tongue), that point hath lain in their light who have translated the Scripture already either out of Greek into Latin, or out of Hebrew into any of them both, as by many translations which we read already, to them that be learned appeareth.

Now as touching the harm that may grow by such blind bayardes° as will, when they read the Bible in English, be more busy than will become them, they that touch that point harp upon the right string and touch truly the great harm that were likely to grow to some folk. Howbeit, not by the occasion yet of the English translation, but by the occasion of their own lewdness° and folly, which yet were not in my mind a sufficient cause to exclude the translation and to put other folk from the benefit thereof, but rather to make provision against such abuse and let a good thing go forth. Nor this letted not,° as I said, the Scripture to be first written in a vulgar tongue. For Scripture, as I said before, was not written but in a vulgar tongue such as the whole people understood, nor in no secret ciphers, but such common letters as almost every man could read. For neither was the Hebrew, nor the Greek tongue, nor the Latin, neither any other speech than such as all the people spoke. And, therefore, if we should lay that it were evil done to translate the Scripture into our tongue because it is vulgar and common to every Englishman, then had it been as evil done to translate it into Greek or into Latin, or to write the New Testament first in Greek, or the Old Testament in Hebrew, because both those tongues were as very° vulgar as ours. And yet should there by this reason also, not only the Scripture be kept out of our tongue, but over that should the reading thereof be forbidden, both all such lay people and all such priests too as can° no more than their grammar, and very scantly that. All which company, though they can understand the words, be yet as far from the perceiving of the sentence in hard and doubtful texts as were our women if the Scripture were translated to our own language.

Howbeit, of truth, seldom hath it been seen that any sect of heretics hath begun of such unlearned folk as nothing could° else but the language wherein they read the Scripture; but there hath always commonly these sects sprung of the pride of such folk as had, with the knowledge of that tongue, some high persuasion in themselves of their own learning besides. To

---

but that . . . minish without diminishing   **sentence** meaning   **bayardes** horses, used here, obviously, as a term of contempt   **lewdness** ignorance **this letted not** this did not prevent   **very** truly   **can** know   **could** knew

whose authority some other folk have soon after, part of malice, part of simpleness, and much part of pleasure and delight in newfangleness, fallen in and increased the faction. But the head hath ever commonly been either some proud, learned man, or at the least, beside the language, some proud smatterer in learning. So that if we should, for fear of heretics that might happen to grow thereby, keep the Scripture out of any tongue, or out of unlearned men's hands, we should, for like fear, be fain° to keep it out of all tongues, and out of unlearned men's hands too, and wot° not whom we might trust therewith.

Wherefore there is, as methinketh, no remedy but if any good thing shall go forward somewhat must needs be adventured.° And some folk will not fail to be naught.° Against which things, provision must be made that as much good may grow and as little harm come as can be devised, and not to keep the whole commodity from any whole people because of harm that, by their own folly and fault, may come to some part. As though a lewd surgeon would cut off the leg by the knee to keep the toe from the gout, or cut off a man's head by the shoulders to keep him from the toothache. There is no treatise of Scripture so hard but that a good, virtuous man, or woman either, shall somewhat find therein that shall delight and increase their devotion. Besides this that every preaching shall be the more pleasant and fruitful unto them when they have in their mind the place of Scripture that they shall there hear expounded. For though it be, as it is indeed, great wisdom for a preacher to use discretion in his preaching, and to have a respect unto the qualities and capacities of his audience, yet letteth that nothing but° that the whole audience may without harm have read and have ready the Scripture in mind that he shall in his preaching declare and expound. For no doubt is there but that God and his Holy Spirit hath so prudently tempered their speech through the whole corpus of Scripture that every man may take good thereby, and no man harm but he that will in the study thereof lean proudly to the folly of his own wit. For albeit that Christ did speak to the people in parables, and expounded them secretly to his special disciples, and sometimes forbare to tell some things to them also because they were not as yet able to bear them; and the apostles in likewise did sometimes spare to speak to some people the things that they did not let° plainly to speak to some others, yet letteth all this nothing° the translation of the Scripture into our own

fain desirous   wot know   somewhat . . . adventured something must be risked   naught injured, led into error   letteth . . . but that in no way prevents   let hesitate   yet letteth . . . nothing yet this in no way prevents

tongue no more than in the Latin. Nor it is no cause to keep the corpus of Scripture out of the hands of any Christian people, so many years fastly° confirmed in faith, because Christ and his apostles used such provision° in their utterance of so strange and unheard mysteries, either unto Jews, pagans, or newly christened folk, except we would say that all the expositions which Christ made himself upon his own parables unto his secret servants and disciples withdrawn from the people, should now, at this day, be kept in likewise from the commons, and no man suffered to read or hear them but those that in his Church represent the state and office of his apostles, which there will (I wote° well) no wise man say, considering that those things, which were then commonly most kept from the people, be now most necessary for the people to know, as it well appeareth by all such things in effect as our Savior at the time taught his apostles apart. Whereof I would not for my mind withhold the profit that one good, devout, unlearned layman might take by the reading, not for the harm that a hundred heretics would fall in by their own willful abuses, no more than our Savior letted for the weal° of such as would be with his grace of his little chosen flock to come into this world and be *lapis offensionis et petra scandali,* "the stone of stumbling and the stone of falling and ruin" to all the willful wretches in the world besides.

Finally, methinketh° that the constitution provincial of which we spoke right now hath determined this question already. For when the clergy therein agreed that the English Bibles should remain which were translated before Wycliffe's days, they consequently did agree that to have the Bible in English was none hurt. And in that they forbade any new translation to be read till it were approved by the bishops, it appeareth well thereby that their intent was that the bishop should approve it if he found it faultless, and also of reason amend it where it was faulty, but if° the man were an heretic that made it, or the faults such and so many as it were more easy to make it all new than mend it—as it happened for both points in the translation of Tyndale.

Now if it so be that it would haply° be thought not a thing meetly to be adventured to set all on a flush at once, and dash rashly out Holy Scripture in every lewd fellow's teeth, yet, thinketh me, there might such a moderation be taken therein as

---

fastly securely   **provision** foresight   **wote** know   **our Savior letted . . . weal** the meaning of this whole clause is that Christ did not hesitate, for the sake of bringing salvation to some, to come into the world and be a stumbling block to many   **methinketh** it seems to me   **but if** unless   **haply** perhaps

neither good, virtuous lay folk should lack it nor rude and rash brains abuse it. For it might be with diligence well and truly translated by some good, Catholic, and well-learned man, or by divers, dividing the labor among them, and after conferring° their several parts together each with other. And after that might the work be allowed and approved by the ordinaries,° and by their authorities so put into print, as all the copies should come whole unto the bishop's hand. Which he may, after° his discretion and wisdom, deliver to such as he perceiveth honest, sad,° and virtuous, with a good monition and fatherly counsel to use it reverently with humble heart and lowly mind, rather seeking therein occasion of devotion than of dispicion.° And providing, as much as may be, that the book be, after the decease of the party, brought again and reverently restored unto the ordinary. So that, as near as may be devised, no man have it but of the ordinary's hand, and by him thought and reputed for such as shall be likely to use it to God's ronor and merit of his own soul. Among whom, if any be proved after to have abused it, then the use thereof to be forbidden him, either forever, or till he be waxen wiser.

THE BURNING OF HERETICS

[The author showeth his opinion concerning the burning of heretics and that it is lawful, necessary, and well done, and showeth also that the clergy doth not procure it, but only the good and politic provision° of the temporalty.°]

The fear of these outrages and mischiefs to follow upon such sects and heresies, with the proof that men have had in some countries thereof, have been the cause that princes and people have been constrained to punish heresies by terrible death, whereas else more easy ways had been taken with them. And, therefore, here will I somewhat (said I to your friend) answer the points which ye moved at your first meeting, when ye said that many men thought it a hard and an uncharitable way taken by the clergy to put men convicted of heresy sometimes to shame, sometimes to death, and that Christ so far abhorred all such violence that he would not any of his flock should fight in any wise, neither in the defense of themselves or any other, not so much as in the defense of Christ himself, for which he blamed Saint Peter, but that we should all live after him in sufferance and patience, so far forth that folk thought, as

conferring collating, comparing   ordinaries bishops in charge of dioceses
after according to   sad serious   dispicion disputation   politic provision
prudent foresight   temporalty the secular order, the laity

ye said, that we should not fight in defense of ourselves against the Turks and infidels. These objections be soon answered.

For neither doth the clergy therein any such thing as is laid and imputed unto them, nor the temporalty neither, albeit with good reason they might yet, had they never indeed fallen so sore to force and violence against heretics, if the violent cruelty first used by the heretics themselves against good Catholic folk driven good princes thereto, for preservation, not of the faith only, but also of the peace among their people. For albeit that forthwith upon the death of Christ in the beginning of the Church, many sects and heresies began (as well appeareth by the Apocalypse of Saint John the Evangelist and the epistles of the Apostle Paul), and after, almost continually, divers heresies sprang in divers places (as we plainly see by the story of the Church, by the books of Saint Jerome, Saint Augustine, Saint Eusebius, Saint Basil, Saint Ambrose, Saint Gregory Nazianzenus, Saint Chrysostom, and many other doctors of the Church), yet in all this time by a long space of many years was there never other punishment done upon them in effect, but only redargucion° and reproving by dispicions, either in words or writing, or condemnations of their opinions in synods and councils, or finally, excommunications and putting out of Christ's flock, saving that they were put sometime to silence upon pain of forfeiture of certain money.

But as I said before, if the heretics had never begun with violence, though they had used all the ways they could to allect° the people by preaching, though they had therewith done as Luther doth now, and as Mahomet did before, bring up opinions pleasant to the people, giving them liberty to lewdness°; yet if they had set violence aside, good Christian people had peradventure yet unto this day used less violence toward them than they do now.

And yet were heresy well worthy to be as sore [punished] as any other fault, since there is no fault that more offendeth God. Howbeit while they forbare violence, there was little violence done to them. And surely though God be able against all persecution to preserve and increase his faith among the people, as he did in the beginning, for all the persecution of the pagans and the Jews, yet is it no reason to look that Christian princes should suffer the Catholic Christian people to be oppressed by Turks or by heretics worse than Turks.

"By my soul," quod your friend," I would all the world were all agreed to take all violence and compulsion away upon all sides, Christian and heathen, and that no man were con-

---

redargucion refutation **allect** attract **lewdness** ignorance, and also loose living

strained to believe but as he could be by grace, wisdom, and good works induced, and then he that would go to God go in God's name, and he that will go to the devil, the devil go with him."

"Forsooth," quod I, "and if it so were, yet would I little doubt but that the good seed, being sown among the people, should as well come up and be as strong to save itself as the cockle, and God should always be stronger than the devil. But yet be heretics and heathen men in two divers cases. For in case the Turks, Saracens, and pagans would suffer the faith of Christ to be peaceably preached among them, and that we Christian men should therefore suffer in like wise all their sects to be preached among us, and violence taken away by assent on both the sides, I nothing mistrust that the faith of Christ should much more increase than decay. And albeit that we should find among us [those] that would for the lewd liberty of these sects draw to the devil, yet so should we find, I doubt not, among them also many a thousand that should be content to leave that beastly pleasure and come to the faith of Christ, as came in the beginning to Christendom out of the pagans, that lived as voluptuously as the Turks do now. But since violence is used on that part, and Christ's faith not there suffered to be preached and taken, he that would now suffer that sect to be preached or taught among Christian men and not punish and destroy the doers were a plain enemy to Christ, as he that were content to suffer Christ [to] lose his worship in many souls on this side, without anyone won in their stead upon the other side. But now if violence were withdrawn on that side, then this way that ye speak of were peradventure between Christendom and Turkey, or pagans, if the world were assented thereunto and could hold it none evil way. For since we should nothing so much regard as the honor of God and increasing of the Christian faith, and winning of men's souls to heaven, we should seem to dishonor God if we mistrusted that his faith preached among other indifferently without disturbance should not be able to prosper. And, believing that it were, we should hinder the profit if we would refuse the condition where there be many more to be won to Christ on that side than to be lost from him on this side. But yet, as for heretics rising among ourselves and springing of ourselves, be in no wise to be suffered, but to be oppressed and overwhelmed in the beginning. For by any covenant with them Christendom can nothing win. For as many as we suffer to fall to them we lose from Christ. And by all them we cannot win to Christ one the more, though we won them all home again, for they were our own before. And yet, as I said, for all that in the beginning, never were they by any temporal punishment of their bodies anything sharply handled till that they began to be violent themselves.

"We read that in the time of Saint Austin, the great doctor of the Church, the heretics of Africa, called the Donatists, fell to force and violence, robbing, beating, tormenting, and killing such as they took of the true Christian flock, as the Lutherans have done in Almayn.° For avoiding whereof, that holy man Saint Austin, who long had with great patience borne and suffered their malice, only writing and preaching in the reproof of their errors, and had not only done them no temporal harm, but also had letted° and resisted others that would have done it, did yet at the last, for the peace of good people, both suffer and exhort the Count Boniface and others to repress them with force, and fear° them with bodily punishment.

"Which manner of doing, holy Saint Jerome and other virtuous Fathers, have in other places allowed. And since that time hath thereupon necessity perceived, by great outrages committed against the peace and quiet of the people in sundry places of Christendom, by heretics rising of a small beginning to a high and unruly multitude, many sore punishments been devised for them, and especially by fire, not only in Italy and Almayn, but also in Spain, and in effect in every part of Christendom. Among which in England, as a good Catholic realm, it hath been long punished by death in the fire. And specially for as much as in the time of that noble prince of most famous memory, King Henry V, while the Lord Cobham maintained certain heresies, and that, by the means thereof, the number so grew and increased that, within a while, though himself was fled into Wales, yet they assembled themselves together in a field near unto London in such wise and such number that the king with his nobles were fain° to put harness on their backs for the repression of them, whereupon they were distressed and many put to execution, and after that the Lord Cobham taken in Wales and burned in London. The king, his nobles, and his people thereupon considering the great peril and jeopardy that the realm was like to have fallen in by those heresies, made at a parliament very good and substantial provisions besides all such as were made before, as well for the withstanding as the repressing and grievous punishment of any such as should be found faulty thereof, and by the clergy left unto the secular hands. For here ye shall understand that it is not the clergy that laboreth to have them punished by death. Well may it be that as we be all men and not angels, some of them may have sometimes either over-fervent mind or indiscreet zeal, or, percase, an angry and a cruel heart, by which they may offend God in the selfsame deed whereof they should else greatly merit.

"But surely the order of the spiritual law therein is both good, reasonable, piteous, and charitable, and nothing desiring the death of any man therein. For at the first fault, he is abjured, forsweareth all heresies, doth such penance for his fault as the bishop assigneth him, and is, in such wise, graciously received again into the favor and suffrages of Christ's Church. But and if he be taken eftsoons° with the same crime again, then is he put out of the Christian flock by excommunication. And because that, being such, his conversation were perilous among Christian men, the Church refuseth him, and thereof the clergy giveth knowledge to the temporalty, not exhorting the prince, or any man else either, to kill him or punish him, but only in the presence of the temporal officer, the spiritualty, not delivereth him, but leaveth him to the secular hand, and forsaketh him as one excommunicate and removed out of the Christian flock. And though the church be not light and sudden in receiving him again, yet, at the time of his death, upon his request, with tokens of repentance, he is absolved and received again."

HERETICS AND THE SECULAR ARM

"Marry," quod your friend,° "but as methinketh, the bishop doth as much as though he killeth him when he leaveth him to the secular hand, in such time and place as he wotteth° well he shall soon be burned."

"I will not here enter into the question," quod I, "whether a priest might for any cause, and if for any, whether then for heresy, without blame of irregularity put or command any man to death, either by express words or under the general name of right and justice. In which matter I could not lack both reason, authority, and example of holy men. But in this matter that we have in hand, it is sufficient that the bishop neither doth it or commandeth it. For I think there will no reason bear it that when the heretic, if he went abroad, would with the spreading of his error infect other folk, the bishop should have such pity upon him that he should, rather than other men should punish his body, suffer him to kill other men's souls. Indeed," quod I,

---

eftsoons a second time **your friend** the other speaker in the dialogue, the messenger, who, according to the fictional design of the work, is supposed to be the spokesman for a friend of More's **wotteth** knows

"there be some as you say that either of high, pretended pity, or of a feigned observance of the counsels of Christ, would not no man should punish° any heretic or infidel either, not though they invaded us and did us all the harm they possibly could. And in this opinion is Luther and his followers, who, among their other heresies, hold for a plain conclusion that it is not lawful to any Christian to fight against the Turk, or to make against him any resistance, though he come into Christendom with a great army and labor to destroy all. For they say that all Christian men are bound to the counsels of Christ, by which they say that we be forbidden to defend ourselves, and that Saint Peter was, as ye rehearsed, reproved of our Savior when he struck off Malchus' ear, albeit that he did it in the defense of his own master and the most innocent man that ever was. And unto this they lay,° as ye said in the beginning, that since that time that Christian men first fell to fighting, it° hath never increased, but always diminished and decayed. So that at this day the Turk hath estraited us very near° and brought it in within a right narrow compass, and narrower shall do, say they, as long as we go about to defend Christendom by the sword. Which they say should be, as it was in the beginning increased, so be continued and preserved only by patience and martyrdom. Thus holily spoke these godly fathers of Luther's sect, laboring to procure that no man should withstand the Turk, but let him win all. And when it should come to that, then would they, as it seemed, win all again by their patience, high virtues and martyrdom, by which now they cannot suffer to resist their beastly voluptuousness, but break their vows and take them harlots under the name of wives. And where they may not fight against the Turk, arise up in great plumps to fight against their even° Christians. It is, I trow,° no great mastery to perceive whom they labor to please that have that opinion.

"And if the Turk happen to come in, it is little doubt whose part they will take, and that Christian people be like to find none so cruel Turks as them. It is a gentle holiness to abstain for devotion from resisting the Turk, and in the meanwhile to rise up in routs and fight against Christian men and destroy, as that sect hath done, many a good religious house; spoiled, maimed, and slain many a good, virtuous man; robbed, polluted, and pulled down many a goodly church of Christ.

"And now where they lay for a proof that God were not contented with battle made against infidels, the loss and minish-ment of Christendom since that guise began, they fare as did once an old sage father fool in Kent at such time as divers men of worship assembled old folk of the country to commune and devise about the amendment of Sandwich haven.

"At which time as they began first to ensearch by reason, and by report of old men thereabout, what thing had been the occasion that so good a haven was in so few years so sore decayed and such sands risen, and such shallow flats made therewith, that right small vessels had now much work to come in at divers tides, where great ships were within few years past accustomed to ride without difficulty; and some laying the fault to Goodwin Sands, some to the lands inned° by divers owners in the isle of Thanet, out of the channel, in which the sea was wont to compass the isle and bring the vessels round about it, whose course at the ebb was wont to scour the haven, which now the sea excluded thence, for lack of such course and scouring, is choked up with sand, as they thus alleged, divers men, divers causes. There started up one good old father and said, 'Ye masters say what ye will, I have marked this matter as well as some other. And, by God, I wot how it waxed nought well enough. For I knew it good, and have marked so I have when it began to wax worse.' 'And what hath hurt it, good father?' quod the gentlemen. 'By my faith, masters,' quod he, 'yonder same Tenterden steeple, and nothing else, that, by the mass, I would 'twere a fair fish pole.' 'Why hath the steeple hurt the haven, good father?' quod they. 'Nay, by Our Lady, masters,' quod he, 'I cannot tell you well why, but I wot well it hath. For, by God, I knew it a good haven till that steeple was builded, and by the Mary mass, I have marked it well, it never throve since.'°

"And thus wisely spake these holy Lutherans, which sowing schisms and seditions among Christian people, lay the loss thereof to the withstanding of the Turks' invasion and the resisting of his malice, where they should rather, if they had any reason in their heads, lay it to the contrary. For when Christian princes did their devoir° against miscreants and infidels, there be stories and monuments enough that witness the manifest aid and help of God in great victories given to good Christian princes by His almighty hand.

"But on the other side, since that the ambition of Christian rulers, desiring each other's dominion, have set them at war

---

inned enclosed   **since** in the original, the old man's speech is heavily sprinkled with dialect forms. It may be interesting to point out that in 1550, in a sermon delivered before King Edward, the renowned Protestant preacher Hugh Latimer refers to More's witty anecdote, and, in fact, recounts the story himself   **devoir** duty

and deadly dissension among themselves, whereby while each hath aspired to the enhancing of his own, they have little forced what came of the common corps of Christendom, God, for the revenging of their inordinate appetites, hath withdrawn His help and showed that He careth as little, suffering, while each of them laboreth to eat up other, the Turk to prosper and so far forth to proceed that if their blind affections look not thereto the sooner, he shall not fail (which Our Lord forbid) within short process to swallow them all. And albeit Christ forbade Saint Peter, being a priest and, under himself, prince of his priests, to fight with the temporal sword toward the impeachment and resistance of his fruitful passion, whereupon depended the salvation of mankind, which affection our Savior had before that time so sore reproved and rebuked in him that he called him therefore Satan, yet is it nothing to the purpose to allege that by that example temporal princes should, without the let° of such spiritual profit and the sufferance of much spiritual harm, suffer their people to be invaded and oppressed by infidels, to their utter undoing, not only temporal, but also of a great part perpetual, which were like of their frailty, for fear of worldly grief and incommodity, to fall from the faith and deny their baptism. In which peril, since Our Lord would not that any man should willfully put himself, and for that cause advised his disciples that if they were pursued in one city, they should not come forth and foolhardily put themselves in peril of denying Christ by impatience of some intolerable torments, but rather flee thence into some other place where they might serve him in quiet, till he should suffer them to fall in such point that there were no way to escape, and then would he have them abide by their tackling like mighty champions, wherein they shall not in such case fail of his help.

"Now albeit so that Christ and his holy apostles exhort every man to patience and sufferance without requiting of an evil deed or making any defense, but using further sufferance and doing also good for evil, yet neither doth this counsel bind a man that he shall of necessity against the common nature suffer another man causeless to kill him, nor letteth not any man from the defense of another whom he seeth innocent and invaded and oppressed by malice. In which case both nature, reason, and God's behest bindeth, first the prince to the safeguard of his people with the peril of himself, as he taught Moses to know himself bounden to kill the Egyptians in the defense of [the] Hebrew; and after, he bindeth every man to the help and defense of his good and harmless neighbor against

let loss, lack

the malice and cruelty of the wrongdoer. For as the Holy Scripture saith, *unicuique dedit deus curam de proximo suo,* 'God hath given every man charge of his neighbor to keep him from harm of body and soul, as much as may lie in his power.' And by this reason is not only excusable but also commendable that common war which every people taketh in the defense of their country against enemies that would invade it, since that every man fighteth not for the defense of himself, of a private affection to himself, but of a Christian charity for the safeguard and preservation of all other. Which reason as it hath place in all battle of defense, so hath it most especially in the battle by which we defend the Christian countries against the Turks, in that we defend each other from far the more peril and loss both of worldly substance, bodily hurt, and perdition of men's souls.

"And now if this be lawful and enjoined also to every private person, how much more belongeth it to princes and rulers, which if they may not upon the peril of their souls, wittingly suffer among the people whom they have in governance anyone to take away another's horse, how may they without eternal damnation suffer other people, and especially infidels, to come in, spoil, and rob, and captive them all? And if they be bounden to the defense, and may not do it alone, what madness were it to say that the people may not help them."

The Supplication of Souls

Toward the end of 1528 there appeared a work, A Supplication for the Beggars, written by a certain Simon Fish and printed on the continent. Fish's book, cast in the form of a petition from the beggars of the realm, is an attack upon the wealth of the clergy and upon the doctrine of purgatory. More's reply, The Supplication of Souls, written around the fall of 1529, defends the clergy against Fish's sweeping charges through the fictional device of using the suffering souls in purgatory as the spokesmen for the orthodox position. It was a device which More seems not to have taken great pains to maintain, and in many places it is clearly More himself speaking out against the man he refers to as the "beggars' proctor."

In the words of one of More's biographers, "We are rather startled when, in More's pages, the souls begin to relate merry tales and to make jokes."

More's Supplication *is approximately ten times the length of Fish's pamphlet.*

CLERICAL CELIBACY

This matter that priests must needs have wives he [Simon Fish, the author of *A Supplication for the Beggars*] bringeth in diversely in three or four places. And, among other, he hath one wherein he showeth, in railing against the clergy, a principal part of his excellent eloquence. For there he useth his royal figure of rhetoric called repetition, repeating often by the whole clergy, "These be they" in the beginning of his clause: "These be they that have made a hundred thousand idle whores in your realm. These be they that corrupt the generation of mankind in your realm. These be they that draw men's wives into incontinency in your realm." And, after divers of such "these be they's," he concludeth and knitteth up the matter with his accustomed vehemence fetched out of Luther's volumes, asking who is able to number the great broad, bottomless ocean sea full of evils that this mischievous and sinful generation bringeth up upon us. As though all the whole clergy were of this condition and no man else but they. But among all his "these be they's" this is one which, as the sorest and the most vehement, he setteth in the forefront of them all: "These be they that by their abstaining from marriage do let° the generation of the people, whereby all the realm at length, if it should be continued, shall be made desert and uninhabitable."

Lo, the deep insight that this beggars' proctor hath in the broad bottomless ocean sea full of evils, to save the grievous shipwreck of the commonwealth. He seeth far farther than ever Christ was ware of, or any of his blessed apostles, or any of the holy fathers of Christ's faith and religion since his holy ascension hitherto, till now that Luther came of late, and Tyndale after him, and spied out this great, secret mystery that neither God nor good man could espy. If their abstaining from marriage should make all the land desert and uninhabitable, how happeneth it that habitation endureth therein so long? For the land hath lasted since the beginning of their abstaining from marriage, ye wot° well, many a fair day. And now if, their abstaining from marriage notwithstanding, the land hath been

let interfere with, prevent   wot know

upholden with the generation of you that are the temporalty°
so long, ye shall likewise hereafter by God's grace and the
help of good prayers for keeping the land from wilderness,
be able to get children still yourself and shall not need to call
neither monks nor friars to help you.

ON PURGATORY

Now if ye consider how late this lewd sect began, which
among Christian men barketh against purgatory, and how few
always for very shame of their folly hath hitherto fallen into
them; and then if ye consider on the other side how full and
whole the great corps of all Christian countries so many hundred years have ever told you the contrary, ye shall, we be very
sure, for every person speaking against purgatory find for the
other part more than many a hundred.

Now if these men will peradventure say that they care not
for such comparison, neither of time with time, number with
number, nor company with company, but since some one man
is in credence worth some seven score; if they will, therefore,
call us to some other reckoning and will that we compare of
the best choice on both sides a certain [number], and match
them man for man, then have we (if we might for shame match
such blessed saints with a sort so far unlike) Saint Austin against
Friar Luther, Saint Jerome against Friar Lambert, Saint
Ambrose against Friar Huskin, Saint Gregory against priest
Pomerane, Saint Chrysostom against Tyndale, Saint Basil
against the beggars' proctor.

Now if our enemies will for lack of other choice help forth
their own part with their wives, then have they some advantage
indeed, for the other holy saints had none. But yet shall we not
lack blessed holy women against these friars' wives. For we
shall have Saint Anastasia against Friar Luther's wife, Saint
Hildegarde against Friar Huskin's wife, Saint Brigid against
Friar Lambert's wife, and Saint Catherine of Siena against
priest Pomerane's wife.

THE REFORMERS CONTRADICT THEMSELVES

Now if these heretics be so stiff and stubborn that rather
than they will confess themselves concluded, they will hold on
their old ways and fall from worse to worse, and like as they
have already against their former promise first rejected reason
and after, law, and then all the doctors and old holy fathers

temporalty the laity

of Christ's Church, and finally the whole Church itself; so if they will at length, as we greatly fear they will, reject all Scripture and cast off Christ and all, now, as we say, if they so do, yet have we left at the worst . . . Luther against Luther, Huskin against Huskin, Tyndale against Tyndale, and finally every heretic against himself. And then when these folk sit in Almaine° upon their bare bench in judgment on us and our matters, we may, as the knight of King Alexander appealed from Alexander to Alexander, from Alexander the drunk to Alexander the sober, so shall we appeal from Luther to Luther: from Luther the drunken to Luther the sober, from Luther the heretic to Luther the Catholic, and likewise in all the remnant.

For this doth no man doubt but that every one of them all, before they fell drunk of the dregs of old poisoned heresies in which they fell a-quaffing with the devil, they did full sadly and soberly pray for all Christian souls. But since that they be fallen drunken in wretched and sinful heresies, they neither care for other men's souls nor for their own neither. And on the other side, if ever they work with grace to purge themselves of those poisoned heresies wherewith they be now so drunk, they will then give sentence on our side as they did before. It were not evil that we showed you somewhat, for example, whereby ye may see what soberness they were in before, and in what drunkenness the devil's draught hath brought them. And in whom should we show it better than in Luther himself, archheretic and father abbot of all that drunken fellowship.

First, this man was so fast of° our side while he was well and sober that yet when he began to be well washed, he could not find in his heart utterly to fall from us. But when his head first began to daze of that evil drink, he wrote that purgatory could not be proved by Scripture. And yet, that notwithstanding, he wrote in this wise therewith, "I am very sure that there is purgatory, and it little moveth me what heretics babble. Should I believe a heretic born of late scant fifty years ago and say the faith were false that hath been holden so many hundred years?" Lo, here this man spake well upon our side. But yet said he therewith one thing or twain that could not stand therewith, and thereby may ye see that he began to reel. For he both affirmed that purgatory could not be proved by Scripture, and affirmed further that nothing could be taken for a sure and certain truth but if° it appeared by clear and evident Scripture. Which two things presupposed, how could any man be sure of purgatory? But the help is that both those points be false. For both is purgatory proved by Scripture, and

Almaine Germany   **fast of** firmly attached to, securely on   **but if** unless

the Catholic faith of Christ's Church were sufficient to make men sure thereof, albeit there were not in all Scripture one text for it, and divers that seemed against it, as we have showed you before.

But here, as we say, ye see how shamefully he staggered and began to reel, howbeit soon after being so dowsy drunk that he could neither stand nor reel, but fell down sow-drunk in the mire. Then like one that nothing remembered what he had said nor heard, nor his own voice, he began to be himself the babbling heretic against whom he had written before, and being not fully fifty years old, began to gainsay the faith of almost fifteen hundred years before his days in the Church of Christ, besides fifteen hundred years three times told among other faithful folk before. For now in his drunken sermon that he wrote upon the gospel of the rich man and Lazarus, whereas he had in his other books before framed of his own fantasy new fond° fashions of purgatory and told them forth for as plain matters as though he had been here and seen them, now in this mad sermon of his he saith plainly that there is none at all, but that all souls lie still and sleep, and so sleep shall until the day of doom. O sow-drunken soul drowned in such an insensible sleep that he lieth rooteth° while the apostles, the evangelists, all the doctors of Christ's Church, all the whole Christian people, and among them Christ himself, stand and cry at his ear that we sely° Christian souls lie and burn in purgatory. And he cannot hear, but lieth still in the mire and snorteth and there dreameth that we lie still and sleep as he doth.

Confutation of Tyndale's Answer

In the spring of 1531 William Tyndale published his Answer Unto Sir Thomas More's Dialogue. *In addition to a chapter by chapter reply to More's 1528* Dialogue Concerning Heresies, *Tyndale defends certain of his New Testament translations rejected by More, and he also attacks the infallibility of the Church and its reliance upon tradition. More took up the chal-*

---

fond foolish   **rooteth** snoring   **sely** poor, innocent

lenge, and the first part of his Confutation of Tyndale's Answer *appeared in 1532, and an additional five books in 1533. The* Confutation *is by far the longest of More's controversial works, a fact largely accounted for by his reprinting lengthy passages from Tyndale's work in order to comment on and reply to them.*

An interesting section of More's work challenges Tyndale's choice of vocabulary in his translation of the New Testament. He was especially concerned with Tyndale's substitutions of congregation *for* church, repentance *for* penance, elders *for* priests, knowledge *for* confession, love *for* charity, *and* favor *for* grace. *A brief sampling of this philological (as well as theological) dispute between the two humanist-trained polemicists is given below, as well as More's famous defense of Erasmus' orthodoxy. Erasmus' name had been brought into the controversy by Tyndale, who asked More why he had not reproved his "darling" for having rendered the Greek* ecclesia *by the Latin* congregatio *in Erasmus' 1516 edition of the New Testament in Latin and Greek.*

In the second chapter Tyndale sayeth that he changed this word *church* into this word *congregation* in the New Testament, where he found this word *ecclesia* in Latin, because the clergy had, he sayeth, brought the people into the ignorance of the true signification of this word *church*, making them understand thereby nothing but the clergy.

First, this is undoubtedly false, whatsoever Tyndale say. For albeit that men call the clergy by the name of the church, as the part ordained of God to be the more spiritual part thereof, yet is there no man, I suppose, so rude° but that he knoweth and so heareth the clergy preach also themselves that of the Church of Christ is every Christian man, and that the whole Church is the whole Christian people, and, therefore, they call it the Catholic Church, that is, universal, by which word never man was, I ween,° so mad to mean only the priests, howsoever boldly Tyndale against his own conscience report himself to every other man's. I would also, because he reporteth him so much to other men's conscience, fain wit° of Tyndale by his own conscience where he had ever heard any priests either preach or write or so much as say the word that only the clergy is the church and none of the church but they. I suppose themselves have not given themselves the name. The word is English, and they teach not every man his mother tongue, as

rude ignorant   **ween** trust, imagine   **wit** know

men teach children their A B C. But the good people have of
old time, though they know themselves also for part of the
church, yet because the church signified a holy name of a
Christian company gathered together in God, have, therefore,
of humility on their own part and reverence toward them,
used to call the clergy by that name, accounting them for the
more godly part of the whole godly company.

And the spiritualty againward° do plainly declare, and ever
have declared in their preaching, that the name is general and
common both to the temporalty and them, and at large they
declare the diverse parts of the church and therein reckon
themselves but for one. And this name so used by the temporalty of their own humility and reverence toward the spiritualty
is not a thing new found, but begun of old, at such time as both
parties were, I ween, somewhat better than I fear me they be
both now.

But now that thing that good folk have of good mind begun
and many hundred years continued, Tyndale, as one of another
sort, would have utterly changed, and rather than laymen
should have any such reverend mind to priests as to call them
the church, he would take it from them both, and, putting
away from both that holy name of *church*, would call them
both by the name of *congregation*, a word without any signification in Christendom any more than among Jews or Turks. . . .

Then he asketh me why I have not contended with Erasmus,
whom he calleth my darling, of all this long while for translating of this word *ecclesia* into this word *congregatio*. And then
he cometh forth with his fete° proper taunt that I favor him
of likelihood for making of his book of *Moria*° in my house.
There had he hit me low, save for lack of a little salt. I have
not contended with Erasmus my darling because I found no
such malicious intent with Erasmus my darling as I find with
Tyndale. For had I found with Erasmus my darling the
shrewd° intent and purpose that I find in Tyndale, Erasmus
my darling should be no more my darling. But I find in Erasmus
my darling that he detesteth and abhorreth the errors and
heresies that Tyndale plainly teacheth and abideth by, and,
therefore, Erasmus my darling shall be my dear darling still.
And surely if Tyndale had either never taught them or yet had
the grace to revoke them, then should Tyndale be my dear
darling too. But while he holdeth such heresies still, I cannot
take for my darling him that the devil taketh for his
darling. . . .

As touching *Moria*, in which Erasmus under the name and

againward in opposition to this   **fete** nasty, foul   **Moria** Erasmus'
Praise of Folly   **shrewd** cunning, insidious

person of Moria, which word in Greek signifieth folly, doth merely touch and reprove such faults and follies as he found in any kind of people, perusing every state and condition spiritual and temporal, leaving almost none untouched, by which book Tyndale sayeth that if it were in English every man should then well see that I was then far otherwise minded than I now write. If this be true then the more cause have I to thank God of amendment. But surely this is [not]° true. For, God be thanked, I never had that mind in my life to have holy saints' images or their holy relics out of reverence. For if there were any such thing in *Moria*, that thing could not yet make any man see that I were myself of that mind, the book being made by another man, though he were my darling never so dear. Howbeit, that book of *Moria* doth indeed but jest upon the abuses of such things, after the manner of the disour's° part in a play, and yet not so far neither by a great deal as the messenger doth in my *Dialogue*,° which I have yet suffered to stand still° in my *Dialogue*, and that rather yet by the counsel of other men than myself. . . .

I say, therefore, in these days in which men by their own default misconstrue and take harm of the very Scripture of God, until men better amend, if any man would now translate *Moria* into English, or some works either that I have myself written ere this, albeit there be none harm therein, folk yet being (as they be) given to take harm of that that is good, I would not only my darling's books but my own also help to burn them both with my own hands, rather than folk would (though through their own fault) take any harm of them, seeing that I see them likely in these days to do.

The Apology of Sir Thomas More

More's controversial writings had, naturally, drawn stinging attacks from his opponents. More set out to defend himself and his methods against these charges in his Apology, *published in 1533, and at least in the beginning of this work this was his aim. It was not long, however, before More turned his atten-*

not missing in original; sense seems to demand it   **disour's** jester's
Dialogue More's *Dialogue Concerning Heresies*   **still** yet

tion to a recent work, A Treatise Concerning the Division Between the Spiritualty and the Temporalty, *by Christopher St. German, a man professing to be a loyal Roman Catholic. The mild, apparently irenic tone of this work seems to have worried More, who regarded St. German's book as a subtly insidious, anticlerical polemic by a man who was secretly in sympathy with the reformers. What started out, consequently, to be but "an incident" in the* Apology *becomes More's central preoccupation throughout more than half the book. More, who refers to his opponent ironically as "the Pacifier," and as "Sir John Some-say" (a reference to St. German's practice of citing "some say" as his authority for his charges), commented on his* Apology *in a later work:*

> So is it now that mine *Apology* is an answer and a defense not only for my former books, wherein the new brethren began to find certain faults, but over that in the selfsame part wherein I touch the "Book of Division" it is an answer and a defense for many good, worshipful folk against the malicious slander and obloquy so generally set forth with so many false some-says in that seditious book.

Christopher St. German defended himself in his Salem and Bizance *(1533), and More returned to the attack in* The Debellation of Salem and Bizance, *published in the same year. More's opponent had the last word in* The Additions of Salem and Bizance, *published in 1534.*

THE FIRST CHAPTER

Sir Thomas More, Knight, to the Christian Readers

So well stand I not (I thank God), good reader, in mine own conceit, and thereby so much in mine own light, but that I can somewhat with equal judgment and an even eye behold and consider both myself and mine own. Nor I use not° to follow the condition of Aesop's ape, that thought her own babes so beauteous and so far passing in all goodly feature and favor, nor the crow that accounted her own birds the fairest of all the fowls that flew.

But like as some (I see well) there are that can° somewhat less than I, that yet for all that put out their works in writing, so am I not so blind upon the other side but that I very well

I use not I am not accustomed to   **can** know

perceive very many so far in wit° and erudition above me, that in such matter as I have anything written, if other men, as many would have taken it in hand as could have done it better, it might much better have become me to let the matter alone than by writing to presume anything to meddle therewith.

And, therefore, good reader, since I so well know so many men so far excel and pass me in all such things as are required in him that might adventure° to put his works abroad, to stand and abide the judgment of all other men; I was never so far overseen as either to look or hope that such faults as in my writing should by mine oversight escape me, could by the eyes of all other men pass forth unspied, but shortly should be both by good and well-learned perceived, and among so many bad brethren as I wist° well would be wroth with them, should be both sought out and sifted to the uttermost flake of bran and largely thereupon controlled and reproved.

But yet against all this fear this one thing recomforted me, that since I was of one point very fast and sure that such things as I write are consonant unto the common Catholic faith and determinations of Christ's Catholic Church, and are clear confutations of false, blasphemous heresies by Tyndale and Barnes put forth unto the contrary, any great fault and intolerable should they none find, of such manner, sort, and kind as the readers should in their souls perish and be destroyed by, of which poisoned faults mine adversaries' books be full.

Fairness To His Opponents

Now will I begin with that point that I most esteem. For of all the remnant of his opponents against him may I little count. But surely loath would I be to misrehearse any man's reason against whom I write, or to rehearse him slenderly.° And in that point undoubtedly they see full well themselves that they say not true. For there is no reason that I rehearse of Tyndale's or of Friar Barnes' either but that I use the contrary manner therein that Tyndale useth with mine. For he rehearseth mine in every place faintly and falsely too, and leaveth out the pith and the strength and the proof that most maketh for the pur-

---

wit mental acuity **adventure** chance, risk **wist** knew **rehearse . . . slenderly** state his arguments meagerly, unfairly. It is true enough that More took great pains to summarize and to quote liberally from the writings of his opponents, so much so, in fact, that a modern editor has found More of great help in the work of establishing a text for some of Tyndale's works. This feature of More's controversial writings, together with an apparent compulsion to let virtually nothing go unchallenged, accounts for the length, repetitiousness, and tedium of the polemical works, especially the *Confutation of Tyndale's Answer*.

pose. And he fareth therein as if there were one that, having day of challenge appointed in which he should wrestle with his adversary, would find the means by craft to get his adversary before the day into his own hands, and there keep him and diet him with such a thin diet that at the day he bringeth him forth feeble, faint, and famished and almost hunger starven, and so lean that he can scant stand on his legs; and then is it easy, ye wote well, to give the sely° soul a fall. And yet when Tyndale hath done all this, he taketh the fall himself.

But every man may well see that I never use that way with Tyndale nor with any of these folk; but I rehearse their reason to the best that they can make it themselves, and I rather enforce it and strength it of mine own than take any part of theirs therefrom.

And this use I not only in such places as I do not rehearse all their own words (for that is not requisite in every place), but I use it also in such places besides, as of all their own words I leave not one syllable out. For such darkness° use they purposely, and Tyndale in especially, that except I took some pain to set out their arguments plainly, many that read them should little wit° what they mean. . . .

Howbeit, glad would I have been if it might have been much more short, for then should my labor have been so much the less. But they will, if they be reasonable men, consider in themselves that it is a shorter thing and sooner done to write heresies than to answer them. For the most foolish heretic in a town may write more false heresies in one leaf than the wisest man in the whole world can well and conveniently by reason and authority soil° and confute in forty. Now when that Tyndale not only teacheth false heresies, but furnisheth his errors also with pretense of reason and Scripture, and instead of reason sometimes with blunt subtleties and rude riddles too, the making open and lightsome to the reader the dark writing of him that would not by his will be well perceived, hath put me to more labor and length in answering than some men would per-adventure have been content to take.

And I sometimes take the pains to rehearse some one thing in divers fashions in more places than one, because I would that the reader should in every place where he fortuneth° to fall in reading have at his hand, without remitting over elsewhere,° or labor of further seeking for it, as much as shall seem requisite for the matter that he there hath in hand. And

sely poor, innocent **darkness** obscurantism **wit** know **soil** damage **fortuneth** happens **without . . . elsewhere** without turning back and looking elsewhere

therein the labor of all that length is mine own, for ease and shortening of the reader's pain.

Gentle Language Cannot Be Used With Heretics

Now come I to them that say I handle Tyndale and Frith and Barnes ungoodly and with uncomely words, calling them by the name of heretics and fools, and so use them in words as though the men had neither wit nor learning; whereas it cannot be denied (they say) but that they be such as every man knoweth well have both.

As for wit and learning, I nowhere say that any of them have none, nor I mean no further but for the matters of their heresies. And in the treating of those they show so little wit or learning either that the more they have, the more appeareth the feebleness of their part and the falsehood of their heresies, if they have any great wit or any great learning indeed, and then for all that, in the defending of those matters with such foolish handling so shamefully confound themselves.

Howbeit of very truth, God, upon such folk as having wit and learning fall wilfully from faith to false heresy, showeth his wrath and indignation with a more vengeance in some part than (as some doctors say) he doth upon the devil himself. For (as divers doctors hold opinion) the fiends be fallen from grace, and therefore have lost their glory, yet God hath suffered them to keep their gifts of nature still, as wit, beauty, strength, agility, and such other like.

And Father Alphonse the Spanish friar told me that the devils be no such deformed, evil-favored creatures as men imagine them, but they be in mind proud, envious, and cruel. And he bade me that if I would see a very right image of a fiend I should no more but even look upon a very fair woman that hath a very shrewd,° fell,° cursed mind. And when I showed him that I never saw none such, nor wist not where I might any such find, he said he could find four or five, but I cannot believe him. Nor verily no more can I believe that the fiends be like fair, shrewd women if there were any such. Nor as the world is, it were not good that young men should ween° so. For they be so full of corage° that were the fiends never so cursed, if they thought them like fair women, they would never fear to adventure upon them once. Nor, to say the truth, no more can I believe neither that the damned spirits have all their natural gifts as whole and as perfect as they had before their fall.

shrewd wicked   **fell** terrible   **ween** think   **corage** ardor

But surely if they have, then (as I said before) God hath on Tyndale, Barnes, and Frith, and those other heretics, more showed his vengeance in some part than he did upon the devil. For, in good faith, God hath, as it seemeth, from these folk taken away the best part of their wits.

For likewise as they that would have builded up the Tower of Babylon for themselves against God had such a stop thrown upon them that suddenly none understood what another said, surely so God upon these heretics of our time that go busily about to heap up to the sky their foul, filthy dunghill of all old and new false, stinking heresies, gathered up together against the true Catholic faith of Christ, that himself hath ever hitherto taught his true Catholic Church; God, I say, who, when the apostles went about to preach the true faith, sent down his own Holy Spirit of unity, concord, and truth unto them with the gift of speech and understanding, so that they understood every man and every man understood them, hath reared up and sent among these heretics the spirit of error and lying, of discord and of division, the damned devil of hell, which so entangleth their tongues and so distempereth their brains that they neither understand well one of them another, nor any of them well himself.

And this that I here say, who so list° to read my books shall find it so true and so plainly proved in many places that he shall well see and say that this is the thing which in my writing grieveth this blessed brotherhood a little more than the length.

And, therefore, where they find the fault that I handle these folk so foul, how could I other do? For while I declare and show their writing to be such (as I needs must, or leave the most necessary points of all the matter untouched), it were very hard for me to handle it in such wise, as when I plainly prove them abominable heretics and against God and his sacraments and saints very° blasphemous fools, they should wene° that I speak them fair.

On Condemning The Faults Of The Clergy

But I perceive well that these good brethren look that I should rebuke the clergy and seek out their faults and lay them to their faces and write some work to their shame, or else they cannot call me but partial to the priests. Howbeit, by this reason they may call me partial to the laymen too. For I never used that way neither toward the one nor the other. I find not yet such plenty and store of virtue in myself as to think it a meetly

who so list whoever is willing   **very** truly   **wene** know part and convenient° for me to play, to rebuke as abominable, vicious folk anyone's honest company, either spiritual or temporal, and much less meet to rebuke and reproach either the whole spiritualty or temporalty,° because of such as are very stark nought° in both.

I dare be bold to say that proud folk be nought, that covetous folk be nought, that lecherous folk be nought, and to speak against open, known thieves, open, known murderers, open, known perjured persons, open, known apostates, open, known, professed or convicted heretics. But surely my guise is not to lay the faults of the naughty to the charge of any whole company, and rail upon merchants and call them usurers; nor to rail upon franklins and call them false jurors; nor to rail upon sheriffs and call them raveners°; nor to rail upon eschetours° and call them extortioners; nor upon all officers and call them bribers; nor upon gentlemen and call them oppressors; nor so forth up higher, to call every degree by such odious names as men might find some of that sort.

And of all degrees specially for my part, I have ever accounted my duty to forbear all such manner of unmannerly behavior toward those two most eminent orders that God hath here ordained in earth: the two great orders I mean of special, consecrated persons, the sacred princes and priests. Against any of which two reverent orders, whoso be so lewd irreverently to speak and malapertly° to jest and rail shall play that part alone for me. And rather will I that these brethren call me partial than for such ill fashion indifferent.

And over this I cannot see what need there were that I should rail upon the clergy and reckon up all their faults. For that part hath Tyndale played, and Friar Barnes both already, and left nothing for me to say therein, not though my mind were sore set thereon. They have with truth and lies together laid the living of bad to bad and good both, in such a vile, villainous fashion that it would make a good stomach to vomit to hear their ribald railing. And yet not against the sacred persons only, but against the blessed sacraments also.

And now would their disciples that I should not speak against their execrable heresies and their despiteful dealing, but if° I should by the way do as they do and help them forth in the same. And herein fare they much like as if there were a sort of villayne,° wretched heretics that, meeting the priests and clerks religious and others going with banners, copes, crosses, and censers, and the sacrament borne about with them upon a

convenient fitting   **spiritualty or temporalty** clergy or laity   **nought** bad, immoral   **raveners** plunderers   **eschetours** financiers   **malapertly** impudently   **but if** unless   **villayne** crude, ignorant, as well as evil

Corpus Christi day, would pick quarrels with them, and first call them all that could come in their villayne mouths, and happely° say true by some, and then catch them all by the heads and throw them in the mire, surplices, copes, censers, crosses, relics, sacrament, and all. And then if any man rebuked their villainous dealing and would step unto the priests and would pull them up and help to wipe the copes, and reverently take up the crosses, the relics, and the blessed sacrament; were it not now well and wisely spoken if one would reprove him that thus did, and say he should not meddle himself in the matter, hot nor cold, but if he would be indifferent and do somewhat on both the sides. And therefore he should, to show himself indifferent, either revile and rebuke the priests, or at the least wise some of them, and souse them somewhat in the mire for the pleasure of them that so served them, or else go by about his other business, and let the matter alone, and neither take up good men out of the mire, nor surplice, cope, nor censer, nor relic, but let them lay the sacrament in the dirt again. Were not this a goodly way? Surely for my part I am not so ambitious of such folks' praise as, to be called indifferent,° will in writing against their heresies help them forth in their railing.

Clergy And Laity Are In Need Of Reform

As for mine own part, look at my *Dialogue*, my *Supplication of Souls*, and both the parts of the *Confutation*, and ye shall clearly see that I neither have used toward the clergy nor toward the temporalty any warm, displeasant word, but have forborne to touch in special either the faults of the one or of the other. But yet have I confessed the thing that truth is: neither part to be faultless. But then, which is the thing that offendeth these blessed brethren, I have not letted,° furthermore, to say the thing which I take also for very true, that as this realm of England hath had hitherto, God be thanked, as good and as laudable a temporalty, number for number, as hath had any other Christian region of the quantity,° so hath it had also, number for number, compared with any realm Christened of no greater quantity, as good and as commendable a clergy, though there have never lacked in any of both the parts plenty of such as have always been nought;° whose faults have ever been their own, and not to be imputed to the whole body, neither of spiritualty nor temporalty, saving that there

---

happely perhaps　　**indifferent** objective, neutral　　**letted** hesitated　　**quantity** same size　　**nought** evil living

have been peradventure on either part, in some such as by their offices ought to look thereto, some lack of the labor and diligence that in the reforming of it should have belonged unto them, which I declare always that I would wish amended, and every man specially labor to mend himself and rather accustom himself to look upon his own faults than upon other men's; and against such as are in either sort found openly evil and nought, and noyous° unto the common weal, as thieves, murderers, and heretics, and such other wretches; the whole corpus of the spiritualty and temporalty both, each with other lovingly to accord and agree, and according to the good ancient laws and commendable usages long continued in this noble realm, either part endeavor themselves diligently to repress and keep under those evil and ungracious folk that, like sores, scabs, and cankers, trouble and vex the body; and of all them to cure such as may be cured, and for health of the whole body cut and cast off the incurable, cankered parts therefrom, observed in the doing evermore such order and fashion as may stand and agree with reason and justice, the king's laws of the realm, the Scripture of God, and the laws of Christ's Church, ever keeping love and concord between the two principal parts the spiritualty and temporalty, lest the dregs of both sorts conspiring together and increasing may little and little grow too strong for both, whereto they might have a fair gap and a broad gate to enter, if they might find the means by craft to sever and set asunder the temporalty against the clergy to strive and so let, as it were, the soul and the body brabble and strive together; and while they study nothing else but the one to grieve the other, the naughty then conspire and agree together and set upon the good people of both.

This hath been hitherto the whole sum of my writing, without any displeasant word used either toward temporalty or spiritualty.°

Defense Against Charges Of Cruelty To Heretics

They that are of this new brotherhood be so bold and so shameless in lying that whoso shall hear them speak and knoweth not what sect they be of shall be very sore abused by them. Myself have good experience of them. For the lies are neither

---

noyous harmful   **spiritualty** the entire preceding passage is directed at Christopher St. German's book on *The Division Between the Spiritualty and the Temporalty*, the mild tone of which had apparently pleased some people. More is anxious to show that he has not contributed to "the division" between clergy and laity by emphasizing the faults of any one group.

few nor small that many of the blessed brethren have made and
daily yet make by me.

Divers of them have said that of such as were in my house
while I was chancellor I used to examine them with torments,
causing them to be bounden to a tree in my garden and there
piteously beaten. And this tale had some of those good brethren
so caused to be blown about that a right worshipful friend of
mine did of late within less than this fortnight tell unto another
near friend of mine that he had of late heard much speaking
thereof.

What cannot these brethren say that can be so shameless to
say thus? For of very truth, albeit that for a great robbery or
a heinous murder, or sacrilege in a church, with carrying away
the pyx with the blessed sacrament, or villainously casting it
out, I caused sometimes such things to be done by some officers
of the Marshalsea or of some other prisons, with which ordering of them by their well-deserved pain, and without any great
hurt that afterward should stick by them, I found out and repressed many such desperate wretches as else had not failed
to have gone further abroad, and to have done to many good
folks a great deal much more harm. Yet though I so did in
thieves, murderers, and robbers of churches, and notwithstanding also that heretics be yet much worse than all they, yet saving only their sure keeping,° I never did else cause any such
thing to be done to any of them all in all my life, except only
twain, of which the one was a child and a servant of mine in
mine own house, whom his father had ere ever he came with
me nowseled° up in such matters, and had set him to attend
upon George Iaye or Gee,° otherwise called clerk, which is a
priest, and is now for all that wedded in Antwerp, into whose
house there the two nuns were brought which John Byrt,
otherwise called Adrian, stole out of their cloister to make
them harlots. This George Iaye did teach this child his ungracious heresy against the blessed sacrament of the altar; which
heresy this child afterward, being in service with me, began to
teach another child in my house, who uttered his counsel. And
upon that perceived and known,° I caused a servant of mine
to stripe° him like a child before mine household for amendment of himself and example of such other.

Another was one who, after that he had fallen into the frantic

saving . . . keeping aside from seeing to it that they were securely locked
up   nowseled instructed, brought up   Gee George Joye, for a time an
associate of Tyndale's, translated the psalter and other portions of
Scripture, authored an attack against More, *The Subversion of More's
False Foundation*, a treatise mainly concerned with More's teaching on
tradition, the "unwritten verities." known after that had come to my
attention   stripe whip

heresies, fell soon after into plain, open frenzy besides. And albeit that he had therefore been put up in Bedlam,° and afterward by beating and correction gathered his remembrance and began to come again to himself, being thereupon set at liberty and walking about abroad, his old fancies began to fall again in his head. And I was from divers good, holy places advertised° that he used in his wandering about to come into the church and there make many mad toys° and trifles, to the trouble of good people in the divine service; and especially would he be most busy in the time of most silence, while the priest was at the secret of the mass about the elevation.° And if he spied any woman kneeling at a form, if her head hung anything low in her meditations, then would he steal behind her, and, if he were not letted,° would labor to lift up all her clothes and cast them quite over head. Whereupon I, being advertised of these pageants and being sent unto and required° by very devout, religious folk to take some other order with him, caused him as he came wandering by my door to be taken by the constables and bound to a tree in the street before the whole town, and there they striped° him with rods therefore till he waxed weary, and somewhat longer. And it appeared well that his remembrance was good enough, save that it went about in grazing till it was beaten home. For he could then very well rehearse his faults himself, and speak and treat° very well, and promise to do afterward as well. And verily, God be thanked, I hear none harm of him now.

And of all that ever came in my hand for heresy, as help me God, saving, as I said, the sure keeping of them°—and yet not so sure neither but that George Constantine could steal away —else had never any of them any stripe or stroke given them, so much as a fillip on the forehead. . . .

But now tell the brethren many marvelous lies of much cruel tormenting that heretics had in my house, so far forth that one Segar, a bookseller of Cambridge, who was in my house about four or five days and never had either bodily harm done him or foul word spoken him while he was in my house, hath reported since, as I hear say, to divers that he was bound to a tree in my garden and thereto . . . piteously beaten; and yet besides that bound about the head with a cord and wrung, that he fell down dead in a swoon.

Bedlam a madhouse   **advertised** informed   **toys** pranks   **secret . . . elevation** the secret is the prayer introducing the most solemn part of the mass, during which the prayers are said silently by the priest; the elevation is that part during which the bread and wine are consecrated   **letted** prevented   **required** requested   **striped** whipped   **treat** act, deal with people   **sure keeping of them** confined, locked up

And this tale of his beating did Tyndale tell to an old acquaintance of his own and to a good lover of mine, with one piece further yet: that while the man was in beating I spied a little purse of his hanging at his doublet, wherein the poor man had (as he said) five marks, and that caught I quickly to me and pulled it from his doublet and put it in my bosom, and that Segar never saw it after. And therein I trow° he said true, for no more did I neither, nor before neither, nor I trow no more did Segar himself neither, in good faith.

But now when I can come to goods by such goodly ways, it is no great marvel though I be so suddenly grown to so great substance of riches as Tyndale told his acquaintance and my friend, to whom he said that he wist well that I was no less worth in money and plate and other movables° than twenty thousand marks. And as much as that have divers of the good brethren affirmed here, nearer home.

And surely this will I confess, that if I have heaped up so much goods together, then have I not gotten the one half by right. And yet by all the thieves, murderers, and heretics that ever came in my hands am I not, thank God, the richer of one groat, and yet have they spent me twain.° Howbeit, if either any of them, or of any kind of people else, that any cause have had before me, or otherwise any meddling with me, find himself so sore grieved with anything that I have taken of his, he had some time to speak thereof. And now since no man cometh forth to ask any restitution yet, but hold their peace and slack their time so long, I give them all plain, peremptory warning now that they drive it off no longer.° For if they tarry till yesterday and then come and ask so great sums among them as shall amount to twenty thousand marks, I propose to purchase such a protection for them that I will leave myself less than the fourth part, even of shrewdness, rather than ever I will pay them.

The Riots Of Evil May Day°

I remember many times that even here in London, after the great business that was there on a May day in the morning, by

trow believe **movables** possessions **and yet . . . twain** the meaning is doubtful: either they have cost me more than I made, which was nothing; or, whereas I have not made a penny, their false rumors would have me spending two **they drive . . . longer** now they are out of luck **Evil May Day** this uprising of the apprentices, mainly directed at foreigners residing in London, occurred in 1517 and is described in some detail by Edward Hall in his chronicle. More, recently entered into the king's service but still popular with his fellow Londoners, was called upon to help quell the riot. The Elizabethan play about More (in which Shakespeare may have had a hand) contains a scene in which More's eloquence wins over the unruly mob.

a rising made against strangers,° for which divers of the apprentices and journeymen suffered execution of treason by an old statute made long before, against all such as would violate the king's safe conduct, I was appointed, among others, to search out and inquire by diligent examination in what wise and by what persons that privy confederacy began. And, in good faith, after great time taken and much diligence used therein, we perfectly tried out at last that all that business of any rising to be made for the matter began only by the conspiracy of two young lads that were apprentices in Cheap. Which after the thing devised° first and compassed between them twain, perused° privily the journeymen first, and after the apprentices of many of the mean° crafts in the city, bearing the first that they spoke with in hand° that they had secretly spoken with many other occupations already, and that they were all agreed thereunto; and that besides them there were two or three hundred of serving men of divers lords' houses, and some of the king's too, which would not be named nor known, that would yet in the night be at hand, and when they were once up, would not fail to fall in with them and take their part.

Now this ungracious invention and these words of those two lewd° lads (who yet in the business fled away themselves and never came again after) did put some others, by their oversight and lightness,° in such a courage and boldness that they wende° themselves able to avenge their displeasure in the night and after either never to be known or to be strong enough to bear it out and go further.

And the like ungracious policy devise now these heretics that call themselves evangelical brethren. Some potheaded apostles they have that wander about the realm into sundry shires, of whom every one hath in every shire a diverse name, and some peradventure in corners here and there they bring into the brotherhood. But whether they get any or none, they let not° to lie when they come home, and say that more than half of every shire is of their own sect. And the same boast Bayfield the apostate, who was after burned in Smithfield, made unto mine own self. But, blessed be God, when he came to the fire he found none very ready to pull him from it.

In Defense Of Laughter

Now come I to the last fault that the brethren find in my books. For as for one more that was showed me within this

---

strangers foreigners **devised** plotted **perused** approached **mean** lower, unskilled **bearing . . . in hand** convincing the first group that they met with **lewd** ignorant **oversight and lightness** imprudence and fickleness **wende** thought **let not** hesitate not

seven night, I not so much esteem as to vouchsafe to answer, that is, to wit, where they reprove that I bring in among the most earnest matters, fancies and sports and merry tales. For as Horace sayeth, a man may sometimes say full soth° in game. And one that is but a layman, as I am, it may better happely° become him merrily to tell his mind than seriously and solemnly to preach. And over this I can scant believe that the brethren find any mirth in my books. For I have not much heard that they very merrily read them.

Conclusion: Would Rather Correct His Own Faults Than Other Men's Errors

And therefore, good Christian readers, as for such further things as I have in my said preface° promised, I propose to pursue at some other further leisure. But first I think it better to bestow some time upon another thing, and leaving for a while both defense of mine own faults and finding of other men's in writing, think better to bestow some time about the mending of mine own in living, which is a thing now for many men more necessary than is writing. For of new bookmakers there are now more than enough. Wherefore that all such as will write may have the grace to write well, or at the least wise none other purpose than to mean well, and as well writers as others to amend our own faults and live well, I beseech almighty God to grant us, and that all folk spiritual and temporal in this world living, and all good Christian souls departed hence and yet not out of pain, may for grace every part pray for other, and all the blessed, holy saints in heaven, both here for grace and there for glory, pray to God for us all. Amen.

From The Dialogue of Comfort

More wrote The Dialogue of Comfort Against Tribulation *in 1534 while in the Tower awaiting execution. He was fearful of death, did everything he could, within the limits of integrity, to avoid it. The death he awaited was a particularly cruel and*

soth truth   **happely** perhaps   **preface** to his *Confutation of Tyndale's Answer*

painful one: The punishment for treason was to be drawn and quartered. Owing to King Henry's intervention on behalf of his onetime friend, More was spared this barbarous punishment. The sentence was reduced to death by beheading.

The Dialogue of Comfort, *as the title indicates, marks More's return to a literary form often used by the humanists in imitation of Plato and Cicero. More's greatest work,* Utopia, *was, it will be recalled, also written in dialogue form, as was his* Dialogue Concerning Heresies. *It is a form which gave More's dialectical mind full play and which also provided the distance and perspective so necessary to a writer like More, for whom control—in life as well as in art—was all. One recalls, in this connection, the possibly apocryphal quip with which More is said to have ended his life, the quip which so scandalized the Protestant historian Edward Hall, who records it in his chronicle: Approaching the shaky stairs to the scaffold, More turned to his warder and said, "I pray you, Master Lieutenant, see me safe up, and for my coming down let me shift for myself."*

In this, More's contribution to the tradition of prison literature, two Hungarians, an uncle and his nephew, are concerned with an impending invasion of Hungary by the Turks. The fictional situation is obviously a thinly veiled allegory in which Hungary suggests or stands for England, and the Turks, the enemies of the Church.

In the three selections which follow, we can observe some of that wit and irony which characterized a younger Thomas More's observations on man's foibles and posturings. The third passage represents the kind of meditation on approaching death with which this work is replete.

OF FLATTERY

Vincent: When I was first in Almaine,° uncle, it happed me to be somewhat favored with a great man of the Church, and a great state, one of the greatest in all that country there. And, indeed, whosoever might spend as much as he might in one thing and other were a right great estate in any country of Christendom. But glorious was he very far above all measure, and that was great pity, for it did harm and made him abuse many great gifts that God had given him. Never was he satiate° of hearing his own praise.

So happed it one day that he had in a great audience made an oration in a certain manner, wherein he liked himself so well that at his dinner he sat, him thought, on thorns till he

Almaine Germany   **satiate** surfeited, satisfied

might hear how they that sat with him at his board would commend it. And when he had sat musing awhile, devising (as I thought after) upon some pretty proper way to bring it in withal, at the last, for lack of a better (lest he should have letted° the matter too long), he brought it even bluntly forth and asked us all that sat at his board's end (for at his own mess in the midst there sat but himself alone) how well we liked his oration that he had made that day. But in faith, uncle, when that problem was once proposed, till it was full answered no man, I ween, ate one morsel of meat more; every man was fallen in so deep a study for the finding of some exquisite praise. For he that should have brought out but a vulgar and a common commendation would have thought himself shamed for ever. Then said we our sentences by row as we sat, from the lowest unto the highest in good order, as it had been a great matter of the commonweal in a right solemn council. When it came to my part (I will not say it, uncle, for no boast), methought, by Our Lady, for my part I quit myself meetly well.

And I liked myself the better because methought my words, being but a stranger, went yet with some grace in the Almaine tongue wherein letting my Latin alone me listed° to show my cunning. And I hoped to be liked the better because I saw that he that sat next me and should say his sentence after me was an unlearned priest, for he could speak no Latin at all. But when he came forth for his part with my lord's commendation, the wily fox had been so well accustomed in court with the craft of flattery that he went beyond me to too far. And then might I see by him what excellence a right mean wit may come to in one craft, that in all his whole life studieth and busieth his wit about no more but that one. But I made afterward a solemn vow unto myself that if ever he and I were matched together at that board again, when we should fall to our flattery, I would flatter in Latin, that he should not contend with me no more. For though I could be content to be outrun of an horse, yet would I no more abide it to be outrun of an ass.

But, uncle, here began now the game. He that sat highest and was to speak was a great beneficed man, and not a doctor only but also somewhat learned indeed in the laws of the Church. A world it was to see how he marked every man's word that spoke before him. And it seemed that every word the more proper it was the worse he liked it for the cumbrance that he had to study out a better to pass it. The man even sweat with the labor, so that he was fain in the while now and then to wipe his face. Howbeit, in conclusion, when it came to his

letted hindered, delayed   **me listed** I was desirous

course, we that had spoken before him had so taken up all among us before that we had not left him one wise word to speak after.

Anthony: Alas, good man: Among so many of you some good fellow should have lent him one.

Vincent: It needed not as hap was,° uncle, for he found out such a shift° that in his flattering he passed us all the many.

Anthony: Why, what said he, cousin?

Vincent: By Our Lady, uncle, not one word. . . . For when he saw that he could find no words of praise that would pass all that had been spoken before already, the wily fox would speak never a word but as he that were ravished unto heavenward with the wonder of the wisdom and eloquence that my lord's grace had uttered in that oration, he set a long sigh with an "Oh!" from the bottom of his breast, and held up both his hands and lifted up his head, and cast up his eyes into the welkin° and wept.

Anthony: Forsooth, cousin, he played his part very properly. But was that great prelate's oration, cousin, anything praiseworthy? For you can tell, I see well. For you would not, I ween, play as Juvenal merrily describeth the blind senator, one of the flatterers of Tiberius the emperor, that among the remnant so magnified the great fish that the emperor had sent for them to show them, which this blind senator (Montanus I trow they called him) marveled of as much as any that marveled most, and many things he spoke thereof with some of his words directed thereunto, looking himself toward his left side while the fish lay on his right side. You would not, I trow, cousin, have taken upon you to praise it so but if° you had heard it.

Vincent: I heard it, uncle, indeed, and to say the truth, it was not to dispraise. Howbeit, surely, somewhat less praise might have served it, by more a great deal than the half. But this am I sure, had it been the worst that ever was made, the praise had not been the less of one hair. For they that used to praise him to his face never considered how much the thing deserved, but how great a laud and praise themselves could give his good grace.

Anthony: Surely, cousin, as Terence saith, such folk make men of fools even stark mad, and much cause have their lords to be right angry with them.

as hap was as chance would have it, as it turned out   **shift** stratagem, device   **welkin** the heavens   **but if** unless

Vincent: God hath indeed and is, I ween. But as for their lords, uncle, if they would after wax angry with them therefore, they should in my mind do them very great wrong, when it is one of the things that they specially keep them for. For those that are of such vainglorious mind (be they lords or be they meaner men) can be much better contented to have their devices commended than amended. And require they their servant and their friend never so specially to tell them the very truth, yet shall he better please them if he speak them fair than if he telleth them truth.

For they be in the case that Martial speaketh of in an epigram unto a friend of his that required his judgment how he liked his verses, but he prayed him in any wise to tell him even the very truth. To whom Martial made answer in this wise:

> The very truth of me thou dost require.
> The very truth is this, my friend dear:
> The very truth thou wouldst not gladly hear.

And in good faith, uncle, the selfsame prelate that I told you my tale of (I dare be bold to swear it, I know it so surely) had on a time made of his own drawing a certain treaty that should serve for a league between that country and a prince. In which treaty himself thought that he had devised his articles so wisely and indited° them so well that all the world would allow them. Whereupon, longing sore to be praised, he called unto him a friend of his, a man well learned and of good worship and very well expert in those matters, as he that had been divers times ambassador for that country and had made many such treaties himself. When he took him the treaty and that he had read it he asked him how he liked it and said, "But I pray you heartily, tell me the very truth." And that he spoke so heartily that the other had weened° he would fain have heard the truth, and in trust thereof he told him a fault therein, at the hearing whereof he swore in great anger, "By the mass, thou art a very fool." The other afterward told me that he would never tell him truth again.

(Book III, Chapter 10)

Let us now consider in like wise what great worldly wealth ariseth unto men by great offices, rooms,° and authority, to those worldly disposed people, I say, that desire them for no better purpose. For of them that desire them for better we

indited composed, written   **weened** thought, imagined   **rooms** offices, position

shall speak after anon. The great thing that they all chiefly like therein is that they may bear a rule, command and control other men, and live uncommanded and uncontrolled themselves. And yet this commodity took I so little heed of that I never was aware it was so great till a good friend of ours merrily told me once that his wife once in a great anger taught it him. For when her husband had no list° to grow greatly upward in the world, nor neither would labor for office of authority, and over that forsook a right worshipful room when it was offered him, she fell in hand with him, he told me, and all-to rated° him and asked him, "What will you do that you list not to put forth yourself as other folk do? Will you sit still by the fire and make goslings in the ashes with a stick as children do? Would God I were a man, and look what I would do!"

"Why, wife," quoth her husband, "what would you do?"

"What? By God, go forward with the best. For as my mother was wont to say (God have mercy on her soul), it is evermore better to rule than to be ruled. And therefore, by God, I would not, I warrant you, be so foolish to be ruled where I might rule."

"By my troth, wife," quoth her husband, "in this I daresay you say truth. For I never found you willing to be ruled yet."

(Book III, Chapter 11)

How many Romans, how many noble courages° of other sundry countries have willingly given their own lives and suffered great, deadly pains and very painful deaths for their countries and the respect of winning by their deaths the only reward of worldly renown and fame? And should we then shrink to suffer as much for eternal honor in heaven and everlasting glory? The devil hath also some so obstinate heretics that endure wittingly° painful death for vainglory, and is it not then more than shame that Christ shall see his Catholics forsake his faith rather than suffer the same for heaven and very glory?

Would God, as I many times have said, that the remembrance of Christ's kindness in suffering his passion for us, the consideration of hell that we should fall in by forsaking of him, the joyful meditation of eternal life in heaven that we shall win with this short temporal death patiently taken for him had so deep a place in our breast as reason would they should, and as, if we would do our devoir° toward it and labor for it and pray therefore, I verily think they should. For then should they so take up our mind and ravish it all another way that as a man

---

list desire   **all-to rated** thoroughly berated   **courages** hearts   **wittingly** consciously, knowingly   **devoir** duty

hurt in a fray feeleth not sometimes his wound, nor yet is aware thereof till his mind fall more thereon, so farforth that sometimes another man showeth him that he hath lost a hand before he perceive it himself, so the mind ravished in the thinking deeply of those other things, Christ's death, hell, and heaven, were likely to diminish and put away of our painful death four parts of the feeling either of the fear or the pain. For of this am I very sure, if we had the fifteenth part of the love to Christ that he both had and hath unto us, all the pain of this Turk's persecution could not keep us from him, but that there would be at this day as many martyrs here in Hungary as have been afore in other countries of old.

(Book III, Chapter 27)

From The English Letters

In 1528 and for several years thereafter, Elizabeth Barton, a nun residing in Kent, claimed to be having religious, prophetic visions. As a result of these visions, she denounced King Henry for his attempts to nullify his marriage with Catharine of Aragon, making dire prophecies about the king's future. Some of Henry's opponents seemed to have aided and encouraged the unsophisticated nun in her denunciations. Thomas More wrote to her, probably some time in 1533, cautioning her to steer clear of political matters in her public statements. She persisted, however, and on April 20, 1534, along with five clerics, she was beheaded for treason.

Thomas Cromwell, who from an early date seems to have been intent upon More's destruction, attempted to implicate ex-Chancellor More in the "conspiracy." The House of Lords, however, convinced of More's obvious innocence, refused to return an indictment against him. In his efforts to clear himself of any suspicion of guilt, More wrote two letters to Secretary Cromwell and one to the king.

The three letters, while interesting in their own right as examples of More's political maneuvering in order to retain his freedom and, ultimately, his life, also provide striking evidence of the textual alteration to which More's writings were often subjected by his early editors. More's nephew, William Rastell, in issuing the great 1557 folio edition of More's English works, printed two of these letters, one of the two he wrote to Cromwell and the one to Henry, but only after he had made certain changes and deletions. The third letter, to Cromwell, he suppressed completely.

Of the three letters following, Rastell neglected to print the first one, although it is known to have been in his possession. The Protestant bishop, Gilbert Burnet, first published the letter in the seventeenth century, accusing Rastell of "fraud" for deliberately having suppressed it. In the first of these letters, as the reader will see for himself, More unequivocally denounces Elizabeth Barton. Rastell, for obvious reasons, was hardly interested in publishing the Catholic martyr's denunciation of the woman who had championed Catharine of Aragon, whose daughter Mary, in 1557, was the ruling monarch of England.

That is not, however, the end of the story connected with these interesting letters.

In the two letters which he did print in the 1557 volume, Rastell made the following changes: 1) Where More had originally written "the wicked woman of Canterbury" (that is, the nun of Kent), and, in another place, "that wicked woman," the editor substituted the neutral phrase "the nun" in both instances. 2) In the letter to Cromwell which he did print, Rastell silently omitted the following passage, which, interestingly, praises Anne Boleyn and acknowledges her to be Henry's lawful queen:

> . . . and this noble woman [Anne Boleyn] really anointed queen [I] neither murmur at it nor dispute upon it, nor never did nor will, but without any other manner meddling of the matter among his other faithful subjects faithfully pray to God for his Grace and hers both, long to live and well and their noble issue too, in such wise as may be to the honor and surety to themselves, rest, peace, wealth, and profit unto this noble realm.

There is still, however, another tale to be told concerning the fate of this same letter. Rastell, in making his deletions, apparently saw no need to omit a clause in which More expresses his opinion on the limitations of papal supremacy. In the passage in question, More, as an example of his loyalty to the king and of his prudence in avoiding a question which had become quite delicate, reveals his own suppression of something he had written which might have offended Henry. Here is what he says in his letter to Cromwell:

Albeit that I have for mine own part such opinion of the pope's primacy as I have showed you, yet never thought I the pope above the general council, nor never have in any book of mine put forth among the king's subjects in our vulgar tongue, advanced greatly the pope's authority. For albeit that a man may peradventure somewhat find therein that after the common manner of all Christian realms I speak of him as primate, yet never do I stick thereon with reasoning and proving of that point. . . . But whereas I had written thereof at length in my *Confutation* before, and for the proof thereof had compiled together all that I could find therefor, at such time as I little looked that there should fall between the King's Highness and the Pope such a breach as is fallen since, when I after that saw the thing likely to draw toward such displeasure between them, I suppressed it utterly, and never put word thereof into my book, but put out the remnant without it, which thing well declareth that I never intended anything to meddle in that matter against the king's gracious pleasure, whatsoever mine own opinion were therein.

Thomas Stapleton, an English exile living at Louvain and an ardent Counter-Reformation polemicist, wrote in 1588 a Latin biography, really a saint's life, of his hero Thomas More. In this work he printed several of More's letters, including this one to Cromwell, but he deleted, without any indication to his readers, the passage quoted above, in which More had expressed his anticentralist views of the papacy.

The three letters which follow were written at approximately the same time, March of 1534. The first, it will be recalled, did not appear in the 1557 edition of More's English works.

The text here is based on Bishop Burnet's transcription of a manuscript copy of the letter in his History of the Reformation, *V, pp. 431–39.*

TO THOMAS CROMWELL

Right Worshipful,

After my most hearty recommendation, with like thanks for your goodness in the accepting of my rude,° long letter, I perceive that of your further goodness and favor toward me, it liked your Mastership to break with° my son Roper° of that, that I had had communication, not only with divers that were

---

rude unpolished   **break with** discuss with   **my son Roper** More's son-in-law, William Roper, who had married his eldest daughter, Margaret. Roper, some twenty years after the death of his father-in-law, wrote a brief biography which he turned over to Nicholas Harpsfield, who made extensive use of it in his biography.

of acquaintance with the lewd° nun of Canterbury, but also with herself; and had, over that, by my writing, declaring favor toward her, given her advice and counsel; of which my demeanor° that it liketh you to be content to take the labor and the pain to hear by mine own writing the truth, I very heartily thank you, and reckon myself therein right deeply beholden to you.

It is, I suppose, about eight or nine years ago since I heard of that huswife° first; at which time the Bishop of Canterbury that then was, God assoil° his soul, sent unto the King's Grace a roll of paper in which were written certain words of hers that she had, as report was then made, at sundry times spoken in her trances. Whereupon it pleased the King's Grace to deliver me the roll, commanding me to look thereon and afterward show him what I thought therein. Whereunto, at another time when his Highness asked me, I told him that, in good faith, I found nothing in these words that I could anything regard or esteem, for saving that some part fell in rhyme, and that God wot,° full rude, else for any reason, God wot, that I saw therein, a right simple woman might, in my mind, speak it of her own wit° well enough; howbeit, I said that because it was constantly reported for a truth that God wrought in her and that a miracle was showed upon her, I durst not nor would not be bold in judging the matter. And the King's Grace, as methought, esteemed the matter as light as it after proved lewd.°

From that time till about Christmas was twelvemonth, albeit that continually there was much talking of her and of her holiness, yet never heard I any talk rehearsed, either of revelation of hers or miracle, saving that I had heard some times in my Lord Cardinal's° days that she had been both with his lordship and with the King's Grace; but what she said either to the one or to the other, upon my faith, I had never heard any one word.

Now as I was about to tell you, about Christmas was twelvemonth, Father Resby, Friar Observant, then of Canterbury, lodged one night at mine house, where, after supper, a little before he went to his chamber, he fell in communication with me of the nun, giving her high commendation of holiness, and that it was wonderful to see and understand the works that God wrought in her; which thing, I answered, that I was very glad to hear it and thanked God thereof.

Then he told me that she had been with my Lord Legate°

lewd can mean ignorant or villainous, or both   of which my demeanor of which conduct   huswife a term of abuse meaning impertinent woman assoil cleanse, save   wot knows   wit mind   lewd bad   my Lord Cardinal Cardinal Wolsey. More succeeded him as chancellor in 1529   my Lord Legate Wolsey, along with his many other offices, was also papal legate *a latere*

in his life and with the King's Grace too, and that she had told
my Lord Legate a revelation of hers, of three swords that God
hath put in my Lord Legate's hand, which, if he ordered not
well, God would lay it sore to his charge. The first, he said, was
the ordering of the spiritualty° under the Pope, as legate; the
second, the rule that he bare in order of the temporalty° under
the king, as his chancellor. And the third, she said, was the
meddling he was put in trust with by the king concerning the
great matter of his marriage. And therewithal I said unto him
that any revelation of the king's matters I would not hear of.°
I doubt not but the goodness of God should direct his Highness with his grace and wisdom, that the thing should take such
end as God should be pleased with, to the king's honor and
surety° of the realm. When he heard me say these words or
the like, he said unto me that God had specially commanded
her to pray for the king. And forthwith he brake again° into
her revelations concerning the cardinal, that his soul was saved
by her mediation, and without any other communication went
into his chamber. And he and I never talked any more of any
such manner of matter, nor since his departing on the morrow
I never saw him after, to my remembrance, till I saw him at
Paul's Cross.°

After this, about Shrovetide, there came unto me a little
before supper Father Rich, Friar Observant of Richmond. And
as we fell in talking, I asked him of Father Resby, how he did?
And upon that occasion, he asked me whether Father Resby
had anything showed me of the holy nun of Kent. And I said
yea, and that I was very glad to hear of her virtue. "I would
not," quoth he, "tell you again that [which] you have heard of
him already, but I have heard and known many great graces
that God hath wrought in her and in other folk by her, which
I would gladly tell you if I thought you had not heard them
already." And therewith he asked me whether Father Resby
had told me anything of her being with my Lord Cardinal. And
I said yea. "Then he told you," quoth he, "of the three swords";
"yea, verily," quod I. "Did he tell you," quoth he, "of the revelations that she had concerning the King's Grace?" "Nay, forsooth," quoth I, "nor if he would have done I would not have
given him the hearing; nor verily no more I would indeed, for
since she hath been with the King's Grace herself and told,

---

spiritualty clergy   **temporalty** laity   **I would not hear of** it was precisely this act of prudence which enabled More to escape indictment for
misprision of treason   **surety** security   **brake again** discussed again
Paul's Cross the nun and those who had aided her publicly confessed
before St. Paul's Cathedral, November, 1533

methought it a thing needless to tell the matter to me or any man else."

And when Father Rich perceived that I would not hear her revelations concerning the King's Grace, he talked on a little of her virtue and let her revelations alone; and therewith my supper was set upon the board, where I required° him to sit with me, but he would in no wise tarry, but departed to London. After that night I talked with him twice, once in mine own house, another time in his own garden at the Friars, at every time a great space, but not of any revelation touching the King's Grace, but only of other mean folk,° I knew not whom, of which things some were very strange and some were very childish. But albeit that he said that he had seen her lie in her trance in great pains and that he had at other times taken great spiritual comfort in her communication, yet did he never tell me she had told him those tales herself; for if he had, I would, for the tale of Mary Magdalene° which he told me, and for the tale of the host, with which, as I heard, she said she was houseled° at the king's mass at Calais—if I had heard it of him as told unto himself by her mouth for a revelation, I would have both liked him and her the worse. But whether ever I heard that same tale of Rich or of Resby or of neither of them both, but of some other man since she was in hold,° in good faith I cannot tell. But I wot well when or wheresoever I heard it, methought it a tale too marvelous to be true, and very likely that she had told some man her dream, who told it out for a revelation. And, in effect, I little doubted but that some of these tales that were told of her were untrue. But yet, since I never heard them reported as spoken by her own mouth, I thought, nevertheless, that many of them might be true and she a very virtuous woman too, as some lies, peradventure,° written of some that be saints in heaven, and yet many miracles indeed done by them for all that.

After this, I being upon a day at Sion talking with divers of the fathers together at the grate, they showed me that she had been with them, and showed me divers things that some of them misliked in her and in this talking. They wished that I had spoken with her and said they would fain see how I should like her. Whereupon, afterward, when I heard that she was there again, I came thither to see her and to speak with her myself. At which communication had, in a little chapel, there were

---

required asked   **mean folk** unimportant, unknown people of low degree
tale . . . Magdalene refers to a letter purportedly written in heaven by
Mary Magdalene. The nun later revealed its true author, an Augustinian
monk   **houseled** communicated, i.e., received the sacrament of the Eucharist   **in hold** in custody   **peradventure** perhaps

none present but we two. In the beginning whereof I showed that my coming to her was not of any curious mind, anything to know of such things as folk talked that it pleased God to reveal and show unto her, but for the great virtue that I had heard for so many years, every day more and more, spoken and reported of her, I therefore had a great mind to see her, and be acquainted with her, that she might have somewhat the more occasion to remember me to God in her devotion and prayers. Whereunto she gave me a very good, virtuous answer, that as God did of his goodness far better by her than such a poor wretch was worthy, so she feared that many folk yet beside that spake of their own favorable minds many things for her, far above the truth, and that of me she had many such things heard that already she prayed for me and ever would, whereof I heartily thanked her.

I said unto her, "Madam, one Helen, a maiden dwelling about Totnam, of whose trances and revelations there hath been much talking, she hath been with me lately and showed me that she was with you, and that after the rehearsal of such visions as she had seen, you showed her that they were no revelations, but plain illusions of the devil, and advised her to cast them out of her mind, and verily she gave therein good credence unto you and thereupon hath left to lean° any longer unto such visions of her own. Whereupon she saith she findeth your words true, for ever since she hath been the less visited with such things as she was wont to be before."

To this she answered me, "Forsooth, sir, there is in this point no praise unto me, but the goodness of God, as it appeareth, hath wrought much meekness in her soul, which hath taken my rude warning so well and not grudged to hear her spirit and her visions reproved." I liked her, in good faith, better for this answer than for many of those things that I heard reported by° her. Afterward she told me, upon that occasion, how great need folk have that are visited with such visions to take heed and prove well of what spirit they come of, and in the communication she told me that of late the devil, in likeness of a bird, was flying and flickering about her in a chamber and suffered himself to be taken; and being in hands suddenly changed, in their sight that were present, into such a strange, ugly-fashioned bird that they were all afraid and threw him out at a window.

For conclusion, we talked no word of the King's Grace or any great personage else, nor, in effect, of any man or woman, but of herself and myself, but after no long communication had, for, or ever we met,° my time came to go home. I gave

left to lean given up leaning   reported by reported about   after no long . . . met we talked briefly, for I had to leave soon after we met

her a double ducat and prayed her to pray for me and mine, and so departed from her and never spake with her after. Howbeit, of truth I had a great good opinion of her, and had her in great estimation, as you shall perceive by the letter that I wrote unto her. For afterward, because I had often heard that many right worshipful folks, as well men as women, used to have much communication with her, and many folk are of nature inquisitive and curious, whereby they fall sometime into such talking, as better were to forbear, of which thing I nothing thought while I talked with her, of charity. Therefore, I wrote her a letter thereof, which since it may be, peradventure, that she brake° or lost, I shall insert the very copy thereof in this present letter. [*Here More gives the full text of the letter he had written to Elizabeth Barton.*]

At the receipt of this letter she answered my servant that she heartily thanked me. Soon after this, there came to mine house the proctor of the Charterhouse at Sheen, and one Brother William with him, who nothing talked with me but of her and of the great joy that they took in her virtue, but of any of her revelations they had no communication. But at another time, Brother William came to me and told me a long tale of her, being at the house of a knight in Kent that was sore troubled with temptation to destroy himself. And none other thing we talked of, nor should have done of likelihood, though we had tarried together much longer. He took so great pleasure, good man, to tell that tale with all the circumstances at length.

When I came again another time to Sion, on a day in which there was a profession,° some of the fathers asked me how I liked the nun. And I answered that, in good faith, I liked her very well in her talking. "Howbeit," quoth I, "she is never the nearer tried by that, for I assure you she were likely to be very bad, if she seemed good, ere I should think her other, till she happed to be proved naught." And, in good faith, that is my manner indeed, except I were set to search and examine the truth upon likelihood of some cloaked evil. For in that case, although I nothing suspected the person myself, yet no less than if I suspected him sore, I would as far as my wit would serve me, search to find out the truth as yourself hath done very prudently in this matter. Wherein you have done, in my mind, to your great laud and praise, a very meritorious deed in bringing forth to light such detestable hypocrisy, whereby every other wretch may take warning and be feared to set forth their own devilish dissimuled° falsehood, under the manner and color of the wonderful work of God; for, verily, this woman so handled herself,

---

brake destroyed   **profession** the taking of the three religious vows— poverty, chastity, and obedience   **dissimuled** dissembled

with help of the evil spirit that inspired her, that after her own
confession declared at Paul's Cross, when I sent word by my
servant unto the proctor of the Charterhouse that she was undoubtedly proved a false, deceiving hypocrite, the good man
had had so good opinion of her so long that he could at the first
scantly believe me therein. Howbeit it was not he alone that
thought her so very good, but many another right good man
besides, as little marvel was upon so good report, till she was
proved naught.°

I remember me further that in communication between
Father Rich and me, I counseled him that in such strange things
as concerned such folk as had come unto her, to whom, as she
said, she had told the causes of their coming ere themselves
spake thereof; and such good fruit as they said that many men
had received by her prayer he and such other as so reported it,
and thought that the knowledge thereof should much pertain
to the glory of God should first cause the things to be well and
surely examined by the ordinaries,° and such as had authority
thereunto; so that it might be surely known whether the things
were true or not, and that there were no lies intermingled among
them or else the lies might after hap to [take] away the credence
of those things that were true. And when he told me the tale
of Mary Magdalene, I said unto him, "Father Rich, that she
is a good virtuous woman, in good faith, I hear so many good
folk so report her that I verily think it true, and think it well
likely that God worketh some good and great things by her. But
yet are, you wot well, these strange tales no part of our creed.
And, therefore, before you see them surely proved, you shall
have my poor counsel not to wed yourself so far forth to the
credence of them as to report them very surely for true, lest
that if it should hap that they were afterward proved false, it
might diminish your estimation in your preaching, whereof
might grow great loss." To this he thanked me for my counsel,
but how he used it after that, I cannot tell.

Thus have I, good Master Cromwell, fully declared you, as
far as myself can call to remembrance, all that ever I have done
or said in this matter, wherein I am sure that never one of them
all shall tell you any further thing of effect, for if any of them,
or any man else, report of me as I trust verily no man will, and
I wot well truly no man can, any word or deed by me spoken
or done touching any breach of my loyal troth and duty toward
my most redoubted sovereign and natural liege lord, I will come
to mine answer, and make it good in such wise as becometh a
poor true man to do, that whosoever any such thing shall say

naught bad   **ordinaries** bishops or archbishops in charge of dioceses

shall therein say untrue. For I neither have in this matter done evil nor said evil, nor so much as any evil thing thought, but only have been glad, and rejoiced of them that were reported for good, which condition I shall, nevertheless, keep toward all other good folk, for the false, cloaked hypocrisy of any of these, no more than I shall esteem Judas the true Apostle for Judas the false traitor.

But so purpose I to bear myself in every man's company, while I live, that neither good man nor bad, neither monk, friar, nor nun, nor other man or woman in this world shall make me digress from my troth and faith, either toward God or toward my natural prince, by the grace of Almighty God. And as you therein find me true, so I heartily therein pray you to continue toward me your favor and good will, as you shall be sure of my poor daily prayer, for other pleasure can I none do you. And thus the blessed Trinity, both bodily and ghostly, long preserve and prosper you.

I pray you pardon me that I write not unto you of mine own hand, for verily I am compelled to forbear writing for a while by reason of this disease of mine, whereof the chief occasion is grown, as it is thought, by the stooping and leaning on my breast that I have used in writing. And this, eftsoons,° I beseech our Lord long to preserve you.

TO HENRY VIII

[February or March, 1533]

It may like your Highness to call your gracious remembrance that at such time as of that great weighty room° and office of your chancellor° (with which so far above my merits or qualities able and meet therefor your Highness had of your incomparable goodness honored and exalted me), ye were so good and gracious unto me as at my poor humble suit to discharge and disburden me, giving me license with your gracious favor to bestow the residue of my life in mine age now to come, about the provision for my soul in the service of God, and to be your Grace's beadsman° and pray for you. It pleased your Highness further to say unto me that for the service which I

---

eftsoons again   **room** synonymous with office   **office . . . chancellor** More had resigned this office in May, 1532, giving poor health as his reason. The king's increasing militancy and impatience on the question of the divorce had, however, made More's position difficult, if not impossible.   **beadsman** one who prays for another

before had done you (which it then liked your goodness far above my deserving to commend) that in any suit that I should after have unto your Highness which either should concern mine honor (that word it liked your Highness to use unto me) or that should pertain unto my profit, I should find your Highness good and gracious lord unto me. So is it now, gracious sovereign, that worldly honor is the thing whereof I have resigned both the possession and the desire, in the resignation of your most honorable office; and worldly profit, I trust experience proveth, and daily more and more shall prove, that I never was very greedy thereon.

But now is my most humble suit unto your excellent Highness, partly to beseech the same, somewhat to tender my poor honesty, but principally that of your accustomed goodness, no sinister information move your noble Grace to have any more distrust of my truth and devotion toward you than I have, or shall during my life give the cause. For in this matter of the wicked woman of Canterbury° I have unto your trusty counselor, Master Thomas Cromwell, by my writing, as plainly declared the truth as I possibly can, which my declaration of his duty toward your Grace and his goodness toward me he hath, I understand, declared unto your Grace. In any part of all which my dealing, whether any other man may peradventure put any doubt, or move any scruple of suspicion, that can I neither tell, nor lieth in mine hand to let,° but unto myself is it not possible any part of my said demeanor° to seem evil, the very clearness of mine own conscience knoweth in all the matter my mind and intent so good.

Wherefore most gracious sovereign, I neither will nor well it can become me with your Highness to reason and argue the matter, but in my most humble manner prostrate at your gracious feet, I only beseech your Majesty with your own high prudence and your accustomed goodness consider and weigh the matter. And then, if in your so doing, your own virtuous mind shall give you that, notwithstanding the manifold excellent goodness that your gracious Highness hath by so many manner ways used unto me, I be a wretch of such monstrous ingratitude as could with any of them all, or with any other person living, digress from my bounden duty of allegiance toward your good Grace, then desire I no further favor at your gracious hand than the loss of all that ever I may lose in this world: goods, lands, and liberty, and finally my life withal,

---

wicked woman of Canterbury the nun, Elizabeth Barton. This is one of the phrases that Rastell, in the 1557 edition, changed to read "the nun." See the introduction to the preceding letter. **let** prevent **demeanor** behavior

whereof the keeping of any part unto myself could never do me pennyworth of pleasure, but only should then my recomfort be that after my short life and your long, which with continual prosperity to God's pleasure our Lord for his mercy send you, I should once meet with your Grace again in heaven, and there be merry with you, where among mine other pleasures this should yet be one, that your Grace should surely see there then that (howsoever you take me) I am your true beadsman now and ever have been, and will be till I die, howsoever your pleasure be to do by me. . . .

Your most humble and most heavy° faithful subject and beadsman,

Thomas More, Knight.

TO THOMAS CROMWELL

Right Worshipful.

After my most hearty recommendation, it may please you to understand that I have perceived by the relation of my son Roper (for which I beseech almighty God reward you) your most charitable labor taken for me toward the king's gracious Highness, in the procuring at his most gracious hand, the relief and comfort of this woeful heaviness in which mine heart standeth, neither for the loss of goods, lands, or liberty, nor for any respect either, of this kind of honesty° that standeth in the opinion of people and worldly reputation, all which manner things (I thank our Lord), I so little esteem for any affection therein toward myself that I can well be content to jeopardize, lose, and forgo them all and my life therewith, without any further respite than even this same present day, either for the pleasure of God or of my prince.

But surely, good Master Cromwell, as I by mouth declared unto you, some part (for all could I neither then say nor now write) it thoroughly pierceth my poor heart that the king's Highness (whose gracious favor toward me far above all the things of this world I have evermore desired, and whereof both for the conscience of mine own true, faithful heart and devotion toward him, and for the manifold benefits of his high goodness continually bestowed upon me, I thought myself always sure), should conceive any such mind or opinion of me as to think that in my communication either with the nun or the friars, or in my letter written unto the nun, I had any other

heavy sad   **honesty** honor

manner mind than might well stand with the duty of a tender, loving subject toward his natural prince, or that his Grace should reckon in me any manner of obstinate heart against his pleasure in anything that ever I said or did concerning his great matter of his marriage or concerning the primacy of the pope. Never would I wish other thing in this world more lief° than that his Highness in these things all three as perfectly knew my dealing and as thoroughly saw my mind as I do myself, or as God himself, whose sight pierceth deeper into my heart than mine own.

For, sir, as for the first matter, that is to wit, my letter or communication with the nun (the whole discourse whereof in my former letter I have as plainly declared unto you as I possibly can), so pray I God to withdraw that scruple and doubt of my good mind out of the king's noble breast and none other wise, but as I not only thought none harm, but also purposed good, and in that thing most in which (as I perceive) his Grace conceiveth most grief and suspicion, that is to wit, in my letter which I wrote unto her. And therefore, sir, since I have by my writing declared the truth of my deed, and am ready by mine oath to declare the truth of mine intent, I can devise no further thing by me to be done in that matter, but only beseech almighty God to put into the king's gracious mind that, as God knoweth the thing is indeed, so his noble Grace may take it.

Now touching the second point concerning his Grace's great matter of his marriage, to the intent that you may see cause with the better conscience to make suit unto his Highness for me, I shall as plainly declare you my demeanor in that matter as I have already declared you in the other, for more plainly can I not.

Sir, upon a time at my coming from beyond the sea where I had been in the king's business, I repaired as my duty was unto the King's Grace, being at that time at Hampton Court. At which time suddenly his Highness, walking in the gallery, brake with me of his great matter, and showed me that it was now perceived that his marriage was not only against the positive law of the Church and the written law of God, but also in such wise against the law of nature that it could in no wise by the Church be dispensable. Now so was it that before my going over the sea, I had heard certain things moved against the bull of the dispensation° concerning the words of the Law Levitical and the Law Deuteronomical to prove the prohibition to be

lief dearly   bull . . . dispensation the papal bull allowing Henry to marry Catharine, the widow of his brother Arthur. The validity or invalidity of this dispensation was the core of the question.

de iure divino,° but yet perceived I not at that time but that the greater hope of the matter stood in certain faults that were found in the bull, whereby the bull should by the law not be sufficient. And such comfort was there in that point as far as I perceived a good season,° that the council on the other part were fain° to bring forth a brief by which they pretended those defaults to be supplied, the truth of which brief was by the king's council suspected, and much diligence was thereafter done for the trial of that point, wherein what was finally found either I never knew or else I not remember.

But I rehearse you this to the intent you shall know that the first time that ever I heard that point moved that it should be in such high degree against the law of nature, was the time in which, as I began to tell you, the King's Grace showed it [to] me himself, and laid the Bible open before me and there read me the words that moved his Highness and divers other erudite persons so to think, and asked me further what myself thought thereon. At which time, not presuming to look that his Highness should anything take that point for the more proved or unproved for my poor mind in so great a matter, I showed, nevertheless, as my duty was at his commandment, what thing I thought upon the words which I there read. Whereupon his Highness accepting benignly my sudden, unadvised answer, commanded me to commune further with Master Fox, now his Grace's Almoner,° and to read a book with him that then was in making for that matter.° After which book read, and my poor opinion eftsoons declared unto his Highness thereupon, his Highness, like a prudent and a virtuous prince, assembled at another time at Hampton Court a good number of very well-learned men, at which time as far as ever I heard, there were (as was in so great a matter most likely to be) diverse opinions among them. Howbeit, I never heard but that they agreed at that time upon a certain form in which the book should be made, which book was afterward at York Place, in my Lord Cardinal's chamber, read in the presence of divers bishops and many learned men. And they all thought that there appeared in the book good and reasonable causes that might well move the King's Highness, being so virtuous a prince, to conceive in his mind a scruple against his marriage, which, while he could not otherwise avoid, he did well and virtuously for the quieting of his conscience to sue and procure to have his doubt decided by judgment of the Church.

de iure divino a matter of divine law, in which case not even the pope could dispense from it   **season** time, while   **fain** willing   **Almoner** one who distributes alms   **book . . . matter** a compilation of learned opinions, gathered from all over Europe, contending that a man might not marry his brother's wife and could not be dispensed therefrom.

After this the suit began, and the legates sat upon the matter, during all which time I never meddled therein, nor was a man meet to do, for the matter was in hand by an ordinary process of the spiritual, whereof I could little skill. And yet while the legates were sitting upon the matter, it pleased the King's Highness to send me in the company of my Lord of London, now of Durham,° in embassy about the peace that at our being there was concluded at Cambrai between his Highness and the emperor and the French king. And after my coming home, his Highness of his only goodness° (as far unworthy as I was thereto) made me, as you well know, his chancellor of this realm, soon after which time his Grace moved me again yet eftsoons to look and consider his great matter, and well and indifferently° to ponder such things as I should find therein. And if it so were that thereupon it should hap me to see such things as should persuade me to that part, he would gladly use me among other of his councillors in that matter, and nevertheless he graciously declared unto me that he would in no wise that I should other thing do or say therein, than upon that that I should perceive mine own conscience should serve me, and that I should first look unto God and after God unto him, which most gracious words was the first lesson also that ever his Grace gave me at my first coming into his noble service. This motion was to me very comfortable and much I longed beside anything that myself either had seen, or by further search should hap to find for the one part or the other, yet specially to have some conference in the matter with some such of his Grace's learned council as most for his part had labored and most have found in the matter.

Whereupon his Highness assigned unto me the now most reverend fathers Archbishops of Canterbury and York, with Master Doctor Fox, now his Grace's Almoner, and Master Doctor Nicholas the Italian friar, whereupon I not only sought and read, and as farforth as my poor wit and learning served me, well weighed and considered every such thing as I could find myself, or read in any other man's labor that I could get, which anything had written therein, but had also diligent conference with his Grace's councillors aforesaid, whose honors and worships I nothing mistrust in this point, but that they both have and will report unto his Highness that they never found obstinate manner or fashion in me, but a mind as toward° and as conformable as reason could in a matter disputable require.

Durham Cuthbert Tunstall, humanist, statesman, bishop, friend of More, whom he commissioned to write against heretics   **only goodness** goodness alone   **indifferently** objectively   **toward** open, tractable

Whereupon the King's Highness being further advertised°
both by them and myself of my poor opinion in the matter
(wherein to have been able and meet to do him service I would,
as I then showed his Highness, have been more glad than of all
such worldly commodities° as I either then had or ever should
come to) his Highness graciously taking in gre° my good mind
in that behalf, used of his blessed disposition in the prosecuting
of his great matter only those (of whom his Grace had good
number) whose conscience his Grace perceived well and fully
persuaded upon that part, and as well myself as any other to
whom his Highness thought the thing to seem otherwise, he
used in his other business, abiding (of his abundant goodness),
nevertheless, gracious lord unto any man, nor never was willing to put any man in ruffle or trouble of his conscience.

After this did I never nothing more therein, nor never any
word wrote I therein to the impairing of his Grace's part, neither
before nor after, nor any man else by my procurement, but
settling my mind in quiet to serve his Grace in other things,
I would not so much as look nor wittingly° let lie by me any
book of the other part, albeit that I gladly read afterward divers
books that were made on his part yet, nor never would I read
the book that Master Abell° made on the other side, nor other
book which were, as I heard say, made in Latin beyond the
sea, nor never give ear to the Pope's proceedings in the matter.

Moreover, whereas I had founden in my study a book that
I had before borrowed of my Lord of Bath, which book he had
made of the matter at such time as the legates sat here thereupon, which book had been by me merely gently cast aside,
and that I showed him I would send him home his book again,
he told me that in good faith he had long time before discharged his mind of that matter, and having forgotten that copy
to remain in my hands, had burned his own copy that he had
thereof at home, and because he no more minded to meddle
anything in the matter, he desired me to burn the same book
too. And upon my faith, so did I.

Besides this, divers other ways have I so used myself that if
I rehearsed them all, it should well appear that I never have had
against his Grace's marriage any manner demeanor whereby
his Highness might have any manner cause or occasion of displeasure toward me, for likewise as I am not he which either
can, or whom it could become to take upon him the determina-
tion or decision of such a weighty matter, nor boldly to affirm
this thing or that therein, whereof divers points a great way
pass my learning, so am I he that among other his Grace's

advertised notified   **commodities** benefits   **in gre** in good grace   **wittingly** knowingly   **Master Abell** Queen Catharine's chaplain

faithful subjects, his Highness being in possession of his marriage and this noble woman royally° anointed queen, neither murmur at it nor dispute upon it, nor never did nor will, but without any other manner meddling of the matter among his other faithful subjects faithfully pray to God for his Grace and hers both, long to live and well and their noble issue too, in such wise as may be to the pleasure of God, honor and surety to themselves, rest, peace, wealth, and profit unto this noble realm.

As touching the third point, the primacy of the pope, I nothing meddle in the matter. Truth it is, that as I told you, when you desired me to show you what I thought therein, I was myself sometime not of the mind that the primacy of that See should be begun by the institution of God, until that I read in that matter those things that the King's Highness had written in his most famous book against the heresies of Martin Luther,° at the first reading whereof I moved the King's Highness either to leave out that point, or else to touch it more slenderly for doubt of such things as after might hap to fall in question between his Highness and some pope as between princes and popes divers times have done. Whereunto his Highness answered me that he would in no wise anything minish° of that matter, of which thing his Highness showed me a secret cause whereof I never had anything heard before. But surely, after that I had read his Grace's book therein, and so many other things as I have seen in that point by this continuance of these ten year since and more have found in effect the substance of all the holy doctors from St. Ignatius, disciple to St. John the Evangelist, unto our own days, both Latins and Greeks so consonant and agreeing in that point, and the thing by such general councils so confirmed also, that in good faith I never neither read nor heard anything of such effect on the other side that ever could lead me to think that my conscience were well discharged, but rather in right great peril if I should follow the other side and deny the primacy to be provided by God, which if we did, yet can I nothing (as I showed you) perceive any commodity° that ever could come by that denial, for that primacy is at the leastwise instituted by the corps of Christen-

---

royally spelled "rially" in the original. Elizabeth Rogers, editor of More's correspondence, modernizes the original to read "really," adding the comment that More's spelling was possibly intended to be ambiguous. The weight of usage lies on the side of taking "rially" to mean "royally." **book . . . against Luther** Henry wrote in Latin a *Defense of the Seven Sacraments*, published in 1521. As a reward for his efforts the pope bestowed upon him and his successors the title of Defender of the Faith, a title still borne by the reigning monarch of England. **minish** diminish, tone down **commodity** benefit

dom, and for a great urgent cause in avoiding of schisms, and corroborated by continual succession more than the space of a thousand years at the least, for there are passed almost a thousand years since the time of holy St. Gregory.°

And, therefore, since all Christendom is one corps, I cannot perceive how any member thereof may without the common assent of the body depart from the common head. And then if we may not lawfully leave it by ourselves, I cannot perceive (but if° the thing were a treating° in a general council) what the question could avail whether the primacy were instituted by God or ordained by the Church. As for the general councils assembled lawfully, I never could perceive but that in the declaration of the truths to be believed and to be standen to,° the authority thereof ought to be taken for undoubtable, or else were there in nothing no certainty, but through Christendom upon every man's affectionate reason, all things might be brought from day to day to continual ruffle and confusion, from which by the general councils, the spirit of God assisting, every such council well assembled keepeth and ever shall keep the corps of his Catholic Church.

And verily since the King's Highness hath (as by the book of his honorable council appeareth) appealed to the general council from the Pope, in which council I beseech our Lord send his Grace comfortable speed, methinketh in my poor mind it could be no furtherance there unto his Grace's cause if his Highness should in his own realm before, either by laws making or books putting forth, seem to derogate and deny not only the primacy of the See Apostolic, but also the authority of the general councils too, which I verily trust his Highness intendeth not, for in the next general council it may well happen that this pope may be deposed and another substituted in his room° with whom the King's Highness may be very well content; for albeit that I have for mine own part such opinion of the pope's primacy as I have showed you, yet never thought I the pope above the general council,° nor never have in any book of mine put forth among the king's subjects in our vulgar tongue, advanced greatly the pope's authority. For albeit that a man may peradventure somewhat find therein that after the common manner of all Christian realms I speak of him as primate, yet never do I stick° thereon with reasoning and proving of that

St. Gregory Pope Gregory the Great, 590–604   **but if** unless   **a treating** under discussion   **standen to** followed   **room** office   **yet never thought I the pope above the general council** Stapleton, in his biography of More, published in 1588, printed this along with several other letters written by More. He deleted this clause, however, from his version of this letter. **stick** dwell

point. And in my book against the Masker,° I wrote not I wot well five lines, and yet of no more but only St. Peter himself, from whose person many take not the primacy, even of those that grant it none of his successors, and yet was that book made, printed, and put forth of very truth before that any of the books of the council was either printed or spoken of. But whereas I had written thereof at length in my *Confutation* before, and for the proof thereof had compiled together all that I could find therefor, at such time as I little looked that there should fall between the King's Highness and the Pope such a breach as is fallen since, when I after that saw the thing likely to draw toward such displeasure between them, I suppressed it utterly and never put word thereof into my book, but put out the remnant without it, which thing well declareth that I never intended anything to meddle in that matter against the king's gracious pleasure, whatsoever mine own opinion were therein.

And thus have I, good Master Cromwell, long troubled your mastership with a long process° of these matters, with which I neither durst nor it could become me to encumber the king's noble Grace, but I beseech you for our Lord's love, that you be not so weary of my most cumbrous suit, but that it may like° you at such opportune time or times as your wisdom may find to help, that his Highness may by your goodness be fully informed of my true faithful mind, and that in the matter of that wicked woman° there never was on my part any other mind than good, nor yet in any other thing else never was there nor never shall there be any further fault found in me, than that I cannot in everything think the same way that some other men of more wisdom and deeper learning do, nor can find in mine heart otherwise to say than as mine own conscience giveth me, which condition hath never grown in anything that ever might touch his gracious pleasure of any obstinate mind or misaffectionate appetite, but of a timorous conscience rising haply° for lack of better perceiving, and yet not without tender respect unto my most bounden duty toward his noble Grace, whose only favor I so much esteem that I nothing have of mine own in all this world, except only my soul, but that I will with better will forgo it than abide of his Highness one heavy displeasant look. And thus I make an end of my long, troublous

---

Masker this refers to More's *The Answer to a Poisoned Book*, 1533 **process** presentation, rehearsal **like** please **wicked woman** the editor of the 1557 edition of the *English Workes*, More's nephew Rastell, substituted the words "the nun" for "wicked woman." The reference is to Elizabeth Barton, the nun of Kent. **haply** by chance

process, beseeching the blessed Trinity for the great goodness ye show me, and the great comfort ye do me, both bodily and ghostly° to prosper you, and in heaven to reward you.

Your deeply bounden,

Tho. More, Knight.

TO NICHOLAS WILSON

Doctor Nicholas Wilson, at one time chaplain and confessor to Henry VIII, could not find it in his conscience to sign the oath admitting Henry's first marriage to Catharine to be invalid. He was, consequently, like More, and at the same time, imprisoned in the Tower. During this time he wrote to More seeking advice as to what he should do about the oath. (He eventually signed it.) More, adhering rigidly to his decision to keep his thoughts to himself and to advise or condemn no one, refused to counsel Wilson. The following is an excerpt from one of the letters More wrote to Wilson, an excerpt which makes clear the morally and legally delicate position More had chosen to occupy.

. . . As touching the oath, the causes for which I refused it, no man wotteth° what they be, for they be secret in mine own conscience, some other peradventure than those that other men would ween° and such as I never disclosed unto any man yet, nor never intend to do while I live. Finally, as I said unto you, before the oath offered unto us when we met in London at adventure, I would be no part taker in the matter, but for mine own self follow mine own conscience, for which myself must make answer unto God, and shall leave every other man to his own, so say to you still and I dare say further that no more you never intended neither. Many things every learned man wotteth well there are in which every man is at liberty without peril of damnation to think which way him list° till the one part be determined for necessary to be believed by a general council. And I am not he that take upon me to define or determine of what kind or nature everything is that the oath containeth, nor am so bold or presumptuous to blame or dispraise the conscience of other men, their truth nor their learn-

---

ghostly spiritually   **wotteth** knows   **peradventure . . . ween** my reasons are possibly quite different from what men think them to be   **which way . . . list** whichever way pleases him, whichever way he decides

ing neither, nor I meddle with no man but of myself, nor of no man's conscience else will I meddle but of mine own. And in mine own conscience I cry God mercy, I find of mine own life, matters enough to think on.

THE MARGARET LETTERS

Among the most moving and revealing documents in the More canon are the letters he wrote from prison to his oldest daughter, his beloved Meg, the wife of William Roper. Over and above their value as sources of information about the state of More's mind and conscience on the great issue which was eventually to lead him to his death, these letters contain passages which can stand comparison with any in the language for what they reveal in quietly eloquent prose of the depths of More's love for his family and friends. These letters, written by a man weakened by illness, dejected by the rigors of imprisonment, and terrified at the prospects of the hideously cruel death he anticipated, disclose a Thomas More who was, nonetheless, filled with a joyous love of life and people. They reveal, in short, a very human Thomas More.

More's refusal to sign the oath of supremacy marked the beginning of the last tragic phase of his career. Imprisonment was inevitable and execution probable. The following letter to his beloved Meg was written in April, 1534, after his refusal, and its tone, unlike that of his other letters to her, is documentary. More, the lawyer and judge, wishes to make a record, to set down in writing his own official version of the incident which was the beginning of the end. This letter contains a defense, rare for the sixteenth century, of the autonomy and sanctity of an individual's conscience.

For a full account of the last fifteen months of More's life, one should consult E. E. Reynolds' The Trial of St. Thomas More *(New York, 1964).*

When I was before the lords at Lambeth, I was the first that was called in, albeit Master Doctor the Vicar of Croyden was come before me, and divers others. After the cause of my sending for [was] declared unto me (whereof I somewhat marveled in my mind, considering that they sent for no more temporal men° but me), I desired the sight of the oath, which they showed me under the great seal. Then desired I the sight of the

temporal men laymen

Act of the Succession,° which was delivered me in a printed roll. After which read secretly by myself, and the oath considered with the act, I showed unto them that my purpose was not to put any fault either in the act or any man that made it, or in the oath or any man that swore it, nor to condemn the conscience of any other man. But as for myself, in good faith my conscience so moved me in the matter that, though I would not deny to swear to the succession, yet unto the oath that there was offered me I could not swear without the jeopardizing of my soul to perpetual damnation. And that if they doubted whether I did refuse the oath only for the grudge of my conscience° or for any other fantasy, I was ready therein to satisfy them by mine oath. Which if they trusted not, what should they be the better to give me any oath? And if they trusted that I would therein swear true, then trusted I that of their goodness they would not move me to swear the oath that they offered me, perceiving that for to swear it was against my conscience.

Unto this my Lord Chancellor° said that they all were sorry to hear me say thus, and see me refuse the oath. And they said all that on their faith I was the very first that ever refused it, which would cause the King's Highness to conceive great suspicion of me and great indignation toward me. And therewith they showed me the roll, and let me see the names of the lords and the commons who had sworn and subscribed their names already. Which notwithstanding, when they saw that I refused to swear the same myself, not blaming any other man that had sworn, I was, in conclusion, commanded to go down into the garden, and thereupon I tarried in the old burned chamber that looketh into the garden and would not go down because of the heat. In that time saw I Master Doctor Latimer come into the garden, and there walked he with divers other doctors and chaplains of my Lord of Canterbury, and very merry I saw him, for he laughed and took one or two about the neck so handsomely that if they had been women, I would have

---

Act of Succession passed in the January-March session of 1534, it nullified Henry's marriage to Catharine, declared valid his marriage to Anne Boleyn; any children born to this marriage were to be the legal heirs to the throne. Elizabeth, the future queen, had at this time already been born to Anne (September, 1533). More had no objection to Parliament's fixing the succession, but the validating and invalidating of marriages was, he felt, beyond the jurisdiction of any secular authority. To sign the oath attached to this Act of Succession was, consequently, to consent to a secular ruler's right to supersede the papacy in spiritual affairs. More, who was certainly no ultramontanist, could not in conscience agree to what he regarded as an illegal usurpation of authority. This was the nub of his disagreement with Henry. **only for . . . grudge of my conscience** only out of ill will **Chancellor** More's successor, Sir Thomas Audley

weened° he had been waxen wanton. After that came Master
Doctor Wilson forth from the lords and was with two gentlemen brought by me, and gentlemanly sent straight unto the
Tower. What time my Lord of Rochester was called in before
them, that can I not tell. But at night I heard that he had been
before them, but where he remained that night and so forth
till he was sent hither, I never heard. I heard also that Master
Vicar of Croyden, and all the remnant of the priests of London
that were sent for, were sworn, and that they had such favor
at the council's hand that they were not lingered° nor made to
dance any long attendance to their travail° and cost, as suitors
were sometime wont to be, but were sped apace to their great
comfort, so far forth that Master Vicar of Croyden, either for
gladness or for dryness, or else that it might be seen (*quod ille
notus erat pontifici*)° went to my lord's buttery bar, and called
for drink, and drank (*valde familiariter*).°

When they had played their pageant and were gone out of
the place, then was I called in again. And then was it declared
unto me what a number had sworn, even since I went aside,
gladly, without any sticking.° Wherein I laid no blame in no
man, but for mine own self answered as before. Now as well
before as then, they somewhat laid unto me for obstinacy, that
whereas before, since I refused to swear, I would not declare
any special part of that oath that grudged° my conscience, and
open the cause° wherefore. For thereunto I had said to them
that I feared lest the King's Highness would, as they said, take
displeasure enough toward me for the only refusal of the oath.
And that if I should open and disclose the causes why, I should
therewith but further exasperate his Highness, which I would
in no wise do, but rather would I abide all the danger and
harm that might come toward me, than give his Highness any
occasion of further displeasure, than the offering of the oath
unto me of pure necessity constrained me.

Howbeit, when they divers times imputed this to me for stubbornness and obstinacy that I would neither swear the oath
nor yet declare the causes why, I declared thus far toward them,
that rather than I would be accounted for obstinate, I would
upon the king's gracious license, or rather his such commandment had as might be my sufficient warrant,° that my declaration should not offend his Highness, nor put me in the danger
of any of his statutes, I would be content to declare the causes

---

weened thought   **lingered** delayed   **travail** hardship   **quod ... pontifici**
that he was known to the archbishop   **valde familiariter** very familiarly
sticking hesitation   **grudged** disturbed   **open the cause** reveal the reason
or rather ... warrant or having received such orders as would sufficiently
protect me

in writing; and over that to give an oath in the beginning, that if I might find those causes by any man in such wise answered, as I might think mine own conscience satisfied, I would after that with all mine heart swear the principal oath too.

To this I was answered that, though the king would give me license under his letters patent, yet it would not serve against the statute. Whereto I said, that yet if I had them, I would stand unto the trust of his honor at my peril for the remnant. But yet it thinketh me,° lo, that if I may not declare the causes without peril, then to leave them undeclared is no obstinacy.

My Lord of Canterbury, taking hold upon that that I said, that I condemned not the conscience of them that swore, said unto me that it appeared well that I did not take it for a very sure thing and a certain, that I might not lawfully swear it, but rather as a thing uncertain and doubtful. But then (said my Lord), you know for a certainty and a thing without doubt that you be bound to obey your sovereign lord your king. And therefore are ye bound to leave off the doubt of your unsure conscience in refusing the oath, and take the sure way in obeying of your prince, and swear it. Now all was it so that° in mine own mind me thought myself not concluded, yet this argument seemed [to] me suddenly so subtle and namely° with such authority coming out of so noble a prelate's mouth, that I could again answer nothing thereto but only that I thought myself I might not well do so, because that in my conscience this was one of the cases in which I was bound that I should not obey my prince, since that whatsoever other folk thought in the matter (whose conscience and learning I would not condemn or take upon me to judge), yet in my conscience the truth seemed on the other side. Wherein I had not informed my conscience neither suddenly nor slightly, but by long leisure and diligent search for the matter. And of truth if that reason may conclude, then have we a ready way to avoid all perplexities. For in whatsoever matters the doctors stand in great doubt, the king's commandment given upon whither side he list soileth° all the doubts.

Then said my Lord of Westminster to me, that howsoever the matter seemed unto mine own mind, I had cause to fear that mine own mind was erroneous, when I see the great council of the realm determine of my mind the contrary, and that therefore I ought to change my conscience. To that I answered, that if there were no more but myself upon my side, and the whole Parliament upon the other, I would be sore afraid to

---

it thinketh me it seems to me **now all . . . that** even though it was true that **namely** especially **upon whither . . . soileth** upon whichever side pleases him resolves all the doubts

lean to mine own mind only against so many. But on the other
side, if it so be, that in some things for which I refuse the oath,
I have (as I think I have) upon my part as great a council and
a greater too, I am not then bound to change my conscience,
and conform it to the council of one realm, against the general
council of Christendom. Upon this, Master Secretary° (as he
that tenderly favoreth me), said and swore a great oath, that
he had liefer° that his own only son (which is of truth a goodly
young gentleman and shall, I trust, come to much worship)
had lost his head than that I should thus have refused the oath.
For surely the King's Highness would now conceive a great suspicion against me, and think that the matter of the nun of
Canterbury was all contrived by my drift.° To which I said
that the contrary was true and well known, and whatsoever
should mishap me, it lay not in my power to help it without
peril of my soul. Then did my Lord Chancellor repeat before
me my refusal unto Master Secretary, as to him that was going
unto the King's Grace. And in the rehearsing his lordship re-
peated again that I denied not but was content to swear to the
succession. Whereunto I said that, as for that point, I would
be content, so that° I might see my oath in that point so framed
in such a manner as might stand with my conscience.

Then said my lord: "Mary, Master Secretary, mark that too,
that he will not swear that neither, but under some certain
manner." "Verily no, my Lord," quoth I, "but that I will see
it made in such wise first as I shall myself see that I shall neither
be foresworn° nor swear against my conscience. Surely as to
swear to the succession I see no peril, but I thought and think
it reason that to mine own oath I look well myself, and be of
counsel also in the fashion, and never intended to swear for
piece, and set my hand to the whole oath, I never withdrew
any man from it, nor never advised any to refuse it, nor never
put, nor will, any scruple in any man's head, but leave every
man to his own conscience. And me thinketh, in good faith,
that so were it good reason that every man should leave me to
mine."

Tower of London

Our Lord Bless You All.

. . . As touching the points of your letter, I can make none
answer, for I doubt not but you well remember that the matters
which move my conscience, without declaration whereof I can

Master Secretary Thomas Cromwell   **liefer** rather   **by my drift** at my
instigation, with my connivance   **so that** provided   **foresworn** sworn
falsely

nothing touch the points, I have sundry times showed you that I will disclose them to no man. And therefore, daughter Margaret, I can in this thing no further, but like as you labor° me again to follow your mind, to desire and pray you both again to leave off such labor, and with my former answers to hold yourself content.

A deadly grief unto me and much more deadly than to hear of mine own death (for the fear thereof, I thank our Lord, the fear of hell, the hope of heaven and the passion of Christ daily more and more assuage) is that I perceive my good son your husband, and you my good daughter, and my good wife, and mine other good children and innocent friends, in great displeasure and danger of great harm thereby. The let° whereof, while it lieth not in my hand, I can no further but commit all unto God. *Nam in manu Dei*, saith the Scripture, *cor regis est, et sicut divisiones aquarum quocunque voluerit, impellit illud,*° whose high goodness I most humbly beseech to incline the noble heart of the King's Highness to the tender favor of you all, and to favor me no better than God and myself know that my faithful heart toward him and my daily prayer for him do deserve. For surely if his Highness might inwardly see my true mind such as God knoweth it is, I would, I trust, soon assuage his high displeasure. Which while I can in this world never in such wise show but that his Grace may be persuaded to believe the contrary of me, I can no further go, but put all in the hands of him, for fear of whose displeasure for the safeguard of my soul stirred by mine own conscience (without insectation° or reproach laying to any other man's) I suffer and endure this trouble. Out of which I beseech him to bring me, when his will shall be, into his endless bliss of heaven, and in the meanwhile, give me grace and you both in all our agonies and troubles, devoutly to resort prostrate unto the remembrance of that bitter agony which our Savior suffered before his passion at the Mount. And if we diligently so do, I verily trust we shall find therein great comfort and consolation. And thus, my dear daughter, the blessed spirit of Christ for his tender mercy govern and guide you all, to his pleasure and your weal° and comfort both body and soul.

Your tender loving father,

Thomas More, Knight.

---

labor urge **let** prevention **Nam . . . illud** Prov. 21:1: For the heart of the king is in the hand of God, and whoever desired the division of the waters, he ordered the same. **insectation** insult **weal** health

Tower of London
1534

The Holy Spirit of God Be With You.

If I would with my writing, mine own good daughter, declare how much pleasure and comfort your daughterly loving letters were unto me, a peck of coals would not suffice to make me the pens. And other pens have I, good Margaret, none here, and, therefore, can I write you no long process° nor dare adventure, good daughter, to write often.

The cause of my close keeping° again did of likelihood grow of my negligent and very plain true word which you remember. And verily, whereas my mind gave me, as I told you in the garden, that some such thing were likely to happen, so doth my mind always give me that some folk yet ween° that I was not so poor as it appeared in the search, and that it may therefore happen that yet eftsoon° oftener than once, some new sudden searches may hap to be made in every house of ours as narrowly as is possible. Which thing if ever it so should hap can make but game to us that know the truth of my poverty, but if° they find out my wife's gay girdle and her golden beads. Howbeit I verily believe in good faith that the King's Grace of his benign pity will take nothing from her.

I thought and yet think that it may be that I was shut up again upon some new causeless suspicion, grown peradventure° upon some secret sinister information, whereby some folk haply° thought that there should be found out against me some other greater things. But I thank our Lord, whensoever this conjecture hath fallen in my mind, the clearness of my conscience hath made my heart hop for joy. For one thing am I very sure of hitherto and trust in God's mercy to be while I live, that as often I have said unto you, I shall for anything toward my prince never take great harm, but if° I take great wrong in the sight of God, I say, howsoever it shall seem in the sight of men. For to the world wrong may seem right sometimes by false conjecturing, sometimes by false witnesses, as that good lord said unto you, which is, I dare say, my very good lord in his mind, and said it of very good will. Before the world also my refusing of this oath is accounted a heinous offense, and my religious fear toward God is called obstinacy toward my prince. But my lords of the council, before whom I refused it, might well perceive by the heaviness of my heart appearing well more ways than one unto them that all sturdy stubbornness whereof obstinacy groweth was very far from my mind. For the clearer proof whereof, since they seemed to take

process account   **keeping** imprisonment   **ween** think   **eftsoon** again   **but if** except   **peradventure** perhaps   **haply** perhaps   **but if** unless

for one argument of obstinacy in me that, refusing of the oath, I would not declare the causes why, I offered with a full heart that albeit I rather would endure all the pain and peril of the statute than by declaring of the causes give any occasion of exasperation unto my most dread sovereign lord and prince.

Yet rather than his Highness should for not disclosing the causes account me for stubborn and obstinate, I would upon such his gracious license and commandment as should discharge me of his displeasure and peril of any statute declare those points that letted° my poor conscience to receive that oath; and would over that be sworn before, that if I should, after the causes disclosed and declared, find them so answered as my conscience should think itself satisfied, I would thereupon swear the oath that I there refused. To this Master Secretary° answered me that, though the King's Grace gave me such a license, yet it could not discharge me against° the statutes in saying anything that were by them upon heinous pains prohibited. In this good warning he showed himself my special tender friend.

And now you see well, Margaret, that it is no obstinacy to leave the causes undeclared, while I could not declare them without peril. But now is it accounted great obstinacy that I refuse the oath, whatsoever my causes be, considering that of so many wiser and better men none sticked° thereat. And Master Secretary, of a great zeal that he bare unto me, sware there before them a great oath that for the displeasure that he thought the King's Highness would bear me, and the suspicion that his Grace would conceive of me, which would now think in his mind that all the nun's business° was wrought and devised by me, he had liefer° than I should have refused the oath that his own only son (which is a goodly young gentleman of whom our Lord send him much joy) had had his head stricken off. This word, Margaret, as it was a marvelous declaration of Master Secretary's great good mind and favor toward me, so was it a heavy hearing to me that the King's Grace, my most dread sovereign lord, were likely to conceive such high suspicion of me and bear such grievous indignation toward me, for the thing which, without danger and peril to my poor soul, lay not in my hand to help, nor doth.

Now have I heard since that some say that this obstinate manner of mine in still refusing the oath shall peradventure force and drive the King's Grace to make a further law for me. I cannot let° such a law to be made. But I am very sure that if I died by such a law, I should die for that point innocent before

---

letted prevented   **Master Secretary** Cromwell   **against** from   **sticked** hesitated   **nun's business** Elizabeth Barton, the nun of Kent. See pp. 242–43.   **liefer** rather   **let** prevent

God. And albeit, good daughter, that I think our Lord that hath the hearts of kings in his hand would never suffer of his high goodness so gracious a prince, and so many honorable men, and so many good men as be in the Parliament to make such an unlawful law, as that should be if it so mishapped,° yet lest I note that point unthought upon, but many times more than one revolved and cast in my mind before my coming hither, both that peril and all other that might put my body in peril of death by the refusing of this oath. In devising where-upon, albeit, mine own good daughter, that I found myself (I cry God mercy) very sensual° and my flesh much more shrink-ing from pain and from death than methought it the part of a faithful Christian man, in such a case as my conscience gave me, that in the saving of my body should stand the loss of my soul, yet I thank our Lord, that in that conflict the spirit had in conclusion the mastery, and reason with help of faith finally concluded that for to be put to death wrongfully for doing well (as I am very sure I do, in refusing to swear against mine own conscience, being such as I am not upon peril of my soul bounden to change whether my death should come without law, or by color of a law), it is a case in which a man may lose his head and yet have none harm, but instead of harm inestimable good at the hand of God.

And I thank our Lord, Meg, since I am come hither I set by° death every day less than other. For though a man lose of his years in this world, it is more than manifold recompensed by coming the sooner to heaven. And though it be a pain to die while a man is in health, yet see I very few that in sickness die with ease. And finally, very sure am I that whensoever the time shall come that may hap to come, God wot° how soon, in which I should lie sick in my death bed by nature, I shall then think that God had done much for me, if he had suffered me to die before by the color of such a law. And, therefore, my reason showeth me, Margaret, that it were great folly for me to be sorry to come to that death, which I would after wish that I had died. Besides that, that a man may hap with less thanks of God and more adventure° of his soul to die as violently and as painfully by many other chances as by enemies or thieves. And, therefore, mine own good daughter, I assure you (thanks be to God) the thinking of any such, albeit it hath grieved me ere this, yet at this day grieveth me nothing. And yet I know well for all this mine own frailty, and that Saint Peter, which feared it much less than I, fell in such fear soon after that at the word of a simple girl he forsook and forswore our Savior.

mishapped unfortunately came to pass   **sensual** still involved with the life of the senses   **set by** account   **wot** knows   **adventure** risk

And, therefore, am I not, Meg, so mad as to warrant myself to stand.° But I shall pray, and I pray thee, mine own good daughter, to pray with me, that it may please God that hath given me this mind, to give me the grace to keep it.

And thus have I, mine own good daughter, disclosed unto you the very secret bottom of my mind, referring the order thereof only to the goodness of God, and that so fully that I assure you Margaret on my faith I never have prayed God to bring me hence nor deliver me from death, but referring all things whole unto his only pleasure, as to him that seeth better what is best for me than myself doth. Nor never longed I since I came hither to set my foot in mine own house, for any desire of or pleasure of my house, but gladly would I sometimes somewhat talk with my friends, and specially my wife and you that pertain to my charge. But since that God otherwise disposeth, I commit all wholly to his goodness and take daily great comfort in that I perceive that you live together so charitably and so quietly; I beseech our Lord continue it.

And thus, mine own good daughter, putting you finally in remembrance that, albeit if the necessity so should require, I thank our Lord in this quiet and comfort is mine heart at this day, and I trust in God's goodness so shall have grace to continue, yet, as I said before, I verily trust that God shall so inspire and govern the king's heart that he shall not suffer his noble heart and courage to requite my true faithful heart and service with such extreme unlawful and uncharitable dealing, only for the displeasure that I cannot think so as others do. But his true subject will I live and die, and truly pray for him will I, both here and in the other world too.

And thus, mine own good daughter, have me recommended to my good bedfellow and all my children, men, women and all, with all your babes and your nurses and all the maids and all the servants, and all our kin, and all our other friends abroad. And I beseech our Lord to save them all and keep them. And I pray you all pray for me, and I shall pray for you all. And take no thought for me whatsoever you shall hap to hear, but be merry in God.

Tower of London
1534

The Holy Spirit of God be with you.

Your daughterly loving letter, my dearly beloved child, was

---

warrant . . . stand guarantee that I will remain steadfast and is, I faithfully assure you, much more inward comfort unto me than my pen can well express you, for divers things that I marked therein but of all things most especially, for that God of his high goodness giveth you the grace to consider the incomparable difference between the wretched estate of this present life and the wealthy state of the life to come, for them that die in God. . . .

And where you write these words of yourself, "But good father, I wretch am far, far, farthest of all other from such point of perfection, our Lord send me the grace to amend my life and continually to have an eye to mine end, without grudge° of death, which to them that die in God, is the gate of a wealthy life to which God of his infinite mercy bring us all. Amen. Good father, strengthen my frailty with your devout prayers." The father of heaven mote° strengthen thy frailty, my good daughter, and the frailty of thy frail father too. And let us not doubt but he so will, if we will not be slack in calling upon him therefor. Of my poor prayers, such as they be, ye may be bold to reckon. . . .

Surely, Meg, a fainter heart than thy frail father hath, canst you not have. And yet I verily trust in the great mercy of God, that he shall of his goodness so stay me with his holy hand that he shall not finally suffer me to fall wretchedly from his favor. And the like trust, dear daughter, in his high goodness I verily conceive of you. And so much the more in that there is neither of us both, but that if we call his benefits to mind and give him oft thanks for them, we may find tokens many to give us good hope for all our manifold offenses toward him, that his great mercy, when we will heartily call therefor, shall not be withdrawn from us. And verily, my dear daughter, in this is my great comfort, that albeit I am of nature so shrinking from pain that I am almost afeard of a fillip, yet in all the agonies that I have had, whereof, before my coming hither as I have showed you ere this, I have had neither small nor few, with heavy fearful heart, forecasting all such perils and painful deaths, as by any manner of possibility might after fall unto me, and in such thought lain long restless and waking, while my wife had weened I had slept, yet in any such fear and heavy pensiveness, I thank the mighty mercy of God, I never in my mind intended to consent that I would for the enduring of the uttermost do any such thing as I should in mine own conscience (for with other men's I am not a man meet to take upon me to meddle) think to be to myself, such as should damnably cast me in the displeasure of God. And this is the least point that

grudge fear   **mote** must (in the sense of hopeful exhortation)

any man may with his salvation come to, as far as I can see, and is bounden if he see peril to examine his conscience surely by learning and by good counsel and be sure that his conscience be such as it may stand with his salvation, or else reform it. And if the matter be such as both the parties may stand with salvation, then on whichever side his conscience fall, he is safe enough before God. But that mine own may stand with my own salvation, thereof I thank our Lord I am very sure. I beseech our Lord bring all parties to his bliss.

It is now, my good daughter late. And therefore thus I commend you to the holy Trinity to guide you, comfort you, and direct you with his Holy Spirit, and all yours and my wife with all my children and all our other friends.

Thomas More, Knight.

Tower of London
May 1535

Our Lord Bless you.
My dearly beloved daughter.

I doubt not but by the reason of the councillors resorting hither, in this time (in which our Lord be their comfort) these fathers of the Charterhouse and Master Reynolds° of Syon, that be now judged to death for treason (whose matters and causes I know not) may hap to put you in trouble and fear of mind concerning me being here prisoner, specially for that it is not unlikely but that you have heard that I was brought also before the council here myself. I have thought it necessary to advertise° you of the very truth, to the end that you neither conceive more hope than the matter giveth, lest upon other turn it might aggrieve your heaviness, nor more grief and fear than the matter giveth of, on the other side. Wherefore shortly ye shall understand that on Friday the last day of April in the afternoon, Master Lieutenant° came in here unto me and showed me that Master Secretary° would speak with me. Whereupon I shifted my gown and went out with Master Lieutenant into the gallery to him, where I met many, some known and some unknown, in the way. And in conclusion, coming into the chamber where his mastership sat with Master Attorney,°

Reynolds More is referring here to several monks who, like More, refused to take the oath, and who were executed on May 4, 1535 **advertise** inform **Master Lieutenant** More's friend Sir Edmund Walsingham **Master Secretary** Cromwell **Master Attorney** Sir Christopher Hales

Master Solicitor,° Master Bedill,° and Master Doctor Tregonnell,° I was offered to sit with them, which in no wise I would.

Whereupon Master Secretary showed unto me that he doubted not but that I had by such friends as hither had resorted to me seen the new statutes made at the last sitting of the Parliament. Whereunto I answered, "Yea, verily. Howbeit, for as much as being here, I have no conversation with any people, I thought it little need for me to bestow much time upon them, and, therefore, I redelivered the book shortly and the effect of the statutes I never marked nor studied to put in remembrance." Then he asked me whether I had not read the first statute of them, of the king being head of the Church. Whereunto I answered, Yes. Then his mastership declared unto me that since it was now by act of Parliament ordained that his Highness and his heirs be, and ever right have been, and perpetually should be supreme head on earth of the Church of England under Christ, the king's pleasure was that those of his council there assembled should demand mine opinion and what my mind was therein. Whereunto I answered that in good faith I had well trusted that the King's Highness would never have commanded any such question to be demanded of me, considering that I ever from the beginning well and truly from time to time declared my mind unto his Highness, and since that time I had, I said, unto your mastership, Master Secretary, also, both by mouth and by writing. And now I have in good faith discharged my mind of all such matters, and neither will dispute king's titles nor pope's, but the king's true faithful subject I am and will be, and daily I pray for him and for all his, and for you all that are of his honorable council, and for all the realm. And otherwise than thus I never intend to meddle.

Whereunto Master Secretary answered that he thought this manner of answer should not satisfy nor content the King's Highness, but that his Grace would exact a more full answer. And his mastership added thereunto that the King's Highness was a prince not of rigor but of mercy and pity, and though that he had found obstinacy at some time in any of his subjects, yet when he should find them at another time conformable and submit themselves, his Grace would show mercy. And that concerning myself, his Highness would be glad to see me take such conformable ways as I might be abroad in the world again among other men as I have been before.

Whereunto I shortly, after the inward affection of my mind,

Master Solicitor Richard Rich, the man whose perjured testimony helped convict More of treason   **Master Bedill** Clerk of the Privy Council   **Tregonnell** a judge associated with the king's efforts to have the marriage to Catharine annulled

answered for a very truth that I would never meddle in the world again, to have the world given me. And to the remnant of the matter I answered in effect as before, showing that I had fully determined with myself neither to study nor meddle with any matter of this world, but that my whole study should be upon the passion of Christ and mine own passage out of this world.

Upon this I was commanded to go forth for a while and after called in again. At which time Master Secretary said unto me that, though I was prisoner and condemned to perpetual prison, yet I was not thereby discharged of mine obedience and allegiance unto the King's Highness. And thereupon demanded of me whether that I thought that the King's Grace might exact of me such things as are contained in the statutes and upon like pains as he might of other men. Whereto I answered that I would not say the contrary. Whereto he said that likewise as the King's Highness would be gracious to them that he found conformable, so his Grace would follow the course of his laws toward such as he shall find obstinate. And his mastership said further that my demeanor in that matter was of a thing that of likelihood made now other men so stiff° therein as they be.

Whereto I answered that I give no man occasion to hold any point one or other, nor never gave any man advice or counsel therein one way or other. And for conclusion I could no further go, whatsoever pain should come thereof. I am, quoth I, the king's true faithful subject and daily beadsman,° and pray for his Highness and all his and all the realm. I do nobody harm, I say none harm, I think none harm, but wish everybody good. And if this be not enough to keep a man alive in good faith, I long not to live. And I am dying already, and have since I came here been divers times in the case° that I thought to die within one hour, and I thank our Lord I was never sorry for it, but rather sorry when I saw the pang past. And, therefore, my poor body is at the king's pleasure. Would God my death might do him good.

After this Master Secretary said, "Well, ye find no fault in that statute, find you any in any of the other statutes after?" Whereto I answered, "Sir, whatsoever thing should seem to me other than good in any of the statutes or in that statute either, I would not declare what fault I found nor speak thereof." Whereunto finally his mastership said full gently that of anything that I had spoken there should none advantage be taken, and whether he said further that there be none to be taken, I am not well remembered. But he said that report should be

stiff stubborn   **beadsman** a person who prays for somebody   **in the case** in such a condition

made unto the King's Highness and his gracious pleasure known.

Whereupon I was delivered again to Master Lieutenant, which was then called in, and so was I by Master Lieutenant brought again into my chamber, and here am I yet in such case as I was, neither better nor worse. That that shall follow lieth in the hand of God, whom I beseech to put in the King's Grace's mind that thing that may be to his high pleasure, and in mine, to mind only the weal of my soul, with little regard of my body.

And you with all yours, and my wife and all my children and all our other friends both bodily and ghostly° heartily well to fare. And I pray you and all them pray for me, and take no thought whatsoever shall happen me. For verily trust in the goodness of God, seem it never so evil to this world, it shall indeed in another world be for the best.

Your loving father,

Thomas More, Knight.

June 1535

Our Lord bless you and all yours.

Forasmuch, dearly beloved daughter, as it is likely that you either have heard or shortly shall hear that the council was here this day and that I was before them, I have thought it necessary to send you word how the matter standeth. And verily, to be short, I perceive little difference between this time and the last, for, as far as I can see, the whole purpose is either to drive me to say precisely the one way or else precisely the other.

Here sat my Lord of Canterbury, my Lord Chancellor, my Lord of Suffolk, my Lord of Wiltshire, and Master Secretary. And after my coming, Master Secretary made rehearsal in what wise he had reported unto the King's Highness what had been said by his Grace's council to me, and what had been answered by me to them at mine other being before them last. Which thing his mastership rehearsed in good faith very well, as I acknowledged and confessed and heartily thanked him therefor. Whereupon he added thereunto that the King's Highness was nothing content nor satisfied with mine answer, but thought that by my demeanor I had been occasion of much grudge°

ghostly spiritually   **grudge** murmuring, agitation, harmful influence

and harm in the realm, and that I had an obstinate mind and an evil toward him and that my duty was, being his subject, and so he had sent them now in his name upon my allegiance to command me, to make a plain and terminate° answer whether I thought the statute lawful or not, and that I should either acknowledge and confess it lawful that his Highness should be supreme head of the Church of England or else to utter plainly malignity.°

Whereto I answered that I had no malignity and therefore I could none utter. And, as to the matter, I could none other answer make than I had before made, which answer his mastership had there rehearsed. Very heavy I was that the King's Highness should have any such opinion of me. Howbeit, if there were one that had informed his Highness many evil things of me that were untrue, to which his Highness for the time gave credence, I would be very sorry that he should have that opinion of me the space of one day. Howbeit, if I were sure that other should come on the morrow by whom his Grace should know the truth of mine innocency, I should in the meanwhile comfort myself with consideration of that. And in like wise now though it be great heaviness to me that his Highness have such opinion of me for the while, yet have I no remedy to help it, but only to comfort myself with this consideration that I know very well that the time shall come when God shall declare my truth toward his Grace before him and all the world. And whereas it might haply seem to be but small cause of comfort because I might take harm here first in the meanwhile, I thanked God that my case was such in this matter through the clearness of mine own conscience that though I might have pain I could not have harm, for a man may in such case lose his head and have no harm. For I was very sure that I had no corrupt affection, but that I had always from the beginning truly used myself to looking first upon God and next upon the king according to the lesson that his Highness taught me at my first coming to his noble service, the most virtuous lesson that ever prince taught his servant. Whose Highness to have of me such opinion is my great heaviness, but I have no means, as I said, to help it, but only comfort myself in the meantime with the hope of that joyful day in which my truth toward him shall well be known. And in this matter further I could not go nor other answer thereto I could not make.

To this it was said by my Lord Chancellor and Master Secretary both that the king might by his laws compel me to make a plain answer thereto, either the one way or the other. Where-

terminate final   **malignity** ill will

unto I answered I would not dispute the king's authority, what his Highness might do in such a case, but I said that verily under correction it seemed to me somewhat hard. For if it so were that my conscience gave me against the statutes (wherein how my mind giveth me I make no declaration), then I nothing doing nor nothing saying against the statute, it were a very hard thing to compel me to say either precisely with it against my conscience to the loss of my soul, or precisely against it to the destruction of my body.

To this Master Secretary said that I had ere this when I was chancellor examined heretics and thieves and other malefactors and gave me a great praise, above my deserving, in that behalf. And he said that I then, as he thought, and at the leastwise bishops did use to examine heretics, whether they believed the pope to be head of the Church and used to compel them to make a precise answer thereto. And why should not then the king, since it is a law made here that his Grace is head of the Church, here compel men to answer precisely to the law here as they did then concerning the pope.

I answered and said that I protested that I intended not to defend any part or stand in contention, but I said there was a difference between those two cases because that at that time as well here as elsewhere through the corps of Christendom, the pope's power was recognized for an undoubted thing, which seemeth not like a thing agreed in this realm and the contrary taken for truth in other realms. Whereunto Master Secretary answered that they were as well burned for the denying of that as they be beheaded for denying of this, and, therefore, as good reason to compel them to make precise answer to the one as to the other.

Whereto I answered that since in this case a man is not by a law of one realm so bound in his conscience, where there is a law of the whole corps of Christendom to the contrary in matter touching belief, as he is by a law of the whole corps, though there happen to be made in some place a local law to the contrary, the reasonableness or the unreasonableness in binding a man to precise answer standeth not in the respect or difference between beheading or burning, but because of the difference in charge of conscience, the difference standeth between beheading and hell.

Much was there answered unto this both by Master Secretary and my Lord Chancellor, overlong to rehearse. And in conclusion they offered me an oath by which I should be sworn to make true answer to such things as should be asked me on the king's behalf, concerning the king's own person.

Whereto I answered that verily I never purposed to swear

any book oath° more while I lived. Then they said that was very obstinate if I would refuse that, for every man doth it in the Star Chamber and everywhere. I said that was true, but I had not so little foresight but that I might well conjecture what should be part of my interrogatory and as good it was to refuse it at the first as afterward.

Whereto my Lord Chancellor answered that he thought I guessed truth, for I should see them and so they were showed me and they were but twain. The first, whether I had seen the statute; the other, whether I believed that it were a lawfully made statute or not. Whereupon I refused the oath and said further by mouth that the first I had before confessed, and to the second I would make none answer. Which was the end of the communication, and I was thereupon sent away.

In the communication before, it was said that it was marveled that I stuck so much in my conscience while at the uttermost I was not sure therein. Whereto I said that I was very sure that mine own conscience so informed as it is by such diligence as I have so long taken therein may stand with mine own salvation. I meddle not with the conscience of them that think otherwise; every man *suo domino stat et cadit.*° I am no man's judge. It was also said unto me that if I had as lief° be out of the world as in it, as I had there said, why did I not speak even out plain against the statute. It appeared well I was not content to die, though I said so. Whereto I answered, as the truth is, that I have not been a man of such holy living as I might be bold to offer myself to death, lest God for my presumption might suffer me to fall, and, therefore, I put not myself forward, but draw back. Howbeit, if God draw me to it himself, then trust I in his great mercy, that he shall not fail to give me grace and strength.

In conclusion, Master Secretary said that he liked me this day much worse than he did the last time, for then he said he pitied me much and now he thought that I meant not well, but God and I know both that I mean well, and so I pray God do by me.

I pray you, be you and mine other friends of good cheer, whatsover fall of me, and take no thought for me, but pray for me as I do and shall do for you and all them.

> Your tender, loving father,
>
> Thomas More, Knight.

---

book oath solemn oath on the Bible   **suo ... cadit** stands and falls as his own ruler   **had as lief** would just as soon

[The following letter, written from the Tower of London on July 5, 1535, the day before his execution, is the last thing Thomas More wrote.]

July 5, 1535.

Our Lord bless you, good daughter, and your good husband, and your little boy, and all yours and all my children, and all my godchildren, and all our friends. Recommend me when you may to my good daughter Cecily,° whom I beseech our Lord to comfort, and I send her my blessing, and to all her children, and pray her to pray for me. I send her a handkerchief, and God comfort my good son, her husband. My good daughter Daunce° hath the picture in parchment that you delivered me from my Lady Coniers; her name is on the back side. Show her that I heartily pray her that you may send it in my name again for a token from me to pray for me.

I like specially well Dorothy Coly,° I pray you be good unto her. I would wit° whether this be she that you wrote me of. If not, I pray you be good to the other as you may in her affliction, and to my good daughter Joan Aleyn° to give her I pray you some kind answer, for she sued hither to me this day to pray you be good to her.

I cumber° you, good Margaret, much, but I would be sorry if it should be any longer than tomorrow, for it is Saint Thomas's Eve, and the utas° of Saint Peter, and, therefore, tomorrow long I to go to God. It were a day very meet and convenient for me.

I never liked your manner toward me better than when you kissed me last,° for I love when daughterly love and dear charity hath no leisure to look to worldly courtesy.

Farewell, my dear child, and pray for me, and I shall for you and all your friends, that we may merrily meet in heaven. I thank you for your great cost.°

I send now unto my good daughter Clement° her algorism

Cecily the youngest of More's three daughters (he also had a son, John) by his first wife, Jane Colt. She was twenty-eight at the time of her father's death. Daunce More's second daughter, married to William Dauncey. She was twenty-nine when her father died. Dorothy Coly Margaret's maid; visited More daily in the Tower   wit know   Joan Aleyn another of Margaret's maids   cumber burden   utas octave. The other feast day referred to is that of Thomas à Becket, who, like More, was also slain by another King Henry for refusing to admit the right of the state to interfere with ecclesiastical matters.   kissed me last for a moving account of More's last encounter with his daughter, see William Roper's (he was Margaret's husband) *Life of Thomas More, Knight*, in *Two Early Tudor Lives*, eds. Richard S. Sylvester and Davis P. Harding, New Haven: Yale University Press, 1962, pp. 251–52.   cost trouble   Clement Margaret Gyge, a member of More's household, the wife of John Clement

stone, and I send her and my good son and all hers God's blessing and mine.

I pray you at time convenient recommend me to my good
son, John More. I liked well his natural fashion. Our Lord bless
him and his good wife, my loving daughter,° to whom I pray
him be good, as he hath great cause, and that if the land of mine
come to his hand, he break not my will concerning his sister
Daunce. And our Lord bless Thomas and Austin,° and all that
they shall have.

my loving daughter More's son John had married Anne Cresacre, More's
ward   **Thomas and Austin** More's grandsons, the sons of John More

Appendixes

I. More's Epitaph

More wrote his own epitaph not once but twice, in verse as well as the prose translated here. The text is inscribed on his tomb at Chelsea, which was damaged during the bombings of World War II; it has been published in Chambers' edition of Harpsfield's life of More. More included this epitaph, in a somewhat different version, in a letter to Erasmus. The epitaph succinctly conveys More's self-evaluation.

Thomas More was born of an honest but undistinguished family in London; he concerned himself to a certain extent in literary efforts; in his youth, after several years as an advocate in the law courts, and having held the office of Under-Sheriff in his native city, he was admitted to the court of the invincible king, Henry VIII, the only king ever to have merited by pen and sword the title of Defender of the Faith; he was received at court, elected to the king's council, knighted, appointed Undertreasurer, Chancellor of Lancaster, and finally Chancellor of England by special royal favor. During this time he was elected Speaker of the House of Commons; in addition, he served as royal ambassador at different times and in a variety of places, the last of which was at Cambrai as an associate and colleague of Cuthbert Tunstall, at that time Bishop of London and soon thereafter Bishop of Durham, a man whose peer in learning, wisdom, and virtue is seldom seen in this world today. There he witnessed as ambassador, to his great joy, the renewal of a peace treaty between the supreme monarchs of Christendom and also the restoration of a long-desired world peace, which peace may the Lord confirm and perpetuate. Such was his conduct while holding these offices that his excellent sovereign at no time found fault with him; he was neither disdained by the nobility nor unpleasant to the populace; rather he was a molester of thieves, murderers, and heretics. His father, John More, was a knight selected by the king as a member of a group of judges known as the King's Bench; he was affable, pleasant, innocent, mild, merciful, honest and upright. Though advanced in age, he was exceptionally vigorous for his time of life; having witnessed the elevation of his son to the chancellorship of England, he considered his stay on earth complete and willingly departed this world for heaven. The son had throughout the lifetime of the father been compared with him and was called the young More, a fact that he found agreeable; now with the loss of his father, as he considered his four children and eleven grandchildren, he began in his own mind to grow old. This feeling was increased by a chest ailment that appeared soon thereafter as a sign of advancing age. Sated with the transient things of this life, he resigned his office, and through the incomparable kindness of the most indulgent prince, may God favor his undertakings, he finally arrived at what had been, almost since childhood, the object of his desires, to have the last years of his life free to gradually retire from mundane affairs and meditate upon the eternity of the life hereafter. He then arranged for the construction of this tomb as a constant reminder of ever approaching death and had the bones of his first wife transferred here. Lest he may have erected this tomb in vain while yet living, and lest he tremble with fear at the thought of advancing death instead of going forth to meet it gladly with a longing for Christ, and that he may find death not really a death for himself but rather the door to a happier life, I beg you, kind reader, pray for him while still he lives and when he is dead.

II. Letter of Erasmus to Ulrich von Hutten

In response to a request from the distinguished German humanist Ulrich von Hutten, Erasmus composed the following biographical sketch of his English friend. Written along the lines of traditional panegyric and filled with rhetorical commonplaces, the document can be read as a humanist manifesto as well as a sincere tribute to a friend of twenty years' standing. The letter was included in a collection of More's Latin writings, the Lucubrationes, *issued at Basel in 1563. Several paragraphs from the opening and the close of the letter have been omitted from the following translation.*

Antwerp
1519

Most illustrious Hutten, you are not alone in the sympathetic understanding, this near-passion, which you bear the talented Thomas More. Many others are moved by the qualities of erudition and true humor which you note in his writing, and in your case the admiration is fully returned. The great pleasure he takes in your work is enough to inspire one to jealousy. It must be an instance of that wisdom of Plato which is the most desirable, possessing as it does a capacity to fire man beyond that of even the most exalted external beauty. Sight is not the exclusive province of the body; the mind's eye too is susceptible to what the Greeks epitomized as love at first sight. Thus it is that men who have never actually exchanged a single word or glance can sometimes become affectionately attached to one another. The appreciation of beauty varies according to the individual and this is true, too, of taste in mind and person— some afford us a relish which others simply cannot inspire; it is as though like minds shared a special affinity.

Your request for a complete picture of More leaves me wishing that my ability to draw him (at full length) could do honor to your sincere entreaty. Time spent in considering so wonderful a friend can only be pleasurable. But it is not every man who can catch the complete More and he may well be particular about the artist for whom he sits. Truly, I cannot imagine More an easier subject than Alexander the Great or Achilles, for his claim to immortality can be no less than theirs. The artistry of an Apelles is here called for, while my strokes, I fear, more closely approximate those of Fulvius or Rutuba, gladiators both. Yet I will attempt a rough sketch based upon the recollection of my intimacy with him during my visits. If you ever chance to encounter him while on foreign service, I fear you will quickly discover what a talentless artist you have charged with this task; you will denounce me as a jealous blindman for offering such a meager account of so many merits.

To begin, then, in that area where you can know least: More is neither tall nor short in build or stature and his limbs are so well proportioned that it is impossible to find any fault there. He is light complexioned, his features having a golden hue that suggests neither sallowness nor ruddiness, admitting rather of a lambency which tints the whole. His hair is auburn touching upon the black, or if you prefer, black touching upon the auburn, and his beard is thin. His eyes are of a blue-gray color interfused with another cast, a type said to denote a happy disposition and, therefore, highly regarded in England, though we prefer black eyes here. No other type, moreover, is said to be so clear and perfect for seeing. His face is a mirror of his nature, reflecting his kindness and a hearty friendliness that holds a hint of ready banter. Though it never approaches foolishness, it is, quite frankly, a face more suggestive of gaiety than dignity or serious gravity. His right shoulder appears slightly more elevated than his left and this trait, most readily apparent in his walk, is not congenital, but like so many of our peculiarities, a product of habit. There is nothing else irregular about him unless one could consider the hands a bit rough in comparison with the rest of his person.

He has been lax about his personal appearance since early youth, never really caring about those things which Ovid considered the only real care. That his youthful charm is still discernible in his present appearance I myself can witness, for I knew him first at about age twenty-three and he is not much past forty now. Of sound health rather than especial vigor, he is equal to any task his station can require, and as his aged father is yet trim and fit, there are good hopes for his long life.

No one in my experience has ever been less fastidious an eater. As a youth he followed his father's example and drank only water, though to spare his fellows' feelings he would sometimes drink it, or the most watery kind of small beer, from a pewter mug. Sometimes, too, in deference to custom he would touch a winecup to his lips when it was passed convivially around the whole table. It is his habit to prefer beef, salt meat, and common fermented bread to the usual delicacies. This doesn't mean, though, that he is averse to harmless bodily pleasure. He does have a special taste for milk pudding and fruit and takes great relish in a bowl of eggs.

His penetrating voice is neither loud nor grave. Lacking soft melody, it better answers the requirements of speaking than those of singing, though he is a great lover of music. His expression is concise and clearly formed and his delivery neither plunges nor halts.

His taste in dress is simple and he foregoes silk, purple, and golden chain whenever the occasion admits. His unconcern for the formalities on which politeness is commonly thought to rest is amazing. Lenient in his demands for protocol, he is none too intent upon observing it himself, either in friendly gatherings or in public. He has the necessary skill and can employ it when he feels it is called for, but generally regards the matter as an effeminacy hardly worthy of a man's time.

The great disdain in which he holds tyranny and his lively interest in equality made court life and intimacy with princes distasteful to him for a time. A court so arranged that it has secured immunity from bustle, dissembling, ambition, luxury, and every disguise of tyranny is not easy to discover. Even the court of the best-mannered and most indulgent Henry VIII could not easily lure him. Free time and leisure are, of course, to his liking, but the degree of pleasure he derives from a vacation is matched by his attentive devotion to the matter at hand when it is again time for business.

The genuine ardor of his friendship seems to show that he was formed for it and born to it, and he isn't one to shrink before Hesiod's injunction against too many friends. Not fastidious here, he is open to any proposal of friendship, solicitous in nurturing such bonds and tirelessly faithful in their maintenance. Should a new companion's faults prove incurable, he finds an occasion to separate where the bonds of friendship can be gently loosed rather than hacked apart. So delighted is he with true friends whose personalities correspond to his own, that friendly intercourse with these form the chief pleasure of his life. He has no relish for the more common genteel diversions of tennis, cards, and dice. Though frequently negligent about his own welfare, no man lavishes more regard upon his friends. Can I say more? To find the perfect model of friendship one need look no farther than More.

The most downcast moods and the most irritating situations, even whole gatherings, are not proof against the infectious sweetness of More's disposition. While his wit was never scurrilous or sardonic, he took such joy in joking from his earliest youth that he often seemed interested in little else. As a boy he performed his own comedies. His appreciation for true wit was such that he was captivated by all ingenious repartee, even barbs aimed at himself. An early diversion with epigram and fondness for Lucian sprang from this taste. It was, in fact, he who prodded me to write *Praise of Folly*, thereby setting a camel to dance, as it were.

There is no occurrence, however grave, in which he is unable to find some delight. The quickness of the bright and learned fires his admiration, while the folly of the dull and unlearned often affords simple amusement. The wonderful flexibility of his taste allows him to tolerate even jesters. The light banter of his own wit encompasses the fair sex, extending even to his own wife. Another Democritus, you could call him, or

more properly, a new Pythagorean philosopher, easily survey-
ing the confusion and commerce of the marketplace.

No one is less servile to public opinion and no one more
influenced by common sense. He is delighted by animal life
and takes a keen interest in the science of its various forms and
distinctions. His home, therefore, abounds with birds and animals, including such comparatively rare guests as monkeys,
foxes, ferrets, and weasels. He further wishes to purchase every
curious thing, foreign or domestic, which catches his eye. He
stocks his home with such wonders and takes vicarious enjoyment when visitors newly discover them.

When his young blood was warm, he did not flee the love of
women, but conducted himself with honor. Instead of exploit-
ing his obvious attractiveness, he derived his satisfaction from
meaningful interrelationship rather than sexual pleasure.

He had plunged into literature early in life and even in his
youth pursued both Greek letters and philosophy. Instead of
applauding these efforts, his father, a lawyer by profession,
cut off his allowance and nearly disinherited the boy for abandoning the traditional family profession. Now the relationship
of law to true learning is extremely vague, but its study does
yield both position and the truest path to fame and fortune
among Englishmen. Certainly, no mean number of their peers
derive from its ranks, and excellence in the field is held to be
possible only after years of intense devotion. His inclination
toward the finer things could hardly dispose our young friend
to undertake such study. In spite of all this, his acuteness and
intellectual capacity enabled him to master the subject thoroughly, even after his excursion into the schools, and he quickly
surpassed those preoccupied solely with the law in both earnings and volume of practice.

The Sacred Fathers, too, received a share of his attentive
energy. While still a young man he delivered well-attended lectures on Augustine's *De Civitate Dei*. Old men and priests
neither disdained nor regretted their lessons from the young
layman. He concentrated diligently upon such religious disciplines as vigils, fasts, and prayers, also, for he was considering the priesthood. This display of wisdom contrasts favorably
with the common practice of plunging headlong into an exact-
ing vocation without the precaution of prior trials. He nearly
took orders, but the attractions of marriage proved so strong
that he determined to be a chaste husband rather than a lewd
priest.

He chose as his bride a young lady of noble birth who had
always dwelt with her family in the country. The comparative
seclusion of her early life enabled him to form her character

in harmony with his inclination. He guided her progress in letters and every kind of music, and just as she was developing into an ideal life companion she was taken by an early death. Not before she gave birth to several children, however, and of these, three girls, Margaret, Alice, and Cecily, and a boy, John, survive today.

Against the advice of friends he abandoned the single life again a few months later to marry a widow. The remarriage was dictated more by the requirements of a young family than by his own whim, and he has been known to allude lightly to his quick and alert little housemistress as "neither a pearl nor a girl." Yet their life together is as sweet and amicable as it could be if she were a ravishing maiden, and his sprightly mildness secures an obedience which harshness couldn't compel. His ability to cajole a no longer young and slightly stubborn woman into setting aside her household affairs long enough for daily practice upon the harp, viol, spinet, and flute is witness to his success. This very mildness effects the banishment of bitter scenes and arguments from the entire household which he rules. He soothes impending crises or acts decisively to nip them in the bud, and in separating anyone from his household, he has never acted in an angry or vindictive manner. The hand of fate seems to have touched his house with joy, for fortune favors its inmates and their honor has never been imperiled.

Few sons ever live in such amity with their own mothers as he has achieved with his stepmother. Each of his father's three wives has been accorded the love due a mother. Having recently met the third, More is prepared to affirm that he has never seen her superior. Neither tiresome nor inattentive, his love for parents, children, and sisters is a true model.

He is a stranger to greed, a free spender of that portion of his property remaining after ample provision has been made for his children. Even when his livelihood still depended on his practice, he considered the welfare of his clients above his own, giving them accurate and amiable advice that stressed the economy of a settlement out of court. To those who, loving a legal battle, could not be persuaded, he outlined the cheapest method of procedure.

He sat for some years as a civil judge in his native city of London. This is a prestigious post involving few duties (meeting as it does only on Thursdays and only before dinner). No judge has disposed of so many cases or surpassed his unimpeachable integrity. It was even his practice to waive the fixed three-shilling fee customarily assessed against both parties to a suit. Such conduct earned him an enviable reputation in the city. It was his decision to rest content in this situation, offering as it did both dignity and protection from public hazard.

He had several times been pressed into service on embassies and his skill in these missions had so impressed King Henry VIII that that monarch could not sit still until he had dragged More to his court. I must say, literally, "dragged" because no one has ever been as eager to get into court as More was to stay out of it. That prince, however, was intent upon establishing about him a circle of learned, serious, intelligent, and honest men, and his most insistent choice was More, with whom he is now so close that he can hardly endure his absence.

There is no wiser counselor for grave matters nor is there an easier companion in pleasant conversation. More provides discreet handling of delicate situations, offering mutually satisfactory solutions. And the man cannot be bribed. What a boon for the world if only Mores were installed as magistrates!

Haughtiness is absent. He finds time to remember his old friends and to return sometimes to his beloved studies, even amid the press of urgent business. The people and those who are his friends are the beneficiaries of his power of office and his influence with the king. His nature has always inclined him to assistance and sympathy, and now that his capacity for good is expanded this is even more in evidence. He renders financial assistance to some, to some he extends immunity, still others advance on his recommendation, and those whom he can't aid in these ways at least receive his counsel. You might well address him as the universal patron of the poor, for no one leaves his door empty-handed. He feels he has secured himself a major advantage when he liberates the downtrodden, or removes stumbling blocks from before the distressed, or reconciles the exiled.

No one gives more quickly or expects less return. His person is as uniquely free from vain pride as his position is susceptible of it.

Let us consider those studies which drew More and myself together. Poetry was the chief concern of his early years. He then struggled to perfect his prose style, working in every form. The results of this endeavor are familiar especially to such as you who always have his books in your hands. Declamations were his favorite exercise, especially those on unresolved subjects, which presented the most intricate challenge to the mind.

Thus, while yet a lad he undertook a dialogue in defense of Plato's principle of complete community, including wife-sharing! He framed a reply to Lucian's *Tyrannicide*, requesting me to provide the opposition, so that he could check his development in that type of writing. In his *Utopia,* he proposed to illustrate the source and spring of political evil, with a special eye toward the England which he knows so well. The recognizable unevenness of style results from the manner and method of its composition. He wrote the second book at a leisurely pace, and then recognizing the need for it, hastily added the first.

He is an unparalleled extempore speaker, marrying the most apt thought to the most felicitous language. His mind seizes and foresees all that is at issue, and his completely furnished memory quickly provides whatever material is needed. One strains one's imagination to envision a sharper disputant, and he often beards the most distinguished theologians in their own dens. John Colet, possessed of a sharp and incisive judgment, is given to saying that while the island abounds in distinguished intellects it contains but one true genius.

More practices a genuine piety, free from taint of superstition and marked by regular prayers, informal and issuing from the heart. His friendly discussions of immortality convey the feeling of sincerity and high personal hopes. Here is the courtier, More, and yet people insist on imagining that real Christians can only be found in monasteries.

These are they whom a discerning king admits into his presence, not simply admits, but invites, nay he forces them in. These are close to his person always as the judges and recorders of his life, as his counselors and traveling companions. He is happy in their company, not in that of degenerate boys, or fops, or exalted grandees, or shifty ministers. The first of these last would entice him to frivolous play, the others goad him into tyranny or hatch some new plot for despoiling the state.

No longer could you be *anticourt,* had you lived at this court; the experience demands a new conception of court life, though I will allow that your prince begs comparison and that such men as Stromer and Copp have the proper sentiments. But what can only two suffice in the face of a host of such distinguished men as Mountjoy, Linacre, Pace, Colet, Stokesley, Latimer, More, Tunstall, Clerk, and their compeers? Any individual among them denotes a world of merit and achievement. There is, of course, a fair chance that our Germany's single star, Albert, will attract to his court men of his own quality and thereby set a fashion that other princes may emulate.

Here, then, is my poor portrait, whose subject shames its artist. You will be even unhappier with it should you chance to meet its subject firsthand. I have at least undone your accusation of neglect and undercut your criticism about the brevity

of my letters, though even this one seemed short in the writing
and will, I trust, not seem overlong in the reading either; our
More's sweetness will see to that. . . .

III. The Death of More
(from
the Paris News Letter)

This account of More's death appeared in the Paris News
Letter, *which was widely circulated throughout Europe and
translated into German, Spanish, and Latin. It is the basis of the*
Expositio fidelis, *a Latin account of the trial and death commonly attributed to Erasmus, which was printed in Basel in
1535 and in Antwerp the following year. The latter was, along
with Roper's* Life, *the most common source of information
about the tragic event. The translation given here is taken from
one of the six French manuscripts (MS. fr. 2981) still extant in
the Bibliothèque Nationale in Paris.*

Sir Thomas More, ex-chancellor of England, was brought
before the judges appointed by the king, on July 1, 1535. After
the denunciations and charges brought against him were read
out to him, the Lord Chancellor and the Duke of Norfolk
turned toward him and spoke as follows:

"You see very well, Sir More, that you have grievously
offended his royal Majesty. Nevertheless we trust that his
clemency and kindness is so great that you will obtain grace
and pardon, if you will only repent and take back that obstinate
opinion of yours which you have so rashly maintained."

More's answer to this was, "My lords, I thank you very kindly
for your good will. My only prayer is that Almighty God may
be pleased to keep me in this just opinion of mine so that I may
persevere in it until I die. As regards the accusations that are
laid to my charge, I doubt that I will have enough intelligence
or memory or eloquence to answer them all, considering their
length and seriousness, and also considering the long time I
have spent in jail, my weakened physical condition, and the
serious illness I am now suffering from."

Hereupon an order was given for a chair to be brought in

for him to sit on. When this was done, he continued his speech as follows:

"As regards the first article, which says that, to show my ill will toward the king, I have always been against his most serene Highness in the matter of his second marriage, I will answer only what I have always said about it, namely, that I followed my conscience, because I neither should nor would hide the truth from my prince. And if I had not acted as I did, I certainly would have been guilty of treachery and disloyalty against him. It was then, for such an error, if you can call it an error, that all my goods were confiscated and I was sentenced to perpetual prison, where I have now been for the last fifteen months. However, I will answer the principal argument on which you base your accusation that I have incurred the penalty laid down by statute in the last Parliament since I've been in prison, namely, that I have maliciously, falsely, and treacherously deprived his Majesty the king of his name, his title, his honor, and his dignity, all of which things have been conferred on him by the above-mentioned Parliament, which accepted him as the supreme head on earth of the Church of England under Jesus Christ. In the first place, in regard to what you object to me, that when the king's secretary and the honorable council of his Majesty questioned me on what was my opinion of this statute, I made no other answer than to say that, being dead to this world, I didn't think about such things, but only about the passion of Jesus Christ, I will tell you now that for such a silence your statute cannot condemn me to death; for neither your statute nor any law in the whole world punishes a man for what he has not said or not done and certainly not for a silence like mine."

To this the king's prosecutor replied that such silence was a proof and a sure indication of malicious thinking against this statute, since every loyal and faithful subject of his Majesty, once he has been questioned about this statute, is bound and obliged to answer definitely and without dissimulation that the statute was good and holy.

"To be sure," answered More, "if it is true what they say in common law that silence gives consent, then my silence has rather strengthened your statute than displayed any contempt for it. And when you say that every faithful subject is bound and obliged to answer, I say to you that, in a matter of conscience, the faithful subject is more bound by his conscience and his soul than by anything else in the world, provided that such a conscience, as is the case with me, does not cause any scandal or incite to a revolution against its lord; and I assure you that I didn't reveal my conscience to a living soul.

"As regards the second article, which says that I acted contrary to this statute by writing eight sets of letters to the Bishop of Rochester in which I warned him against your statute, I have indeed a most marvelous desire to hear these letters read in public. But since, as you say, these letters have been burned by the bishop, I will gladly tell you what was in them. Some of them were about intimate things connected with our long-standing friendship. One of them contained my answer to the letter in which he asked me what and how I answered at the time of my first trial in the Tower concerning the statute in question, and my answer to this was that I had formed my own conscience on the matter and I likewise suggested to him that he should form his for himself. Really now, and I swear it on my soul's salvation, this is all there is in the letters in question, and for them I cannot be sentenced to death.

"As regards the third article, which says that in my trial before the council I answered that your statute was like a two-edged sword, because a person couldn't keep it without losing his soul nor break it without losing his life, which is the same answer according to you given by the Bishop of Rochester, and that's why it seems that we had come to an agreement on the matter, my answer to that charge is that I was speaking only conditionally: that is to say, if the said statute were like a two-edged sword, how could a man so act as not to incur one or the other of the two dangers? What sort of answer the Bishop of Rochester might have given, I have no idea. If he answered as I did, that came about because we think alike and have been taught alike and not because we had come to an agreement on this point. And believe me I have never done or said anything with malicious intent against your statute. But it may very well be that somebody has maliciously spoken about me to his Grace, the king."

At this point one of the court attendants called in twelve men according to the custom of the land, and they were handed the above-mentioned articles and told to consider them and pass judgment on whether Sir Thomas More had maliciously broken the above-mentioned statute or not. They withdrew for a quarter of an hour and then came back into the presence of the princes and judges and pronounced "Gylti," which means, "sentenced to death or deserving death." Immediately, sentence was pronounced by my lord the chancellor according to the tenor of the new law.

When this was done, More began to speak in this manner: "Well: Now that sentence of death has been passed on me, and God knows how, I will freely speak about your statute to relieve my conscience. I say that I have been studying this matter for seven years, but I have never read in any doctor approved by the Church that a secular prince can or ought to be the head over things spiritual."

Right here his speech was interrupted by the Lord Chancellor, who said, "Sir Thomas More, you wish to be esteemed wiser and of a better conscience than all the bishops, the whole nobility, and everybody else in the kingdom."

To this More replied, "My lord, for one bishop that you have on your side, I have more than a hundred holy ones on my side; and for one parliament, and God knows what it is, I have all the general councils for the past thousand years; and for one kingdom, I have France and all the other kingdoms throughout Christianity."

Then the Duke of Norfolk said to him, "Now, More, we see very clearly your malice."

And More answered, "My lord, what I am saying I feel compelled to say, simply to explain and make clear my conscience and to satisfy my own soul, and in doing this I call God above as my witness, who is the sole searcher of the human heart. And I say further that your law is an evil one, for you yourselves have professed and sworn never to do anything against the Church, which throughout the world is one, unique, undivided, and intact, and you by yourselves, without the consent of all other Christians, have no authority whatsoever to make a law or pass an act of Parliament contrary to this unity of Christianity. I know very well indeed for what reason you have sentenced me. It is because I have never been willing so far to give my consent in this matter of the king's marriage; but I have great confidence in God's kindness and mercy, and I hope that just as Saint Paul, as is written in his life, persecuted Saint Stephen, and is now his friend in paradise, so too we may, all of us, no matter what our disagreements may have been in this world, in the next be united together in perfect charity. At this point I pray that God will save the king and keep and give him good counsel."

As they were bringing More back to the great Tower and before he entered it, one of his daughters, named Margaret, seized and overcome with great grief and sorrow for her father, forced her way right through the crowd of archers and satellites, and without any respect for the people there or the public place she was in, rushed up to her father and threw her arms around his neck, holding him tightly in her embrace without being able to say a word. And then her father, with the permission of the archers, spoke to comfort her:

"Margaret, have patience, do not torment yourself. It is the will of God. You have known the secret desire of my heart for a long time."

Then she stepped back some ten or twelve feet, but again she came forward to take him in her arms, and he, without shedding tears and without any change in his face or voice, simply told her to pray to God for his soul.

The following Wednesday he was decapitated in the great square in front of the Tower. He spoke little before his execution. He only begged the bystanders to pray to God for him, promising that he, for his part, would pray for them. Afterward he exhorted them and earnestly begged them to pray to God for the king so that he might have good counsel, and finally he protested that he died the king's good servant but God's first.

MERIDIAN CLASSICS You'll Enjoy

**Buy them at your local
bookstore or use coupon
on next page for ordering.**

Interesting Reading from MERIDIAN CLASSICS

More MERIDIAN CLASSICS You'll Enjoy

(0452)

☐ **DEMOCRACY: An American Novel by Henry Adams.** With a Foreword by Henry D. Aiken. Vote buying and fixed elections, slanderous competition, preposterous graft—this is the Washington of the 1870s that Henry Adams reveals in his famous novel. The story of two people who aspire to power, here is an incisive exposé of corruption, in individuals and in government ... an entertaining caricature of government life that may be seen to have its application even today. (006511—$3.50)

☐ **SARTORIS by William Faulkner.** Foreword by Robert Cantwell and Afterword by Lawrance Thompson. A brilliant dissection of a decaying social class, and a vivid evocation of both the physical landscape and psychological climate of the South, *Sartoris* introduces many of the key themes, places, and characters of the Faulkner canon. (006465—$3.50)

☐ **THE SATYRICON by Petronius.** Translated and with an Introduction by William Arrowsmith. A classic of comedy, this is a superbly funny picture of Nero's Rome as seen through the eyes of Petronius, its most amorous and elegant courtier. *The Satyricon* is the hilarious tale of the pleasure-seeking adventures of an educated rogue, Encolpius, his handsome serving boy, Giton, and Ascyltus, who lusts after Giton—three impure pilgrims who live by their wits and other men's purses. (006538—$2.95)

☐ **A HAZARD OF NEW FORTUNES by William Dean Howells.** With an Afterword by Benjamin DeMott. A memorable portrait of an era and a profoundly moving study of human relationships, this novel centers on the conflict between a self-made millionaire and a fervent social revolutionary—a conflict in which a man of goodwill futilely attempts to act as mediator, only to be forced himself into a crisis of conscience. (006503—$3.95)

All prices higher in Canada.

Quality Fiction from PLUME